Surrounded

Stanford Studies in Middle Eastern and Islamic Societies and Cultures

Surrounded

Palestinian Soldiers in the Israeli Military

Rhoda Ann Kanaaneh

Stanford University Press

Stanford, California

Stanford University Press
Stanford, California

©2009 by the Board of Trustees of the Leland Stanford Junior University.
All rights reserved.

Printed in the United States of America on acid-free, archival-quality paper

Library of Congress Cataloging-in-Publication Data

Kanaaneh, Rhoda Ann.
  Surrounded : Palestinian soldiers in the Israeli military / Rhoda Ann Kanaaneh.
      p. cm.--(Stanford studies in Middle Eastern and Islamic societies and cul-
tures)
  Includes bibliographical references and index.
  ISBN 978-0-8047-5858-1 (cloth : alk. paper)
  1. Soldiers, Palestinian Arab--Israel. 2. Israel--Armed Forces--Minorities. 3. So-
ciology, Military--Israel. 4. Palestinian Arabs--Israel. 5. Israel--Ethnic relations.
I. Title. II. Series.
  UB419.I75K35 2009
  355.0089'927405694--dc22   2008028599

Typeset by Bruce Lundquist in 11/13.5 Adobe Garamond

To Malaika and Laiali

Contents

1 Israel's Arabs   1

2 Embattled Identities   9

3 Conditional Citizenship   27

4 Material Upgrade   35

5 Military Ethnification   51

6 The Limits of Being a Good Arab   61

7 Broken Promises   69

8 Boys or Men? Duped or "Made"?   79

9 Blood in the Same Mud   91

Afterword Unsettling Methods   113

   Acknowledgments   129

   Notes   133

   Bibliography   183

   Index   203

Surrounded

1

Israel's Arabs

WHO ARE THE PALESTINIAN ARABS IN ISRAEL? They are Samih al-Qasim, whose Arabic poetry has chronicled and spirited the intifadas. They are 'Azmi Bishara, the parliamentarian, whose demands for a state of all its citizens made international headlines and earned him an exile of sorts. They are filmmaker Elie Sulieman, whose films have been canonized as Palestinian "struggle" cinema. They are Asel Asleh, the nineteen-year-old who was shot by an Israeli policeman—in the neck from behind—during the October 2000 uprising. And they are 'Abir Kobati, the telegenic contestant on a popular Israeli reality television show, who refused to stand for the Israeli Jewish national anthem.

But they are also Sayed Kashua, whose command of Hebrew and eloquence in his second language, as if it were his "mother tongue," have made his books popular among Israeli Jews.[1] They are the manager of the Maccabi Sakhnin soccer team, who says he is proud to represent Israel in matches abroad. They are Ishmael Khaldi, a veteran of the Israeli military who tours American campuses sponsored by the Israel on Campus Coalition, singing the praises of the state. And they are Taysir al-Hayb who volunteered to serve in the Israeli military and shot and killed Tom Hurndall, a British activist in the International Solidarity Movement.

Technically speaking, Palestinians living inside the 1948 borders of Israel, unlike those living in the Occupied Territories or in the Diaspora, are citizens of the state of Israel. Numbering about 12 percent of Palestinians globally, they are largely descendants of the relatively few Palestinians who were not exiled outside the borders of the emerging state of Israel during the 1948 war. Nearing 1.25 million people, these Palestinians today find themselves a minoritized 18 percent of the Israeli population.

The answer to the question of "who are they?" of course depends on whom and when you ask. Ask Israeli Jews. Some might tell you they are the fortunate beneficiaries of Israeli rule, fully equal citizens. With the exception of some bad apples, they are supposedly happy living in the modern democratic and Jewish state and are, of course, no longer Palestinians but "Arabs of Israel." Or some might say they are ungrateful, violent fanatics who continue to constitute a threat to the state and need to be tightly controlled. The image of Palestinians in Israel vacillates between that of docile subjects, who lead rural traditional lives in villages that make excellent destinations for exotic tourism, and that of the enemy within, the lurking demographic threat, contaminating Jewish culture and constituting a key part of the problem in the Israeli-Arab conflict.

Ask Palestinians in the West Bank city of Nablus or Rafah refugee camp in Gaza, and they might tell you that Palestinians inside Israel are largely traitors, collaborators, and people co-opted en masse whom they sometimes call *Arab al-Shamenet*, or "sour cream Arabs." Shamenet is an Israeli-made creamy yogurt. The term *Arab al-Shamenet* mocks Palestinians in Israel as soft, addicted to this modern, Hebrew-named, Israeli-made product, and accepting of their dependency on Israel. Alternatively, they are seen as victims of a different form of the same colonial system that Palestinians in the West Bank and Gaza are subjected to. " '48 Arabs," as they are sometimes called, are *samidun*, steadfast.

Ask Palestinians in Israel about themselves, and you will also get a range of performances of diffidence, acquiescence, and contradiction. One twenty-year-old Palestinian told me: "We are doing the best we can, nobody has figured out the perfect answer. If we knew how to bring back Palestine, don't you think we all would do it?" Palestinians inside Israel number over a million, and like many minority groups, they have learned—been forced to learn—to maneuver through a complex system, straddle multiple zones, and take on an array of contradictory challenges. They are constantly negotiating, experimenting with different strategies, being silent, being brash—or in the words of writer Kashua—they are "Dancing Arabs."

The state tries to define them on the one hand not as a single national minority but as a fractured collection of ethnic and religious groups: Druze, Bedouin, Christian, and Muslim. On the other hand, it frequently lapses into categorizing them all in relation to the core Jewishness of the state as "non-Jews." Indeed, the state policy of differentiation is constantly collapsing under the weight of larger Zionist imperatives, such as the appropriation of Arab land. The Druze are defined as a special and loyal minority who are conscripted into the military. Yet, like all other Arabs, they are subject to having their land expropriated for the good of the (Jewish) state. Given this schizophrenic treatment, state attempts to differentiate between subgroups seem half-baked.

The line between Palestinians inside Israel and Palestinians in the West Bank and Gaza, or those in nearby Arab countries, is also a line that is constantly drawn, erased, and redrawn, blurring, fading, and reemerging. By virtue of multiple wars and generations of subjection to different state powers, and with divergent and shared histories, Palestinians inside Israel are both linked to other Palestinians and disconnected from them. Sixty years of living in the state of Israel has made them into contradictory subjects: they are formally citizens, but inferior ones, struggling, marginalized, feared by the state yet largely Hebrew-speaking, passport-carrying, and bureaucracy-engaging. On Israeli independence day, or the Palestinian day of the Nakba or Catastrophe, some of them have been pressured into experimenting with waving the Israeli flag—non-Jews awkwardly holding up the large star of David, hoping that somehow the flag will protect them, bring them closer to the fold of the Jewish state. Others suffer the consequences of waving Palestinian flags, while still others forgo flag waving altogether.

All Palestinians in Israel, however, are forced at some level—sometimes mundane, at other times more profound—to engage in absurd and contradictory practices similar to the waving of the Israeli flag. This might be as simple as the legal requirement to carry ID cards at all times—cards covered with blue plastic embossed with a menorah on the outside and a nationality entry on the inside reading Muslim, Christian, Bedouin, or Druze (to be distinguished from Jewish, and never "Palestinian" or simply Israeli).[2] Palestinians inside Israel are constantly required to work within and show allegiance to a state that by definition views them as outsiders. They are forced to deal with a state that problematizes their very existence within its borders and prioritizes members of another religion, but constantly requires compliance, acquiescence, and paperwork.

A Snapshot

Consider the following snapshots. As an Arab student in Israel, you are required to study Hebrew, while your Jewish peers do not have to study Arabic. You are taught about Jewish literature and history, not Palestinian literature and history, and the security services oversee the appointment of your teachers. Upon graduating—if you make it that far—from an underfunded high school, you are not conscripted into the military as your Jewish counterparts are, unless you are Druze.[3] Because of your ethnicity you are "spared" the three years of mandatory service (or two if you are a woman), as well as all the benefits that are tied to that service. When you apply to a university—none of which is Arab in Israel—your Jewish co-applicants are given preference because they have completed military service. The student loans and scholarships available to you are inferior because you have not served in the military. The faculty club on campus is a former Palestinian home from a village erased from Israeli existence and even Arabic literature is taught in Hebrew.[4] You pick up an Israeli newspaper and the help-wanted ads call for veterans. You must pay extremely high taxes on privately owned land (the majority of Jews lease land from the state and do not own it privately) and all the forms are in Hebrew and everything is stamped with stars of David and menorahs. You likely live in one of the three main regions where Arabs now live—the Galilee, the Triangle, or the Naqab. Your village might be only occasionally marked on maps, or altogether unrecognized. The road signs to it, if there are any, are in Hebrew. Occasionally Arabic, usually misspelled, is added. If your village is recognized, its zoning maps were created by planners with the explicit goal of maximizing Jewish land and population. In mixed cities, where you are minoritized, Arabic street names have been changed to the Hebrew names of Zionist leaders or biblical figures. Housing prices in your neighborhood might be driven up by "gentrification-as-Judaization" and developers want to turn the old mosque down the road into a shopping mall.[5] You might work in construction, where "Arab work"[6] is the term used for inferior workmanship, or you might work as a doctor in a hospital where patients often express a strong preference for Jewish doctors. You might work as a cook in a Jewish restaurant opened in an old Arab home evacuated in 1948. Or you might be internally displaced yourself and employed doing renovation work on your relatives' former home that was emptied of your relatives and is now occupied by Jews.

Even if you are lucky enough not to encounter any individual prejudice—which is widespread—there is little room for doubt that you are at best, a second-class citizen. How do Palestinians deal with this? Which of the multitude of violations of their rights and identities that they face simply by existing in this colonized space do they decide to challenge? Moments after they are born, their nationality is registered in the hospital, and the marginalization begins.[7] Some of it becomes routinized and no longer given much thought since it would be nearly impossible to challenge every aspect of it. Other aspects of marginalization are of greater consequence—to income, opportunities, work options and conditions, travel, mobility, access. And yet, Palestinians in Israel have continued to play largely by the state's rules, in the state's game, despite—or perhaps also because of—decades of losing at that game.

The legal system in Israel has allowed and even mandated much of the injustice against Palestinians, from land expropriation to torture of political prisoners.[8] Palestinian rapper Tamer Nafar chants, "I broke the law? No, no, the law broke me."[9] Yet time and again Palestinians turn to that very same legal system to seek redress. This attempt to hold state institutions to their best conceivable potential began early after the establishment of the state. For example, after brutal military sweeps of the relatively few remaining Arab cities and villages in 1949, Palestinian residents cabled petitions to the Military Administration objecting to the behavior of soldiers during the sweeps.[10] Regional planning committees have the explicit goal of expanding Jewish land control and settlements in the Galilee and the Naqab. Yet Palestinians submit appeals and write letters to such committees in the hopes of keeping their land. The police shot and killed thirteen unarmed Palestinians, twelve of them citizens, during demonstrations in October 2000. Palestinians then placed their hopes on a government-appointed commission to hold the police accountable (none of the mildly reformative recommendations of this committee were carried out).[11] Two hundred thousand Palestinians live in villages not formally recognized by the state because it wants to relocate them to more concentrated locations (where they will occupy less land), and thus they do not receive water, electricity, education, or health care. Members of these communities then create nongovernmental organizations that attempt to advocate—through the usual Israeli channels—for formal recognition of their villages.

In his award-winning novel *The Secret Life of Saeed*, Palestinian writer Emile Habiby calls his protagonist Saeed a pessoptimist—a combination of pessimist and optimist. Luckless Saeed "saves his life by succumbing to the side that has the power."[12] Not unlike Saeed, most Palestinians inside Israel play by the unfair rules of the state's game. This is mostly because they lack other options. But it is also because somewhere in the Israeli story there is a promise, as fleeting, misleading, and unactualized as it is, of democracy. The Palestinian struggle to be included in the state—baffling as it is given repeated disappointments—seems to constitute the core of democracy in Israel (to the extent that it exists), rather than the state's practices or institutions. Time and again, Arabs try to succeed in a game in which they desperately grasp at rules that promise them contingent rewards, even as many other rules fundamentally foreclose that possibility.

A Military With a State Attached

Palestinian citizens who serve in the Israeli security forces are an extreme and rare example of this trend.[13] Mostly products of underfunded and badly staffed schools, with limited opportunities because they are Arab and don't serve in the military, they decide, of all things, to serve in the military, Border Guard, or police.[14] Numbering only a few thousand, they represent less than one percent of the Palestinian population.[15]

Military service lies at the extreme of a continuum of Palestinian strategies that range from collaboration and informing all the way to armed struggle against the state, with many different shades in between. The choice of soldiering is unpopular and rare and soldiers are considered traitors by the majority of Palestinians. But it is no coincidence that it is to the military that this small group turns in order to push the boundaries of their citizenship. For Israel is a military democracy at best. A Palestinian journalist friend put it this way: "Israel is not a country with a military and intelligence service attached to it, but a military and intelligence service with a country attached to it." Military service has enormous symbolic and material significance in Israel and has been a key institution in creating a sense both of Jewish belonging and of Palestinian marginalization.

Given the colonial settler history of the establishment of the state, "Israeli society was from the outset a 'war society' needing loyal and trained human power to help with the military effort."[16] The military has played a central nation-building role.[17] As the "workshop of the new nation," universal (read Jewish) conscription was used to create and socialize a new type of Jew.[18] Service in the military and participation in "the ritual of security" is a "second Bar Mitzvah," a crucial rite of passage to full Israeli citizenship that indoctrinates cohort after cohort of Israeli Jewish youth.[19]

This clearly does not apply to Palestinians living inside Israel. Indeed, the "holy quartet" of "Jewishness, masculinity, military service and collective membership" in Israel is actually defined against Palestinians.[20] The military "melting pot" excludes—first and foremost—Arab citizens.[21] According to Israel's "ethnic state security map," non-Jews are in fact *the* source of insecurity.[22] The state actively uses the criterion of military service to exclude most Arab citizens, while Jewish citizens who do not serve in the military can still reap the benefits available through alternative national service.[23] The ideal of universal conscription of Israeli Jews went hand in hand with the exemption of Palestinian citizens, creating an exclusive, imagined "community of warriors."[24] Equal citizenship rights for Palestinians are thus constructed as contingent on equal duties—military duties—which the state largely limits to Jews.[25] Discrimination against "non-conscriptable" Palestinian citizens is hence justified by linking it to their non-service in the military.[26]

It may be argued, however, that Jewish security requires and depends on the embodiment of Arabs as a source of insecurity in order to justify the continued centrality of the security apparatus. If Arab ethnicity

functions in Israel as a signifier of insecurity and illegality, and membership in the military as a signifier of security, then the Arab soldier in the
military is a security- and law-enforcer who must fight against the very
insecurity and illegality he (note the masculine pronoun) embodies and
of which he cannot entirely rid himself.[27] This attribution of insecurity to
all non-Jewish Arabs is an abiding framework for state management of all
of its Arab population, soldiers and otherwise.

The small group of men (and a few women) that is the focus of this
book offers a unique perspective on citizenship in Israel. These people
express at some level the hope of inclusion through military service. They
put Israel to a critical test: are these "good Arabs" who will go to almost
any length to become Israeli, allowed into the fold?[28]

2

Embattled Identities

EARLY ON IN MY STUDY I wrote to a prominent Israeli academic asking for his suggestions regarding my research on Palestinians serving in the Israeli armed forces. He emailed me back:

> I don't know what . . . you're talking [about]. Except [for] about a dozen . . . volunteers no Palestinians serv[e] in the Israeli military. Druze and Circassians are drafted and several hundreds of Bedouins (and perhaps some Arab Christians) serv[e] as volunteers. However [to the best of my] knowledge none of them perceived themselves as "Palestinian." If you're searching for ARABS in the Israeli military, this is another issue.

This brief note reflects the complex and contentious politics of naming when it comes to Palestinians living inside the 1948 borders of Israel. Although "Palestinian" is at one level a subcategory of the larger regional identity "Arab," there is potentially more meaning to one's choice of terms.

According to an Amazon book reviewer, an earlier book of mine was biased against the Israeli government because I refer "to Israeli-Arabs as 'Palestinians'—a label that is not only inaccurate but also deliberately offensive to Israelis." According to the reviewer, "in today's context, the term 'Palestinians' refers strictly to residents of the West Bank, Gaza, and displaced refugees outside of Israel. . . . Labeling Israeli-Arabs as

'Palestinians' is deliberately degrading to Israeli citizens, who consider Galilee Arabs to be of their own."[1]

This view is not atypical. It has roots in the fact that the state of Israel has historically avoided the term "Palestinian" because of the implied recognition of the existence of such a national group and its rights. Rather it has attempted to categorize Palestinians as divided into groups: Druze, Bedouins, Christians, and Muslims. This is an explicit policy articulated from early on, as in the conclusions of a 1949 Interministerial Committee on the integration of Arabs into the Jewish state: the committee decided that the best approach to Arabs should be to prevent them from coalescing into a single group and "the best way to deal with minorities was 'to divide and subdivide them.'"[2]

Israeli authorities attempted to consolidate their power by "feeding and reinforcing confessional loyalties until they eclipsed national feelings" and exacerbating inter-group tensions, disputes, and rivalries.[3] One of the ways these special minorities were created and re-created was through the military. Palestinian Druze historian Kais Firro argues that Israel's segmentation policy is intended to produce "good Arabs" (Druze, Bedouins, Christians, and a few others) in opposition to "bad Arabs" (the rest).[4] To put it very simply, the state has created a hierarchy within the Arab community: Druze are at the top, followed by Bedouins, and then Christians, with the remaining majority of non-Druze, non-Bedouin Muslims at the bottom as the least-favored type of citizen. By calling these groups Druze, Bedouins, Christians, and Arabs, the state tries to imply that the Druze, Bedouins, and Christians are other than Arab—or, as one Israeli journalist put it, "Arab lite."[5]

Druzification

This segmentation policy has singled out the Druze—8 percent of the Arab population in Israel—as a separate group to be Druzified and de-Arabized. Starting with the 1936 Arab rebellion, Zionists developed links with the Druze communities in Palestine and Syria, as part of their strategy of building alliances with non-Arab and non-Sunni Muslim communities against Arab nationalism. The continued Israeli cultivation of a so-called natural and "endemic animosity" between the Druze and the

Muslim majority prepared the way for the neutral or pro-Zionist stance most Druze in Palestine took during the 1948 war.[6] A "Minorities Unit" consisting of Druze and Bedouins who were used for sweeps of emptied Palestinian villages and in the expulsion of returned refugees exacerbated tensions between the Druze and other Palestinians.[7]

In 1956, Israeli government officials and a narrow elite of sixteen Druze leaders agreed upon mandatory military conscription for Druze men.[8] The purpose of this conscription is documented in the state's archives: it aimed to cut the ties between the Druze and other Arabs.[9] Initially there was strong opposition to conscription and only about a quarter of the Druze men called up appeared voluntarily.[10] But this opposition was mostly broken through a combination of persuasion and force.[11]

A year after the introduction of mandatory conscription, the Ministry of Religious Affairs gave the Druze a new status as an independent religious community rather than a sect of Islam.[12] Since then, Druze must register themselves with the Ministry of the Interior as being of "Druze nationality" rather than Arab. In 1961, the Druze religious leadership was recognized as an independent religious council and in 1963 the council was given autonomy in religious and family matters.[13] A separate Druze heritage was created whereby, for example, the state changed and separated Druze and Sunni Muslim religious holidays and ceremonies. This newly engineered heritage was taught in a separate Druze educational system created in 1976 to solve lingering "identity problems" among the Druze.[14]

Government efforts to deepen divisions between the Druze and other Arabs in Israel have included the extension of special benefits to the Druze: for instance, the selection of a relatively large number of Druze to run for parliament on government-controlled lists, the designation of some Druze villages as "development towns" with more generous budget allocations, and the appointment of Druze to government ministries and Jewish party organs.[15] The benefits also include the employment option of career military service, which has become an important source of financial security for roughly 30 percent of employed Druze citizens.[16]

Despite the special benefits Druze receive as a loyal minority, they continue to be treated as Arabs in most of their interactions with the state. For Druze villagers, inequalities with Jews in terms of land confiscation, municipal budgets, education, and employment, as well as discrimination in the army are constant reminders of their immutable Arabness in the eyes of the state.[17] The extensive confiscation of Druze land has led to calls among the Druze for a "Carmel intifada" (referring to the Carmel region, where several key Druze villages are located).[18] The privileging of the Druze is thus largely rhetorical and their de-Arabization is "deliberately incomplete."[19]

Bedouin Brothers-in-Arms

Another group in the Arab community that has been targeted by the state segmentation policy is the Bedouins.[20] Stereotyped as "nonpolitical" and "disinclined to follow political ideas or groups that might commit them to action not conducive to their tenuous existence," Bedouins have been figured as rootless nomads and "movable objects" that can be "easily evacuated from any given piece of land" when the state needs it.[21] As with the Druze, a few Bedouin leaders were cultivated during the pre-state period to secure their collaboration during the 1948 war.[22] Some cooperating families were allowed to remain within the emerging borders of the state though they were often relocated. However, unlike Druze villages, which were mostly spared expulsion, the Bedouin population of the Naqab was reduced by the end of 1948 to roughly one-fifth of its original size and in the Galilee to one-third.[23]

In line with its policy of dividing the Palestinian community, Israel has tried to emphasize divisions between Bedouins and other Palestinians and required the former, for example, to register their nationality on their ID cards as Bedouin rather than Arab.[24] Some Bedouins, particularly those from "friendly" tribes, are encouraged to volunteer to serve in the Israeli armed forces. Although the percentage of volunteers is small, Bedouins are celebrated as warriors and friends of the Jews in both popular and official discourse.

Even more than for the Druze, however, the benefits of this special relationship with the Jewish state have remained elusive. Military rule (imposed on most Palestinian communities until 1966), for example, was applied most harshly to the Naqab Bedouins.[25] In 1951, Israeli authorities physically evicted two-thirds of the remaining Naqab Bedouins and transferred them to a closed reservation area.[26] The state confiscated most of their land, prevented their flocks from grazing, and implemented a policy of "concentration by choice" that forced many Bedouins to settle in townships. To date, seven such townships have been established, saddled with an economic infrastructure that can only support landless migrant laborers.[27] All seven of the townships were among the eight poorest places in Israel in 2003.[28] There are plans for three more townships to absorb the remaining Naqab Bedouins, a population of 70,000, who have refused to move. This latter group of residents live in villages unrecognized by the government, and thus are denied basic services such as water, electricity, permanent housing (or with housing subject to demolition), health care, schools, roads, and an elected local government.[29] The same holds true for the unrecognized villages of the Galilee Bedouins, where residents are pressured to give up their land and relocate to designated townships.

As special allies of the state, Bedouins who serve in the military (a small minority) are described as the Jews' brothers-in-arms. Generations of them have served as trackers in the military and dozens have been killed in action. Yet Bedouins' crops on land the state claims as its own are burned with toxic chemicals. Their high fertility rates loom exceptionally large in the Israeli fears of the Arab demographic time bomb. Their economic status is the lowest and their unemployment rates are the highest in the country.[30] State officials voice their fears of a "Bedouin intifada," and view Bedouins as lawless trespassers and criminal "foreigners" invading state land and hence subject to the "expulsion of intruders" law.[31]

Other Special Minorities

To a lesser degree, Christians—10 percent of the Arab community—have also been identified as somehow other than Arab. The state has followed in the French (in Syria and Lebanon) and British traditions of trying to manipulate them along sectarian lines.[32] During the 1948 war, a small number of Christian villages were spared or returned after church officials with European connections appealed on their behalf. Christian (and Druze) returnees appear to have been less vulnerable than Muslims in terms of whether they would be allowed to remain.[33] Although there is no declared policy of recruiting Christians, rumors of preference for hiring Christians in the police force are widespread. And conflicts between Christians and Muslims are used as opportunities to recruit Christians into the military.

The state has also developed special ties with certain villages, often isolated ones, such as the cluster of villages near Jerusalem—Abu Ghosh, Bayt Naquba, and 'Ayn Rafa. Starting in 1919, some Abu Ghosh leaders collaborated with pre-state Jewish forces and were renowned for helping Zionist intelligence and military forces.[34] Abu Ghosh was one of the few Palestinian villages in the Jerusalem area whose residents were not expelled by Israeli forces during the 1948 war, although the majority of their lands were confiscated for Jewish use.[35] The residents of Bayt Naquba and 'Ayn Rafa were expelled from their villages, but subsequently some of them who remained in Abu Ghosh were allowed to resettle nearby.

A seemingly higher-than-average number of residents of these villages volunteer to serve in the security apparatus. Recently, a special Abu Ghosh commando unit was established with sixty "highly motivated" volunteers, and sixty more waiting to be enlisted.[36] Despite this atypical history vis-à-vis the state, these villages share with other Palestinian communities a pattern of "disenfranchisement and underdevelopment."[37]

Are They "Normal"?

Palestinians are a religiously and residentially diverse group; the terms "Druze," "Bedouin," "Christian," and "Muslim" are certainly used within the Palestinian community. And they are terms that I inevitably use to refer to the men and women I interviewed. However, these labels have been given different valences by the state's segmentation policy. As official state categories, they function as "an authoritative tune to which most of the population must dance"—all the more so among the small group of volunteers in the military.[38] This segmentation policy has produced new expressions of identity among the soldiers I interviewed. In addition to a few who call themselves "Palestinian" or "Palestinian Arab," other individuals call themselves "Israeli Arab," "Christian Israeli," "Muslim Arab," "Arab Bedouin," "Israeli Bedouin," "Zionist," "Arab formerly of Palestinian origin," or explain that "My identity card is Israeli, I'm an Arab, [and] Palestinian, but not all the time." These responses are clearly contextual; as might be expected, my own identification as Palestinian likely influenced the answers I heard.[39] But beyond my interviews, I found soldiers identifying in multiple and often contradictory ways.

Hasan al-Hayb is the mayor of the northern Bedouin village of Zarazir, a longtime member of the right-wing Zionist Likud Party, and a former officer in the Israeli army. Although he defined himself to me simply as "Israeli," he was widely cited among the soldiers I interviewed as having given an impassioned speech in which he insisted on a "Palestinian Arab" identity. This speech was delivered at the funeral of four Bedouin soldiers killed in service with the Israeli army by Palestinians near Gaza. Addressing the large funeral gathering that included many Jewish military and state officials, Mr. al-Hayb called on Israeli leaders to refrain from seeking revenge for the death of the four soldiers by essentially highlighting their shared identity with their killers from across the Green Line.[40]

Another of the soldiers I interviewed pointed out the flawed nature of my question on identity:

> Frankly, "How do you identify yourself?" is not a good question. It depends on where I am. If I am at the tax office or in the [Jewish] mall I'm not going to go around shouting, "Hey, look at me, I'm a Palestinian." I'm not stupid. There, I identify myself as an Israeli Arab. If you ask me here in my village among the people of the village, I'll tell you I'm a Palestinian Arab. Everybody tailors his answer to the situation he is in. This is the reality.

One of the policewomen I interviewed similarly highlighted the geographically specific and instrumentalist nature of national identity: "Being [a Palestinian] nationalist and patriotic *in this region* is stupid and ridiculous. It gets you nowhere" (emphasis added). Although national identities and loyalties are often regarded as primordial, these statements suggest that they are also recognized as contingent and shifting.

Messy Contradictions

These "bad Palestinians," as some might view them (or "good Arabs" as the state defines them), spoke extensively about contradictions, hesitations, dilemmas, regrets, and changes of mind. One of the men

I interviewed started out as an officer in the Arab Liberation Army, the irregular Arab volunteers who fought against Zionist forces during the 1948 war. His village of origin was one of the many emptied during the war, making him a refugee. After the war, he continued to "infiltrate" into Israel to visit his family, who now lived in a surviving village, and was repeatedly imprisoned and deported. Over the course of his many encounters with the military, this man eventually struck a deal whereby he would serve in the Israeli Border Guard and eventually receive Israeli residency.[41] When his commanding officer wanted to orient him to the area he would be patrolling, the soldier told him he was already familiar with it: "I've crossed this area so many times on foot." Part of his new job was to guard against "infiltrators" such as himself. Later, during the first intifada, he refused to sign on for a new contract after he was redeployed from the Lebanese border to the heart of Arab East Jerusalem.

As a former Druze officer who is now a leader in the movement to eliminate the Druze military draft put it, "Humans do not make free choices. Depending on their perceptions of the opportunities before them, they can put their eggs in different baskets." Writer Amitav Ghosh argues that the idea that individuals owe loyalty to a single political entity is probably historically recent, linked to the birth of the nation-state. Yet human loyalties "are, and always have been, diverse. People are capable of being faithful to many things at once: not just to their families, their kin, their compatriots. But also to their masters, their servants, their friends, their colleagues, and, sometimes, even their enemies."[42]

Such messiness is particularly easy to discern in colonial contexts. Indians in the British Indian Army were necessarily conflicted: "Emblazoned on the walls of the Indian Military Academy were the words 'The honour, welfare and safety of your country comes first, always and every time.' And yet what was the country to which a colonial soldier owed his allegiance? There was no political entity to which Indian soldiers could give their undivided, heartfelt allegiance."[43] The parallel with the allegiances of Palestinians in the Jewish state of Israel is easy to draw; the colonial history of the establishment of the state and its continued definition as a Jewish state make Palestinian allegiance to it inherently contradictory.

Asel Asleh, a teenager from my hometown of 'Arrabi, once reflected in a group email to his comrades on his experience at a Jewish–Arab "peacemakers" camp:

> For 40 days . . . I learnt about those people that I lived with. Now I know who my friends are. In a few years from now they will become soldiers. They will go to the army to protect their families. But will they stay the same? Will they be the same Edi or Tzachi that I knew? . . . What will happen if they become like those soldiers? And the duty will call them for what they call "protection"—what then?[44]

Two-and-a-half years later, Asel was shot and killed near his home by an Israeli policeman during the October 2000 mass demonstrations by Arab citizens. Also shot dead were twelve other young Palestinians, eleven of them citizens of Israel, not to mention scores of Palestinians in the West Bank and Gaza Strip.[45] The demonstrations began in protest against Israel's violent suppression and killing of demonstrators in the Occupied Territories at the beginning of the second intifada and lasted several days. They also became directed against the police's use of lethal force against Palestinian citizens. Palestinians in Israel felt that they were still "at square one," with the state treating them as a threatening fifth column.[46] Asel's reflections did not rule out the scenario of his death, but what he did not ponder was that an Arab might have been "that soldier."

Many people from the nearby town of Sakhnin initially believed that the policeman who killed two young men from the village, Walid Abu Saleh and 'Imad Ghanaim, might have been an Arab. This turned out not to be the case, but the fact that Sakhnin residents found this rumor credible shows that an Arab policeman or soldier was considered capable of firing on Arab citizens.[47] An Arab policeman from Dayr al-Asad suspected of killing one of the Arab citizens was forced to leave his village for fear of possible retaliation by the victim's family. In the village of Jatt, Arab patrolman Murshad Rashad killed another of the Arab citizens. He fired a rubber bullet from close range at twenty-one-year-old Rami Jarra that penetrated his face.[48] Beyond the October 2000 events, an Arab soldier shot Iman al-Hams, a thirteen-year-old school girl from Gaza, "pumping multiple M-16 bullets into [her] . . . at close range while she lay in a gully."[49] The reputation of Arab soldiers in the West Bank and Gaza is actually that of the most brutal Israeli soldiers of all.

Like many other Palestinians, Asel saw Israel's security ethos and system as major obstacles dividing Arabs and Jews. Yet at least fifteen of Asel's fellow villagers, some of them his classmates, at some point chose to enlist in this security system.[50] Although the military officially acknowledges that the number of recruits among Bedouins, for example, declined after October 2000, several young men from Asel's and my hometown of 'Arrabi joined after the Israeli police had killed the thirteen Palestinians in Israel, including two boys killed from our very village.[51]

Fadi, a soldier from 'Arrabi who was in the army during these events, described how he feared for his safety in the village at the time and tried to keep a low profile. He stopped wearing his uniform or carrying his gun when in the village. He described how his superiors promised him housing in one of the nearby Jewish settlements—a privilege not allowed to an Arab under normal circumstances.[52] Yet Fadi also feared for his safety in Jewish areas; even in military uniform he was not safe from the communal violence that was taking place. Many soldiers, among them Fadi, told stories of attacks on Arabs, including uniformed Arab policemen and soldiers, by angry Jews at a mall near Haifa and in Tiberias. Those attacked reportedly included the brother of high-profile 'Omar Sawa'id, the Bedouin soldier captured by Hezbollah that month and hailed as an Israeli hero. Like his physical safety in October, Fadi's loyalties and sense of belonging were complicated.

Hani, another man I interviewed, had completed three years of basic service in the army and then joined the police force, where he had worked for the last five years. He stressed that "I continue to support and vote for the Communist Party. I've never stopped supporting it and its ideals of peace and equality. Even when my friends from the party stopped talking to me, or even stopped saying hello to me when I passed them on the street, I still support their party because I believe in what it says." Hani is aware that the Communist Party has repeatedly condemned Palestinian enlistment in the army. At some level, Hani ideologically condemns himself.

My interview with another soldier, Shafiq, illustrates the contradictions implicit (and sometimes explicit) in strategies of identification. Shafiq is from a village known as a stronghold of Palestinian nationalism, with martyrs (a term many Arabs use to describe any Palestinian killed in the Israeli–Palestinian conflict) both from Land Day in 1976 (strikes to protest government-planned, massive land confiscations) and from October 2000. Shafiq's family was politically marginal: his father served in the army for seventeen years, and all five of his sons became career soldiers or policemen. During the annual Land Day protests, a routine stop on the marchers' path is Shafiq's family home, where shouts of "Shame, shame to the agents of colonialism!" (Arabic, *kul il-khizy w-kul il-ʿār la-ʿumalāʾ il-ʾistiʿmār*) can be heard and an occasional stone even pelts the front door. But Shafiq is not an outsider in his village. He lives there, he bought land from a respectable family there, he married the daughter of another local mainstream family, he has friends there, he shops there, and so on. Yet his strategies of identification set him apart:

> I consider myself a Zionist. I studied history in high school and I read the history of the Jews and of Zionism and that encouraged me to go down this path. I entered the army with the motivation of defending the state, the law. I am an individual in this state, and it is my right to defend everything in it.

After minimal prodding from me, however, Shafiq admitted that his military service was not perfect:

> My service had some negative aspects, in some periods. It depends on the leadership at the time. If their horizons are wide, then they don't differentiate between Jew and non-Jew. But if someone comes along bringing ideas from his home, then he discriminates. Such people behave as though they don't believe or trust what you tell them, and that is very difficult for me psychologically. But I never gave up and I fought and enlisted those around me to change the bad things [such as discrimination], and in many cases, I won.

To my surprise, Shafiq sometimes sounded more mainstream than one would expect from an "agent of colonialism":

> It is very easy to see that there are no Arab officers at the very highest rank. This is because the state is still considered Jewish. If it were a secular democratic state for all its citizens, then there could be an Arab commander-in-chief or an Arab president. But recently some Druze have reached very high ranks, ranks we could not dream of before. These men are privy to many of the secrets of the state. It is not unrealistic that in ten, fifteen, or twenty years there will be real decision makers in this state who are Arab.

Shafiq emphasized that "I am very different from my father [who had also served in the army]. He is very attached to the idea that he is Arab and Muslim. I am more open. That stuff doesn't matter to me. I'm a human being just like anyone else, that's all that matters."

In these few sentences, Shafiq presented a variety of positions: desire for a secular democratic state of its citizens, allegience to Zionism, criticism of the Jewishness of the state, an understanding of citizenship as defined by participation in military secrets and war, a view of racism as private rather than institutional, and finally, a self-identification that is humanistic rather than nationalist or religious. These contradictory positions succeed to different degrees and in different contexts in allowing Shafiq to "make sense" to me as well as to people in his village. Both Shafiq and Hani consider themselves to be "nationalists"—a word that always means different things to different people in different places.

Gentle Force

The soldiers I interviewed were clearly aware that their soldierly duties are repugnant to most Palestinians. When one mediator told a soldier that I was interested in studying Arabs serving in the Israeli military, his immediate response was defensive: "Why? We don't harm anyone." In my opinion, one of the less successful ways Arab soldiers tried to sanitize their military or police service was by stressing their efforts to be "fair" and "good" to Arabs while performing their duties. Yet many of these duties were, by their community's definition inherently unfair to Arabs.

All the soldiers I interviewed claimed not to harm anyone unnecessarily and not to carry out their missions brutally. Some even argued that they were being patriotic by monitoring and moderating the excesses of their Jewish comrades.[53] I heard several stories from men in the Border Guard of shooting in the air rather than at "infiltrators" who had come across the Lebanese border; they didn't kill despite their orders to do so. Fadil urged me to use a picture of him (see Figure 1), sitting in his jeep, pouring cold water from his canister for a thirsty Palestinian woman on a hot day. The photograph was taken in Gaza during a deployment of Palestinian troops under the Oslo Accords. The image was clearly cherished by Fadil, who otherwise spoke of nightmares from the "things you see in the army but have to keep quiet about."

FIGURE 1 *Soldier giving water to a Palestinian woman in Gaza. Photographer unknown.*

Bassam told me how, while he was stationed at the border crossing with Gaza, he often helped Arabs, especially Arab women, cross into Israel for work:

> The other [Jewish] soldiers didn't speak Arabic and the women couldn't speak Hebrew. So we would intervene to work things out. Often, we would let the women pass on our own personal responsibility. They would always thank us, and shower us with blessings. When they returned in the evening they would often bring us boxes of fruit from their work [as seasonal fruit pickers]. We were swimming in guavas the whole season.

Some policemen stressed their generosity in assisting friends and acquaintances in "dealing with traffic tickets" or getting out of trouble with the law—practices of personal influence or corruption known as *wasṭa*, long fostered by the state as part of its segmentation policy.[54] Among the soldiers I interviewed, this emphasis on making a kinder, gentler military force was stretched the farthest by Mahmud, a young man who served for three years in a unit trained to go undercover as Arabs, infiltrate Palestinian areas, and capture wanted individuals. As an Arab somehow going "undercover" as an Arab, he seemed to find redemption in the smallest gestures: he described how, during night raids on homes, he would always carry some candy in his pocket to calm down the terrified children of raided households.[55] These deployments, as unsuccessful as they may have been, illustrate the conflicted position these soldiers find themselves in.

Exceptional Soldiers?

Human rights lawyer Hassan Jabareen notes that in Israeli security institutions, "Arabs are asked to prove their loyalty to the Jewish collective in Israel and not to the state as a neutral actor. It is thus a loyalty to another people."[56] Many of my interviewees argue that this is not unique to security institutions, which are only a microcosm of the state as a whole: "How do you think you can get ahead as a schoolteacher? By teaching the poetry of Samih al-Qasim or Mahmoud Darwish? No, you have to lower your head and march with the flow. It's the same with the national health insurance system, the same everywhere." Another soldier insisted that there are no "pure" or "clean" Arabs in Israel, since "we all pay taxes which are eventually used to buy tanks and warplanes. Even the Arabs in the other countries, they sell their gas; it's that gas that makes the Israeli tanks in Gaza go." Another told me: "How can that man criticize us when he is [a construction worker] building Jewish homes on stolen Arab land? He built fifty stories in Tel Aviv." A widely circulated rumor had it that a major supplier of cement for the illegal wall being built to physically imprison Palestinians in the Occupied Territories was a member of the Palestinian National Authority. While these arguments can be used to depoliticize, and thus justify, any behavior, they also highlight the deeply contradictory position Palestinians in Israel find themselves in.

These contradictions are particularly visible among the soldiers, but thoroughly transcend that group. Mohammad Abu al-Hayja is the founder of the Association of Forty, an organization fighting for the rights of the Arab unrecognized villages in Israel. But he was also a construction worker in the now-Jewish village of Ein Hod from which his family was displaced in 1948. He thus participated in the process of transforming the homes of his former village into refurbished homes, galleries, and restaurants for the Zionist Dada artists who now occupy the village.[57] Women displaced from al-Birwe village had to work as cheap laborers for Jewish bosses on their own confiscated land.[58] My relative Abu-'Atif is employed by the Jewish National Fund to guard olive orchards, including his own orchards confiscated from him by the government. He sees to it that nobody harms the trees or the crops that others planted on the land he still contests.[59] These contradictions are of course not limited to Palestinians inside Israel. Palestinians in the West Bank and Gaza Strip have, for example, been placed in the conflicted position of "building other people's homes"—of working as construction laborers on Jewish settlements.[60]

Identity is malleable not only among marginal groups such as the soldiers. A sample of Palestinian university students in Israel in 1989 gave the following responses to the question "How would you define yourself?": "Palestinian in Israel," 43.5 percent; "Palestinian Arab," 25.7 percent; "Israeli Palestinian," 10.6 percent; "Palestinian Arab in Israel," 5.5 percent; "Palestinian," 4.5 percent; "Arab," 4.1 percent; "Israeli," 2.7 percent; "Other," 2.1 percent; "Israeli Arab," 1.4 percent.[61] Significantly, the term "Palestinian" appears in some form in 88.4 percent of the responses. Yet the data also suggest that there is rarely consensus on self-definitions. Surveys conducted by the Israeli Institute for Peace Research at Givat Haviva show strong fluctuations in the responses of their sample of Arabs in Israel: 63.2 percent of those interviewed found the term "Israeli" appropriate to their self-identity in 1995, compared to 32.8 percent in 1999.[62] The fact that the political scene includes a sizable "Israeli Arab" camp that preaches integration with Jewish Zionist parties, accepts Arabs' junior status in them, and "emphasizes the Israeli component of the Arabs without demanding that the State modify its character" illustrates the wide spectrum of strategies—often contradictory—that Palestinians have chosen.[63]

These strategies change over time. Hisham Naffa', a journalist and activist of Druze origin who served two years in prison because of his refusal to enlist, explained to me:

> I don't consider national identity essential or natural, but when you have a policy aiming deliberately at dividing and ruling, as in the policy to produce a non-Arab Druze identity, then you are imposing something that's only in

the interest of the Jewish majority. . . . After Oslo and with access to the world of satellite channels, all of a sudden, people—including hard-core [Druze] Likudniks who said for many years "the Druze are not Arabs," "the Arabs are our enemies"—are today saying "we are Arabs and we are Muslims." They have made a full about-turn. They want to get a piece of the Oslo pie.

In the West Bank and Gaza Strip, as inside the Green Line, "collaboration" and "loyalty" cannot be treated as uncomplicated categories. During the first intifada, Palestinians in the Occupied Territories often took severe measures against those suspected of questionable loyalties or of "collaboration" with the occupier. It was reported that 777 Palestinians were killed by other Palestinians on suspicion of collaboration between 1987 and 1993.[64] Oddly enough, Palestinians working as policemen under Israeli rule were not automatically included in this category. At the outbreak of the intifada in 1987, the grassroots Unified National Command of the Uprising ordered all Palestinians in the territories serving in the Israeli police force to resign. The few who did not agree and who worked as active collaborators in security matters were targets of violence—at least seven of them were killed during the intifada. Those who resigned in response to the appeals and warnings were rarely harmed. The PLO even compensated all the policemen who resigned, providing them with monthly salaries. Former policemen and officers in the Israeli police were even appointed to senior positions under the Palestinian National Authority: a former officer in the Israel police, for example, was appointed to head the Palestinian police committee in Gaza.[65]

That these Arab identities are messy, contradictory, and conflicted should not be interpreted as a sign of an identity crisis. Rather, they are standard and human loyalties are generally more complicated than they appear. Dominant identities such as that of "Israeli Jew" are also not free of contradiction.[66] The recently prominent Israeli Jewish "refuseniks" who have declined to serve in the West Bank and Gaza Strip were attacked by other Israelis as part of a fifth column or as anti-Semites. Some Israeli Jewish soldiers from lower socioeconomic backgrounds, especially Mizrahi (Oriental or Eastern Jewish) soldiers, consider their earnest privileged fellow soldiers as dupes of the state.[67] Russian Jewish men continue to value their evasion of the state, and gay Israeli Jewish men negotiate the disjunctures between their sexuality and national identifications.[68] These examples show that national identity and its relationship to the state, to borders, to ethnicity, to gender, class, and sexuality are, more often than not, "embattled."

Israeli television Channel 2 broadcast a documentary on the soccer team of Tuba, a Bedouin village in the north. In the middle of the final match against the team from Migdal (now a Jewish town), national and football tensions escalated. Tuba soccer fans stopped waving the Israeli flag they carried at the beginning of the match and deliberately folded it away in front of the camera. These Tuba fans, like the Arab Likudniks, activists, and soldiers mentioned above, demobilize and remobilize Palestinianness, Arabness, and Israeliness in various combinations. Their mobilizations are informed at some level by the "basket" at hand—not being harassed at a mall, "getting somewhere" *in this region*, or wanting a piece of the Oslo pie—the parameters of which are often set by the state.

The question then becomes: how effective are these different performances and what have the various strategies achieved? What have the strategies of integration into a Zionist state afforded the "Israeli Arab" political parties? What have Palestinian soldiers gained? While departing from a narrow nationalist paradigm, such questions are not necessarily apolitical or judgment free. My findings do not attempt to mask my personal opposition to military service, but rather present a more serious engagement with this issue than accusations of "collaboration" allow. In any case, in posing these questions, the incredible creativity of the marginalized in trying to escape that marginality becomes apparent. Trying so many different strategies, they attempt to work their way out, under, over, and through the limits they face.

3

Conditional Citizenship

IF YOU HAPPEN TO BE BORN TO A JEWISH MOTHER almost anywhere in the world, you automatically gain the right to Israeli citizenship. You are entitled to immigrate to and settle in Israel with the aid and assistance of the state.[1] An almost sacred law in Israel, the Law of Return, guarantees you this. If you are born to non-Jewish parents in Israel, then your citizenship is regulated by a different set of laws. In order to be a citizen, one of your non-Jewish parents must be an Israeli citizen. If you are unlucky enough to have a Palestinian parent from the Occupied Territories, your chances of getting Israeli citizenship are close to zero.

For Palestinians in Israel, citizenship is "a conditional privilege to be conferred by the state."[2] Because the state represents the Jewish collective, all Palestinians are considered essentially alien; their rights to citizenship or equality are not rights at all—in the sense of rights present at birth.[3] Rather, they are contingent privileges to be potentially partially dispensed (or withheld) by the state, based on its satisfaction that individual Palestinians have fulfilled particular conditions, usually service in the military or security apparatus.

Tiered "Martial Citizenship"

There are dozens of Bedouins in the southern Naqab region who are not considered Israeli citizens and remain stateless. Some of them have served in the Israeli military. Of these soldiers with no citizenship, some have never left the borders of the country. Others were removed outside the borders of Israel in the early 1950s and then subsequently "infiltrated" back and were allowed to join the military. In 1998, a large group of Bedouins from the 'Azazma tribe attempted to return to the Naqab—some 800 of them were thrown back into Sinai in Egypt, but a few who could prove they had served in the army or helped the Israeli state in other ways were allowed to remain. They were given no status but were "allowed to be illegals."[4]

A publication of the Ministry of Defense admits that in "not a few instances" Bedouins who had served in the military for years did not receive a certificate of military completion, while others discovered upon submission of administrative requests that they were not Israeli citizens.[5] Assistants to Talab al-Sani', an Arab Parliament member from the Naqab, told me that their office often receives appeals for help from "people who have served in the military, are still serving, and carrying a weapon, and at the same time don't have citizenship."

The Association for Civil Rights in Israel has been involved in advocating for these stateless Bedouins to receive residency or citizenship. Their efforts have been largely unsuccessful. The association has used a number of arguments to try to persuade Israeli officials and the public.[6] Perhaps the most effective strategy emphasizes that these individuals (or their fathers or brothers) have served in the military and therefore deserve to be helped. A recent article in *Haaretz* discusses the case of Shtewi Srahin,

> one of dozens of Azazma former scouts who served in or worked for the army in the 1970s. Not only do they receive no pension or aid from the military, they don't have Israeli identity cards, they don't have health insurance, they don't get National Insurance stipends. . . . They were Israeli enough for the IDF [Israeli Defense Forces]. Just not Israeli enough to get identity cards.[7]

Of all the legal and humanitarian arguments used to advocate for this group, the one that they have served in the military and therefore should be rewarded with some rights receives the most sympathy from the Israeli Jewish public. With this conception of "martial citizenship," the argument that their relatives who have not served in the military should also be accorded the same status is summarily dismissed.[8]

Some ID-less men who had served in the military hired private lawyers and managed to negotiate individual arrangements with the government to grant them residency or citizenship. Their story is not unlike that of the man who started out as an officer in the Arab Liberation Army during the 1948 war, and then after becoming a refugee, made his way into the Israeli Border Guard. He was able, after years of struggle, multiple imprisonments, deportations, and "re-infiltrations" to strike an individual bargain whereby he was granted citizenship in exchange for his service. Individual arrangements such as this are part of the ad hoc patronage system common in the military. Although a few soldiers have been granted citizenship or residency, this has been done without legislation or the setting of legal precedence for such a right.

Not only are citizenship rights granted to Palestinians based on the satisfaction of certain conditions, but the reverse is also true: Palestinians in Israel can be stripped of their citizenship—as unequal as it is—if they are considered to have broken certain conditions. On September 9, 2002, then interior minister Eli Yishai revoked the citizenship of Nihad Abu Kishik, a Palestinian citizen accused (though not convicted) of aiding a suicide bomber.[9] It is noteworthy that a previous interior minister declined to revoke the citizenship of Yigal Amir, an Israeli Jewish citizen convicted of assassinating Prime Minister Yitzhak Rabin, because such a decision would be an extreme and drastic measure.[10]

Another example of the linking of citizenship to military service is the recent easing of Israel's restrictive immigration policy for (non-Arab) non-Jews who complete military service. In 2003, immigrants who self-identify as Jews but are not recognized as such by traditional Jewish law (usually because their mothers are not Jewish) were granted citizenship if they served at least twelve months in the military.[11] The Jewish Agency applauded the move, noting that these individuals had "completely fulfilled their military obligations. Many, who were killed and wounded, paid a heavy price for their right to return to their homeland."[12] Unlike state-recognized Jews, whose citizenship is automatic, those the state does not consider Jewish (but who are not Arab) must pay a price to potentially acquire this status.[13]

Another reform granted citizenship to the children of foreign migrant laborers (who are not Jewish and not Arab) who complete military service. Their parents and younger siblings would be granted only temporary residency, with the latter becoming eligible for citizenship upon completion of military service. Bondi Paebon, the nineteen-year-old son of Thai workers in Israel, exclaimed, "Enlisting means that my life is beginning."[14]

Other countries similarly link citizenship to military service. For example, a large contingent of "green card forces" who serve in the United States military are allowed to speed up the process of acquiring American citizenship in exchange for military service.[15] In the Israeli case, however, immigration reforms do not apply to all noncitizens. Palestinian noncitizens are specifically excluded from them and have no legislated access to military-contingent citizenship. They are legally barred from this system and, as I have stated, are only rarely granted access through individual ad hoc arrangements, as the few stateless Bedouins who gained citizenship were able to do.

Rights and Jewish Duties

Some might argue that although citizenship is automatically granted to Jews in Israel, they in return must shoulder the burden of performing mandatory military service. This model of rights in exchange for duties is held up as the legitimate basis for the two-tiered citizenship system in Israel: privileged Jewish citizenship is justified by the military duties Jews must perform, while the weaker, more circumscribed citizenship of Palestinians is linked to their release from military duties. In other words, Palestinians don't have equal duties, so it stands to reason that they don't have equal rights. This makes basic rights accorded to Jews conditional for Palestinians. It also ignores the fact that Palestinians as a group were never asked whether they wanted to serve in the military; their exemption has been the state's choice.

Many Jewish women—some 40 percent of draft-age Jewish women—are granted exemptions from military service. These exemptions are framed as alternative contributions to the Jewish nation. Women are exempt, for example, if they are pregnant or have children. Their contributions are conceived of as reproducing the Jewish nation.[16] As former parliament member Geula Cohen put it, the Jewish woman "is a wife and a mother in Israel, and therefore it is of her nature to be a soldier, a wife of a soldier, a sister of a soldier, a grandmother of a soldier—this is her reserve service. She is continually in military service."[17]

Starting soon after the establishment of Israel, the state also granted many religious Jews, known as Haredim or ultra-Orthodox, exemptions from military service and instead paid them to complete their religious studies.[18] This is in part a product of the fact that religious Jews are seen as offering an alternative contribution to the Jewish nation.[19] Since the only attribute common to the Jewish nation is the Jewish religion, if Zionism is to purport to speak for that nation, it acutely needs the bearers and symbols of religion to legitimate itself.[20] Not only are Haredi men exempt from military service in exchange for their spiritual and symbolic contributions, but they are also accorded many benefits similar to those granted to Jews who have completed military service.

While this exemption has been periodically debated in Israel, it remains very much intact. Some of the legal challenges to it drive home precisely the fact that what is at stake in discussions of Israeli citizenship are contributions to the Jewish nation and not to a neutral state. In a 1983 High Court case, an Arab citizen argued that the granting of social benefits to yeshiva students similar to those received by citizens who have served in the military in effect discriminates against Arabs who do not receive such benefits.[21] The court responded by defending the vital contribution of yeshiva students to Zionist goals, comparing its importance to that of performing military service.[22] The court insisted that the case involved two groups (Arabs and ultra-Orthodox) that were unequal from the start, thus justifying different treatment.[23] Whereas religious Jews were incorporated into the community of citizens by exemption from military service, the same principle of military exemption was used to exclude Palestinian citizens.[24] Debate on military service and its alternatives in Israel makes it clear that the service in question is to the Jewish collective.

In another High Court case, two non-religious Jewish members of parliament requested that yeshiva students be subject to the military draft.[25] They argued for this on the ostensibly comprehensive grounds of the violation of the principle of equality of all citizens. Yet they did not request the conscription of Palestinian citizens. The court, in turn, did not note the absence of Palestinians in the case nor did religious leaders.[26] Apparently, equality of all citizens means equality of all Jewish citizens only.

Professor Raphael Israeli of the Hebrew University has testified to an official commission that the state must adopt a citizenship test revolving around an individual's willingness to serve Zionist ideology. Only those who pass the test should be given the rights of citizenship.[27] This specific recommendation has technically not been implemented, but it reflects the principle underlying much of political discourse and practice in Israel. It captures the contingency of Palestinian citizenship and the hierarchal access to rights. Palestinians are not part of the unmarked "all citizens" and are excluded from the definition of the common good. Palestinian demands for equal rights are dismissed by pointing to their unequal duties, duties they have no role in choosing and that are imposed on them by the narrow ethno-religious definition of the state as a state of and for the Jews. This logic unsubtly places the blame for discrimination against Arabs on Arabs themselves.[28]

After the deaths of thirteen Arabs at the hands of Israeli police in October 2000, the Or Commission of Inquiry was established and eventually made a series of recommendations for reforms "designed to reassure Arab citizens that they were valued by their state." Subsequently, the Sharon government followed up by creating another panel, this time called the Lapid Committee, packed with "rightwing cabinet ministers, many of whom had objected to the establishment of the Or Commission in the first place."[29] The Lapid Committee proceeded to ignore almost all of Or's recommendations and proposed instead "that Arab citizens should be required to perform some kind of national service, in parallel to the military service currently done by some Jews, before considering their claims for equal rights."[30] Even this recommendation was quickly forgotten by the government.[31]

Similar suggestions for creating some kind of alternative service/duties for Arabs in Israel have abounded. In the 1988 elections "three right-wing Jewish political parties demanded that national service for Palestinian citizens become a condition for their enjoyment of full citizenship."[32] In 1997, Amnon Rubenstein, a parliament member considered leftist in Israel, (unsuccessfully) proposed a Social and Community Volunteer Service Law to regulate national service for Palestinian citizens.[33]

National service has thus been a recurring theme—never fully implemented, but used as a sort of threat to Palestinian citizens. The Jewish
majority has not required military or national service of Palestinian citizens, while using their absence as a justification for Jewish privileges.

In 1996 the Association for Civil Rights in Israel filed a petition
on behalf of a Jewish man and two Arab women requesting that they
be allowed to volunteer for national service, then limited only to Jewish
women.[34] The association argued that the petitioners' request to serve in
national service arose from the desire "to feel a sense of belonging and
make a contribution to society."[35] The petition continues: "a person who
has not served in the military or performed national service is destined to
encounter many obstacles and hardships, such as the denial of state benefits, difficulties in being accepted at work places, and social stigma."[36]
The solution proposed by the association was to introduce the option of
national service as an (inferior) alternative to military service. Arab organizations pointed out that to have a human rights organization raise this
issue reinforces the dominant connection between rights and duties and
further weakens the civil status of the majority of Palestinians who would
not opt to perform voluntary national service.[37]

National service is not considered equivalent to military service and
is unlikely to garner those who complete it equal rights. Even among
those who perform military duties, there is a hierarchy of privileges, with
combatants placed at the top.[38] The same Association for Civil Rights in
Israel that argued for national service to improve the lot of Arabs, advocated in another case just two years earlier the right of Jewish women to
be included in an air force pilot's course during their military service.[39]
The message transmitted in this latter case was that "equal and complete
citizenship is dependent on contribut[ing] to the military and on proximity to it."[40]

Pilot national service programs have been implemented in a number of Palestinian villages, and have periodically become the subject of
discussion there.[41] The Arabic press has raised a wide range of objections—including that it will ultimately lead to military service, that the
principle of rights should not be contingent on duties, that the promise
of equality through service cannot be believed because conscripted Druze
have failed to attain equality, and that national service is a ploy by the

government to spend even less money in Arab communities by using national service recruits to provide basic services there. However, the most common Palestinian objection to national service is captured by a commentary titled "Serving Which Nationality and Which Nationalism Exactly?!" It points to the absurdity of the requirement that non-Jews serve Jewish national goals that marginalize them by definition.[42] Proposals for national service for Arabs figure them not as indigenous people who were forced to become a minority in Israel, but as outsiders to the state needing to legitimate their citizenship.[43]

It is within this context of contingent rights for non-Jews in exchange for duties to the Jewish nation that Palestinians join the Israeli military. The Ministry of Defense makes the following promise to all soldiers about to complete their three years of military service: "After you have fulfilled your duty to the state, the administration of the Ministry of Defense feels it is our duty and deep privilege to help you integrate into social and economic life."[44] The promise of improved rights for Arab soldiers is widely repeated in Israel. Colonel Arik Regev tried to convince soldiers who were unsure about signing up for five additional years of service after the 1967 war by saying "whoever serves during this period with the regular army will have a right in the state like the rights of a prime minister."[45]

An Arab policewoman I interviewed framed her service as follows: "Some people say, 'Let me take first, then I'll give.' I don't know if I'm right, but I'm saying I want to give first before I can ask to take. Maybe I'm naïve, but isn't it better to improve [used Hebrew, *nishaper*] our situation in the meantime?"[46] Even critics of military service for Arabs accept this linkage to some extent. A social worker told me, "They are crazy if they expect Arabs to serve in the military when we are second- or third-class citizens. Equal duties come after equal rights, not before." While they do not represent the entire spectrum of Palestinian opinion, both the social worker and the policewoman closely associated rights with duties, although they differed in the order in which they placed them.

4

Material Upgrade

> The truth is we want the wages, the
> benefits from the state, the land.
>
> *Hatim, from Kufur Kanna,*
> *served in the military for three years*

SOLDIERING IN THE ISRAELI MILITARY IS DANGEROUS, perhaps even more so for Arab soldiers, whose fatality rates are claimed to be higher. It is also unpopular—Arab soldiers are widely criticized in their communities as traitors. They serve in the military of a state that colonized them and that is fighting other Palestinians only a few miles away. So why do hundreds of Arabs volunteer to join the Israeli security apparatus?

To a large extent, the answer is economics. Despite the political nature of the decision, the majority of soldiers I interviewed argued that material conditions were their primary motivation. Major political events such as the Oslo agreements in the 1990s, the October 2000 killings of unarmed Palestinian citizens, or the death of co-villagers do not appear to be clearly linked to a change in the number of Arab volunteers. I asked Haitham, a middle-aged policeman from the Abu Ghosh area near Jerusalem, what effect he thought the Oslo Accords had on the number of Arabs volunteering for the military and police. I thought that optimism for a possible peace settlement between Israel and the PLO at that time might have meant a slight increase in the number of Palestinian citizens joining the Israeli military. But Haitham explained to me that "Oslo is not relevant. Those who are looking for work don't think about that kind of thing." The few statistics available on the number of Arab volunteers over the years do not suggest an overwhelming correlation between Arab enlistment rates and particular political events.[1] Haitham put it simply, "They ask me, 'Why do you work for the police?' I say the pay is 5,000 shekels a month. Find me a job that pays 6,000 a month and I won't work for the police."

Work for the Unemployed

The explanation of Fadi, a young soldier in his second year of service, of how he became a soldier is similar to many of the other narratives I heard during my research. Fadi recounted how after graduating from high school, he searched for work in vain even though he had successfully completed his matriculation exams. He then worked with his father in construction for two years, at the end of which they went bankrupt. It is only then that he turned to the possibility of joining the military. He was in love with and engaged to Layla but had limited economic prospects. Like many Arabs in the region, Layla's parents would not let their daughter get married until her prospective husband had built a house. Having no land to inherit, Fadi would have to buy a piece of property to build on. In addition to the approximately $100,000 it would cost to build a house, the market rate for the standard legal-sized plot in Fadi's village was about $70,000. Such steep property prices are the result, as Fadi himself points out, of the government's explicit policy of limiting the physical expansion of Arab communities, thus making what little land that is zoned residential rare and expensive: "They don't want Arab villages to grow and develop, but I'm going to grow and develop."[2] Military service promised to lighten this financial burden significantly.

> I want to guarantee my future—I want a plot of land. I'm going to finish my three years [of service] and that's it. Once I get a certificate of discharge, that's it. I want that piece of paper with a stamp on it in my hand. . . . There is this book they give you when you finish service and it has all the details of your rights. . . . The list includes a permit to build and two types of loans. Then I can march into the village municipality and just point to a piece of land on the map. I can choose where I want it . . . and I'll have the highest priority of anyone in the village. . . . My fiancée has always wanted to continue her education. Now she can enroll at the army's expense.

His future father-in-law told me that Fadi "has no options; he tried find-ing other work but couldn't. Like every man, he wants to build his future and start a family, and this is the way he found. He might regret it later, but now he is forced to take this economic opportunity."

Fadi's narrative centers on his failure to find other work and his need for land and housing assistance. This is not surprising given that Arab citizens of Israel fare significantly worse than their Jewish counterparts on all economic indicators. Using the United Nations' Human Devel-opment Index, the Arab minority in Israel ranks sixty-sixth, forty-three slots below the general ranking of Israel.[3] The "economic opportunity" of soldiering is a product of state policies that include the confiscation of Arab lands (including some of the land previously owned by Fadi's fam-ily), Ministry of the Interior planning that seeks to Judaize seized land, discriminatory employment policies, segregated and hierarchical educa-tion systems, differential treatment by welfare agencies, and the linking of citizenship rights to military service.[4]

The majority of the soldiers I interviewed, though not all, saw their decision to join the military not as a first choice but, lacking other alter-natives, as a necessity. An older retired soldier, Sharif, presented his path to soldiering as a last resort:

> I worked six or seven years in a kibbutz as an agricultural worker, in the chicken coop, and then there was a lot of unemployment in Israel and they fired me. I tried to start my own coop with a local entrepreneur. Running a chicken coop is easy and makes a large profit. A neighbor who had a job in the Ministry of Agriculture worked hard to get me a permit to open one. But they told him it is impossible to have a chicken coop permit in an Arab village. I went down with him so I could meet with the director; maybe I could figure something out with him. He told me, "What do you want? Cows? Goats? Okay. But a chicken coop? No way." This is because they wanted only [the government company] Tnuva to sell eggs and chickens. I wanted to open a big, officially approved chicken coop with 10,000 or 12,000 birds, but I spent the whole unemployment period [used Hebrew, *mitun*] without work.[5] Then I went to Tel Aviv to work as a construction worker, but it wasn't enough for my family. I almost gave up on life. I figured I have to do some permanent work, I don't care what the people in the village say. . . . God had mercy on me.

Haitham, the policeman from the Abu Ghosh area who said "Oslo is not relevant," also explained his turn to policing as a necessity:

When I finished elementary school in the '60s we could either study in Jerusalem, in the north or in the Triangle. There were no high schools here. I went and registered at the Freir School in Nazareth. But they wanted 1,000 liras for tuition. My family simply didn't have that much. I had paid 60 liras for admission and lost it. I was forced to enter a professional school in Jewish Jerusalem and that's how I made my way into police mechanics. Any Arab who is financially comfortable does not go into the military or police. The only reason they join is that there is nowhere else to go. People who are educated look for alternative ways to organize their future. Find me one guy who is educated who wants to go to the military. You won't find any.[6]

Since the establishment of Israel and the destruction of Palestinian agriculture, construction wage labor has been one of the primary sources of income available to Arab citizens. The bosses are mostly Jewish and the work is physically challenging and low-paid. It is not surprising then that the image of the struggling beleaguered construction worker haunts many of the men I interviewed. For instance, 'Imad, who became a teacher thanks to a military-subsidized program, said:

I have to tell you that I was very influenced when I was young by what I saw around me. I saw how my father, who never went to the army, worked so hard. He worked as a laborer and would come home tired, totally exhausted. He was a construction worker; he basically built the Plaza and Jordan River Hotels. The other men in our neighborhood who were employed [in the military] would come home relaxed and clean and organized. I knew when I was in high school that I had to continue my studies so I wouldn't have to suffer like my father, and the Bedouin [educational military] track was heaven-sent. . . . But education by itself is not enough. My best friend graduated as an engineer with honors. He hadn't served in the military, and every time he went to a company to apply for work they'd say he needed military service. It makes you feel screwed. So instead of sitting in an office, he works in construction. I am not as smart as he is, so I would be even worse off without military service.

While the majority of the soldiers I interviewed constructed an economic narrative around their decision to join the military, the degree of economic need and ambition at stake varied. Often it was basic, as in the desperation expressed by Halima, a widowed mother originally from a West Bank village, who for eleven years cleaned schools—a job considered socially degrading. She supplemented this by picking wild thistles, which she would painfully clean of their thorns and sell to neighbors to eat: "We lived a very difficult life. We had one room and nine children and life was very hard. . . . I worked a lot. Then my husband died. My son had no alternative."

But not all of the soldiers I interviewed came from backgrounds of poverty. For some, soldiering satisfied middle-class aspirations. Some soldiers emphasized basic benefits available through the military, such as a stable income, payments for children's school supplies at the beginning of each year, and medical, dental, car, and life insurance. Others mentioned luxuries, such as the offer of a five-day all-inclusive hotel stay every year, gifts on the holidays, a 22 percent discount at the Mashbir department store chain, and a 50 percent discount on movie tickets.[7]

The Benefits

Soldiers who perform basic service (called "mandatory" even though for non-Druze Arabs it is performed voluntarily) receive a stipend.[8] Career soldiering is considered by many of the men I interviewed a stable and reasonable source of income. In some Bedouin communities with high rates of military service and poverty, the term used for military service is *mitwazzif*—meaning simply "employed."

Beyond the stipends and salaries, military service promises a host of other material benefits to those who complete a minimum term. Anyone who has performed basic service for at least twelve months in the military, Border Guard, or police force (or any woman who has served twelve months of national service) is defined by the Ministry of Defense as a "released soldier."[9] This status of "released" qualifies the individual and his or her family for a wide range of financial assistance in the areas of education, professional training, housing, and starting a business, as well as exemption from or reduction in municipal property taxes, credit points on income tax calculations, free driving courses, and so on.[10]

Employers in Israel routinely give preference to applicants who have completed military service and discriminate against those who have not—in other words, most Arabs. This is true for security-related positions such as guard work or work in weapons factories, but also for many other jobs where military experience is irrelevant. Arab soldiers are well aware of this. One former soldier who succeeded in securing lucrative work in heavy equipment told me, "I dare you to find a good job that doesn't require completion of military service. . . . Look at the job listings in the [Hebrew] newspapers; most of them require service."[11]

Released soldiers have the additional advantage of free access to guidance counselors, occupational psychologists, and courses on how to apply for a job and how to start a business.[12] They can take their time in order to find an appropriate job since they are entitled to a year of unemployment pay.[13] Special incentive grants encourage them to work in jobs designated by the Ministry of Labor as "needed."[14] Overall, the employment field in Israel is designed for (mostly Jewish) citizens who have completed military service.

At a more informal level, military service can facilitate employment by allowing Arab soldiers some access to social networks that include wealthy and influential people. The Ministry of Defense bulletin for soon-to-be released soldiers encourages them to "ask your fellow unit members about job opportunities."[15] A middle-aged former soldier, Mahir, told me how

> by chance, I ran into a guy I knew from reserve service [used Hebrew, *milu'im*] who worked in the City Council in Haifa and he gave me the job I have now. Service in the military can open many doors, in terms of trade, commissions, becoming a representative of a company, and others. Because you've served in the military, you find Jews more willing to give you work, and there is more trust.

'Imad, who had served through the Bedouin military educational track, told me:

> During reserve services, you mix with all kinds of people—the garbage collector, and the drug addict, and the doctor all serve together. You get to make a lot of contacts. I once served with the central district bank director, and we enjoyed our conversations. These contacts can be helpful later on. You are not automatically equal after service. You have to use your wits, to eat the other person up with your words, to advance yourself.

Military service thus offers Palestinians an opportunity to try to access, though perhaps not join, the old boys' network.

Just as employment is geared toward citizens who have completed military service, the same can be said for higher education. In addition to offering released soldiers special study grants and scholarships, various universities in Israel give them different preferences, such as priority in admission to "needed" fields of study. At Haifa University, released soldier applicants were given preferential access to dormitories.[16] Students called up for reserve duty receive special consideration in the scheduling of classes, in exams, and in grades. Israeli universities regularly set the minimum age of admission based on the assumption that applicants have completed their mandatory military service, thus forcing non-serving Arab students to wait up to three years after high school before becoming eligible to apply.[17] However, the enrollment age requirements do not apply to Jewish students who have elected to defer their military service in order to study.[18] These deferrers also receive various preferences.

Arabs who serve in the Israeli military qualify for some of these benefits (although for non-Druze Arabs, service is voluntary and therefore they are ineligible for deferrer's status). Yet only a few of the soldiers I interviewed mentioned the preferences universities give to veterans as a major attraction of military service. Most of them in fact were not able to obtain a postsecondary education—some did not even complete high school. That so few Arab veterans are able to obtain a higher education explains the creation of special programs offering subsidized studies to specific ethnic groups in combination with a reduced period of military service. In the Bedouin military educational track, basic training is followed by free education at a teacher's college in exchange for teaching at an Arab school in military uniform with reduced pay for a period thereafter. The group of soldiers I interviewed included a few graduates of this track. An additional program, called Flame, promises to soon allow minority soldiers one year of study-leave after two years of mandatory service.[19]

More prominent in the soldiers' narratives was their ability to lease state land at significantly discounted prices in select locations.[20] For example, in 2002 the Israel Lands Administration awarded a 90 percent discount on the price of leasing lands to released soldiers in 423 small towns in the Galilee and the Naqab, none of which were Arab, to encourage Jewish settlement in those areas.[21] Other lease discounts have been made available in some Arab locations. The size of the price reduction varied. Soldiers reported discounts ranging from 90 percent on a $100,000 plot, to 50 percent on a $25,000 plot, while others pointed out that such arrangements were not available at all in their villages. A discounted lease is a key attraction for Palestinians, whose land has been subject to confiscation and restrictive zoning. Large subsidies are also available for any digging on the plot. Fadi, the young soldier who claimed to have joined the military for the land discount, put it simply: "A construction worker will toil all his life and won't be able to buy a plot of land, but a soldier can comfortably get one in three years." Released soldiers are also entitled to housing assistance and favorable loans.[22]

Becoming a State Man

Beyond specific entitlements, the overall benefits of military service for Palestinians are captured by the concept of becoming a state man. Over and over, I heard that when one joins the military, one becomes *misudar*, Hebrew for "organized," or less literally "made" or "set up." One young soldier told me, "When I joined, my family was so happy, my father couldn't believe it—life in the military is very organized [used Hebrew, *misuderit*]. You become a state man [Hebrew, *'ish medinah*]. A soldier is a state worker and he is *misudar* for all his life. He can go out for retirement when he is young, and there is something to depend on [Hebrew, *yesh mah lismokh 'alav*]."

A border patrolman with fourteen years of service explained how joining helped beyond providing a salary. He told me his family needed money and

I had already borrowed money from my uncle to buy a piece of land and couldn't ask him for more. I worked in construction, but the pay was very meager and there wasn't much work. God had mercy on me and I found this job. No matter what the situation, my monthly salary was there. My wages are guaranteed and are not in the hands of a contractor who will tell me "Today I don't have it. Come back tomorrow." When I signed up for the Border Guard, the goldsmith in [a nearby city] immediately gave me a loan because he knew

I would be *misudar* and would get a good check every month—not like a laborer who might not be paid for months at a time. This is a huge help.

In addition to the regularity and stability of military work, many of the soldiers I interviewed highlighted that being a "made" soldier in a sense facilitates "key transactions with the state."[23] This is particularly important for Palestinians whose normal expected course of life—owning land, building homes, expanding families—puts them in conflict with the Judaizing goals of the state. While transactions are facilitated on a case-by-case basis and appear informal, they are part of a larger system of clientalism and patronage fostered by the state. A Ministry of Defense publication clearly states that historically, "appropriate rewards" to Arab soldiers has not necessarily meant money, but has involved connections instrumental in gaining soldiers permits for movement (required during the Military Administration period from 1948 to 1966), grazing-land leases, water lines, and job appointments after release.[24] Thus military service is rewarding in that it involves the lifting of some of the burdens and punishments that non-serving Arabs are subjected to, not on an automatic by-rights basis, but at the individually negotiated level.

It is not a coincidence that Fadi wants "that piece of paper with a stamp on it" in his hand. The Ministry of Defense reminds released soldiers to obtain a certificate of release because "generally, you will be asked to show it at work interviews, educational institutions or for professional training."[25] Soldiers widely perceive certificates of military service as instrumental to opening various doors before them—even if not all the way.

A retired soldier I interviewed, Ahmad, used his status as a soldier to seek basic services such as electricity and water for his home. Although Ahmad lived in a small but recognized village, his access to these necessities was limited. Military service changed that.

In eleven years I did many things for the family: licenses, buildings, telephone lines, electricity, water. I started going to government offices and finding someone who'd listen. At first, my extended family objected to me joining the military, but when they understood that I was doing it for a purpose, to advance the family, they accepted. My uncles had tried to get a water pipe to our neighborhood for so long—they knew how important this was.[26]

In addition to fettered access to basic services, Arab citizens also suffer high property taxes. As mentioned earlier, such taxes are imposed on private land, primarily owned by Arabs, making it burdensome to keep, with the goal of bringing it under the control of the state or para-state Jewish organizations.[27] Military service has helped some soldiers manage this financial burden as well. According to Sharif, a soldier from a recognized Arab village, he benefited from joining the military because he needed to

> license my house and to get rid of the tax debt I owed. When I wanted to close my tax file, they [tax officials] advised me to go to the army. After I enlisted I went to the tax office—I told the man, tomorrow I am going to Lebanon [with the army], and I don't know if I will come back or not. He signed away the debt on the spot. Out of over 100,000 shekels I ended up paying 2,000. I showed them my army card and they immediately said, *Sa'* [Hebrew for "Go"]. This state is a Mafia.

Another area of potential patronage involves Palestinian physical mobility in Israel. While movement permits are no longer required as they were during the Military Administration period, Palestinians are regularly delayed by security checks or turned away from private institutions by security guards. According to a young policeman from the Triangle: "In a security [used Hebrew, *biṭaḥon*] place, they don't search me. At a checkpoint, they don't give me trouble. At clubs [Hebrew, *mo'adonim*] where they don't let Arabs in, I show my card and the bouncer shakes my hand [Hebrew, *loḥets yad*]."

Potential Patronage

Historically the very recruitment of Arab soldiers relied on a system of personal patronage in which individual collaborating shaykhs or leaders offered members of their families to the military and guaranteed their trustworthiness. As a veteran from Tuba described it: "The shaykh shook hands, and we were employed."[28] More recently, this has evolved into the requirement of two formal recommendations for new volunteers. At ethnically specific recruiting centers, such as the run-down Bedouin one in Bir al-Sabi' (see Figure 2), the help of particular patrons is offered and sought. While Bedouins can sign up in other recruiting offices, according to staff members, "everyone knows Farid [the head of the center], and this office gives them more help." Personal connections thus continue to be key for soldiers from the get-go.[29]

The military continues to hold some recruitment ceremonies and military celebrations in the private homes of key patron shaykhs and leaders, rather than in public or state spaces. Many soldiers told me of individual favors done for them by particular officers, and of government officials agreeing to grant special requests contingent on the person's "cooperation with the Shabak," the General Security Service, usually by informing on neighbors and fellow Arab residents. A retired soldier from an unrecognized village in the Naqab was told "if you bring us one of your sons [to serve in the military], we'll give you a six-month grazing permit."

"Minority" soldiers themselves seem encouraged to nurture similar relationships of patronage and influence with other Arabs.[30] Several of the policemen I interviewed in fact seemed to define the public good

FIGURE 2   *Entrance to the Bedouin recruiting center at Bir al-Sabi'.*
Photograph by author.

(or the good of citizens, *ṭovat il-izraḥ*, as one of them put it in Arabized Hebrew) in this narrow sense of forgiving traffic violations and tax debts. According to a volunteer policeman from the Triangle region: "I have a friend who had a huge fine that he had to pay. I talked to the Jewish officer and I told him, 'Leave him alone, he's a friend.' And he did leave him alone. Sometimes there is a checkpoint near our village, and we see lawbreakers [used the Arabized Hebrew term *'ovrīm il-ḥok*]. If I know them, I let them go. So there is give and take." Many other interviewees made similar claims.[31] This definition of the public good is not surprising given that Palestinians have been incorporated into the state through a system of collaboration that gives some financial and symbolic benefits to those who collaborate, including authority over compatriots.[32]

Patronage can also be rewarded at the village level. One soldier explained that "villages that have many men who have served [in the military] get more money, and the state lottery [used Hebrew, *mif'al ha-payis*] invests more there. . . . When in '95 one guy from our village died [in service], Benyamin Eliezer came out. When he saw the state the village was in, he told his staff [in Hebrew] 'What's going on friends? I feel like I'm entering the West Bank.' And within a week the streets were being paved." The mayor of the Arab village of Mashhad hired Ze'ev Hartman, a right-wing Jewish politician, as a consultant. His stated goal (after stopping the absorption of more Arabs in the nearby Jewish city of Upper Nazareth) was to recruit village residents for service in the military and thus enable changing

> Mashhad in the next three years into a Swiss village in terms of roads and infrastructure. We will make the village green . . . and open a center for geriatric care that will be the only one of its kind in the area. . . . I'm working within the council of Mashhad to recruit young men for the army, and so far I've recruited seven men for the Border Guard and the Giv'ati Unit. I also deal with matters concerning released soldiers and struggle so that each of them will receive half a dunam of land so that every Arab knows that any person who sympathizes with the state will receive all their rights.[33]

The benefits of patronage depend on the strength of the relationship between the individual soldier and state officials, on the tact of the soldier, and the generosity of the patron. Nothing is guaranteed. One policeman and former soldier, Jarir, mocked the supposed naïveté of some Arab recruits:

> Some men think that because we did military service, that we did something big for the state and they have to take care of us.[34] No mister, there are thousands of soldiers [used Hebrew, *ḥayalim*] arriving every day and being discharged every day. You can't come and act like you are owed a big favor.[35] . . . And then they are surprised and complain "look, the state threw us aside." They should have known this from the beginning.

Patronage is limited to the persons involved and is not highly variable. The official history of the Bedouin in the military praises one of the commanders of the trackers unit for his personal assistance to individual soldiers: "One day he received an emergency call from a few trackers to their home, and when he arrived, he found himself clashing with the people of the Green Patrol" who planned to confiscate and sell tens of thousands of the Bedouin soldiers' goats.[36] The commander stopped them and the herds were spared in this instance. But the general policy of reducing Bedouin herds and Judaizing their land remained intact.[37] Similarly, demolition orders against a career captain's home in Rahat in the Naqab were apparently rescinded after "the intervention of some senior IDF officers," but neither the dire land conditions in the township nor the criminalization of the Bedouin presence on so-called national land was altered.[38]

Making the Most of It

Yusif is a young military recruit from a northern village who goes by the Hebrew version of his name, Yosi. His mother apparently tries to take advantage in every way she can of the fact that her son serves in the army. According to her fellow villagers, she thinks that her son's service entitles her, for example, to cut in line at understaffed government offices. A postal clerk related that "whenever there was a long line at the post office, that woman would come to the counter, to the front of the line, saying 'I'm Imm [mother of] Yosi, I'm Imm Yosi.' She thinks that if her son is in the military that all of Israel would know and that she can cut to the front of the line."[39]

Rather than being misguided, Imm Yosi seems to be an astute observer of the Israeli system of patronage for its so-called good Arabs. Such pushiness seems necessary. The details of many of the official benefits are convoluted and constantly changing, and involve massive bureaucracies. Throughout the guidelines for released soldiers' benefits are suggestions that soldiers should contact various offices to obtain current details and forms. One soldier, Fuad, told me, "You are entitled to a lot of things that you don't know about. You have to go out and look for them. They don't just come to you. Nobody sends you a letter saying 'come take this money.' No, you have to run after them for it." In addition to the confusing details of formal entitlements, the system of patronage and the special benefits negotiated by individual soldiers through their Jewish patrons feed conflicting rumors about what benefits are available to Arab soldiers. Fuad opines, "Maybe we don't deal with institutions correctly, we don't demand things in the correct way. There are only a few exceptions of Arab men who have been able to take advantage of military service to really advance in life. Those are men with rare abilities. Most men just manage to get by."

In addition to the uncertainty generated by the patronage system, Arab soldiers are structurally disadvantaged in pursuing their benefits. Part of this is linguistic—Hebrew is their second language, which makes navigating the system more challenging. But it is also "social," as illustrated by the story of a man from Maghar village who had served in the Border Guard for seven years and was killed in 1982 in a service-related driving accident, the details of which remain vague. According to the family, the Ministry of Defense sent a social worker during the mourning period with forms for the illiterate wife to sign giving up her rights and benefits. The family did not realize it was entitled to benefits until their son enlisted several years later.[40] The deceased's wife claims: "This story did not and would not happen to a Jewish family."[41]

Arab soldiers are also at a political disadvantage. While some told me their service helped them be more assertive in their interactions with the state, others argued that being in the military made soldiers act more cautiously. Those who are unwilling to do all that is asked of them in the military automatically feel like they are underperforming and subject to suspicion, and so become less demanding. This is true, for example, of

Hasan, a young man who refused to be stationed in the West Bank and left the military soon thereafter: "A friend from my unit advised me to go down to Tel Aviv and check because I am entitled to many things. But I don't want anything from them. I just want them to leave me alone." Dahish, a Druze veteran, told me that land confiscations in Druze villages have been extensive, but have met with relatively less protest there than in other Arab villages "because they are all in the military and are afraid to raise their heads. The state controls them more. I know this because I've felt it." As many interviewees emphasized, bureaucratic skill and persistence are required of all soldiers, Jews and Arabs, in order to obtain many benefits. However, it appears that Jewish soldiers in a Jewish state are better positioned to get what is due them.

In a *Saturday Night Live* skit from the early 1990s, comedian Eddie Murphy is sitting on a bus in "white-face." As soon as the last black person gets off the bus, music comes on, money is distributed, champagne is popped and the party begins. Murphy comically discovers the exclusive world of white privilege in America. Though in a completely different context where the politics of skin color are more complicated, the soldiers in my study are trying to get on the bus of Jewish privilege. But in Israel, no one waits for the Arabs to get off—in clear view to all, Jewish privilege, especially vis-à-vis military service, is flaunted rather than hidden.

In this tiered citizenship system, Arab soldiers try to get more rights and benefits than other Arabs are allowed. Ali, a former soldier, is particularly eloquent on this point:

> [Military service] gives you some things, and makes other things easier, but it doesn't reach the level of equality. We are, like the rest of the Arabs in Israel, screwed.[42] But they provide this door for us. If you get employed [in the military], the door will open. . . . But it doesn't open all the way. . . . Right after I was released I went to the center in Tel Aviv to see what I was entitled to. When I boarded the bus, everyone was looking at me differently.

On his way to obtain his benefits, their limitations were already apparent.

5

Military Ethnification

SOON AFTER THE FIRST MINORITIES UNIT was established in the Israeli military, a deadly fight broke out between the unit's Druze and Bedouin soldiers. Military authorities attributed this clash, known as the Nesher Incident, to preexisting animosity between the Druze and Bedouins. However, the fighting reportedly broke out as a result of disagreements over guard duty and leave rotations—these were formally divided and organized by the military along Druze-versus-Bedouin lines. According to one of the soldiers involved: "Who is it that stirred up the Druze? The Jews promoted sedition among us."[1] Druze and Bedouins were then placed in separate units.

The recruitment of Arabs into the Israeli military does not aim simply at adding their strength to the ranks. Beyond "military utility," their selective recruitment fits well with the policy of dividing and subdividing the Arab population.[2] This segmentation is also practiced within the ranks. Categorization as Bedouin, Druze, Muslim, or Christian (versus Jewish) is paramount within the so-called melting pot of the Israeli military. A sign on the door of the Bedouin recruitment center in Bir al-Sabi' states that enlistment "strengthens the identification between the Bedouin sector and the state/IDF." This sectoral view of soldiers and citizens informs unit structure, assignments, promotions, and benefits in the military.

Units of Difference

Until the 1970s, all Arabs were placed in segregated units under the command of Jewish officers. Not only were their units separate, but for Bedouins in the south, their official status in the military was also different. They were initially recruited as "civilian IDF workers" and only in 1978 were some of them upgraded to regular soldiers.[3] Well into the late 1970s, Bedouin units were assigned tents while the rest of the soldiers were housed in buildings.[4] Since the 1970s, "minority" soldiers have been allowed positions outside segregated units (but not in the air force or in intelligence), and all units were officially opened in 1991. But the largely segregated units continue to exist and "minority" soldiers continue to be directed primarily to them. In ordered to be accepted for service, Arab volunteers are often required to make advance commitments to serve in frontline field units, usually farther from home and with higher casualty rates.[5] Many elite combat units, the air force, and intelligence remain closed to them.

There are currently three minority units in the Israeli military: the Druze unit, now called the Sword Battalion, the Bedouin Desert Reconnaissance Battalion, and the Bedouin Trackers units. Although Arabs are now officially allowed to join any unit, roughly 80 percent of Bedouins in the Naqab, for example, join one of the two Bedouin units.[6] According to Colonel Ganon, onetime commander of the Trackers unit in the southern border area, "They are more successful there. . . . It is easier for them."[7] There are no Jewish or Druze trackers in the Israeli military—apparently only Bedouins have the "natural ability" and "instinct" necessary for the job.[8] Bedouin applicants are thus limited by the fact that the concept of "tracker" and that of "Bedouin" are so intertwined in the military that it is difficult to separate one from the other.[9]

Druze are also primarily placed in the Druze unit. In 1953 the commander of the Druze unit objected to a proposal to integrate Druze soldiers into regular units because they "suffer from feelings of inferiority and suspicion that they will not be able to overcome while being in the same unit with Jewish soldiers" and added that "it appears to me that also for security reasons, it is desirable that they be in a separate unit to make supervising them more effective."[10] Just as the Bedouin are stereotyped as naturally suited for tracking, Druze men are often Orientalized as "'natural' warriors suited to the infantry or certain combat units."[11] In

2001 Sergeant Husam Janam had to petition the Supreme Court because his demand to transfer out of the Druze infantry unit had been denied. In practice, the ability of Arab soldiers to join other units continues to be severely curtailed.[12]

The continued predominance of "minorities units" highlights that such soldiers are not just Israeli soldiers, but "minority" Israeli soldiers, since "Israeli" on its own is used to mean Jewish.[13] Arabs who serve in the Israeli military are seen not as individuals, but as members of particular minority groups.[14] An official history of Bedouins in the military, for example, describes an early attempt by a Bedouin soldier to complete a paratrooper course. On his first parachute jump he became too frightened to jump. As a result of his individual failure it was decided at the time that no Bedouin would be allowed to join the paratroopers.[15]

The minority units are ethnically marked by the military. Official ceremonies for the Druze Battalion, for example, are held at Druze religious sites and Druze officer graduations are scheduled on the religious holiday of Nabi Sh'ayb. When the Druze unit was established, its flag borrowed the five colors of the Druze religious symbol with the addition of a star of David. When the unit was renamed the Sword Battalion in 1987, it adopted a new emblem with the Islamic crossed swords protecting a star of David below.

Not only are the minorities units communally labeled as either Bedouin or Druze, but they have been in a constant struggle to prove themselves to the military establishment, and are put in competition with one another.[16] The very idea of creating a Bedouin combat unit in fact arose in the late 1980s in part out of competition with the Druze combat unit. According to a Ministry of Defense authorized account, the shaykh who advocated establishing the unit reportedly argued, "If in the IDF there is a unit consisting of members of the Druze community, there should also be room for a Bedouin unit there."[17]

This ethnic competition is also illustrated by the experiment of placing Ethiopian immigrants with the Trackers in 1991. These immigrants were stereotyped as hailing from rural backgrounds that the Israeli military establishment imagined would equip them, like the Bedouins, with so-called natural tracking skills. Bedouins in the unit felt threatened by this project and feared being replaced.[18] The Ethiopian immigrants themselves supposedly preferred other units that would offer better job opportunities after release and the experiment failed.[19]

Beyond official minorities units, several of my interviewees described unofficial yet seemingly sanctioned ethnic controls and nepotism. According to a Muslim policeman:

> The Druze control the Border Guard [used Hebrew, *mishmar gvul*], and the Tiberias [police] station is in the hands of the Christians. . . . If someone from a different group tries to come in, they find a way to get rid of him. Everyone knows from his background what unit he will be successful in. . . . There is often competition between policemen. The other time, a Druze policeman informed [Hebrew, *hilshin*] on me falsely, to try to get rid of me. He didn't want a non-Druze to work in his unit. There are many who think that way.

Second-Class Warriors

Soldiers consider majority-Jewish units more prestigious than minority ones, which are plagued by a "lack of pride."[20] For example, as the state's official history of Bedouins in the military notes, tracking is widely considered "an inferior profession," with diminished opportunities for advancement as well as for employment after release.[21] The automatic assignment of Bedouins to the Trackers has aroused resentment.[22] One particularly bitter veteran commented on the limited use of Bedouins in the military: "They have us shining shoes. You know how close we get to the air force? They have us sitting on F16s shooing away the pigeons."

Many soldiers I interviewed echoed the sentiment that such units offer limited opportunities for advancement. In the words of Ammar,

> I was supposed to go into the special minorities unit, but I kept on pushing to be in the Giv'ati [Brigade] with the Jews. It was very difficult, but I did not give up. I found that being with them, I learned more, and saw more things and better things. It is well known that the Bedouin unit stays in the same location all the time, and for me it was better to move around to get more experience.

Jewish majority units are often preferred, particularly ones considered to have more Ashkenazi or European Jews. Jawad, an ambitious young soldier, explained to me the particular Jews Arab soldiers should seek to associate with: "Why would I want to get close to the Mizrahim? They fare just as poorly as we do.[23] I would be wasting my time. I don't need to serve in the army for that. If I'm going to advance I have to build relationships with the big Ashkenazis."

The lower status of the minorities units is also related to the perception that they are placed on the front lines. Many Druze claim that more Druze were killed in Israel's war in Lebanon in the 1980s than their overall percentage in the military, and that they are assigned particularly dangerous policing jobs in the West Bank and Gaza.[24] A Bedouin soldier reminded me: "The trackers are the first to get hit. And the Arabs in general, they use them as the barrel of the cannon."[25] It is hard to assess the accuracy of this perception given that the military closely guards relevant data. However, while Jewish units get regularly reassigned to different locations, the Bedouin Desert battalion, for example, has long been confined to the same dangerous post at the Rafah crossing in the south. After the death of five soldiers in the battalion, an editorial in the Hebrew *Haaretz* newspaper delicately raised the question of "whether the assignments and missions given to [this] unit are not derived from the [lower] social status of the soldiers who serve in it."[26]

Bedouin Tracks, Druze Memorials

In addition to the ethnic organization of units, particular posts within the military are reserved for members of particular ethnicities. Samir, a Bedouin veteran, explained:

> They sent me to an officers' [training] course and they assigned a psychotechnic exam on the Adha holiday [the largest Muslim holiday of the year], and I still got a very high score.[27] But because the military is divided, the Bedouin area [used Arabized Hebrew, *il-mirḥav il-badawi*] did not have an open position [Hebrew, *tekin*] that year. The officer in charge tried to help me and told me to wait a year, that maybe next year there would be an opening.

Samir decided not to wait for a Bedouin opening and eventually returned to civilian work.

Promotions in the military are said to often involve ethnic considerations. It was widely known that the sons of certain notable families the state was trying to cultivate would advance in the minority units. According to Farid, a Christian policeman: "There are people with college degrees [used Hebrew, *to'ar rishon*] who don't get promoted, and men who aren't worth a shekel but their relatives are so and so and they are the ones that get promoted." Sons of notable Druze families were promoted in the Druze unit, and sons of notable Bedouin families were promoted in the Bedouin unit—again as part of the Israeli policy of segmentation, including along clan and family lines. This became part of the impetus for soldiers from non-influential families to lobby for the opening of other units where they could have a chance at advancement.

The continuing divisions in the Israeli military are also evident in the creation of ethnically specific benefits such as the Bedouin educational military track. Memorials to soldiers follow the same ethnic logic—a memorial to the Fallen Bedouin near Battouf Valley in the Galilee includes a wall and database of Bedouin names as well as so-called Bedouin cultural artifacts, such as an old threshing board and plow.[28] A Jewish journalist described the monument as being "reminiscent of a wave in the cloth of a Bedouin tent."[29] (See Figures 3 and 4.) A separate Druze military cemetery in 'Isifya similarly uses the state "vocabulary of stone slabs" to recognize specifically Druze sacrifices to the Jewish state.[30]

FIGURE 3 *Bedouin Warrior Junction. Photograph by author.*

FIGURE 4 *Bedouin Memorial Wall. Photograph by author.*

Recruiting Divisions

Given this history of official military segmentation, it is not surprising that expressions of intergroup hostility and prejudice among Arabs were rarely censured in the military. In my interviews, a few soldiers described their objections to placement with particular groups—the prejudice shaping these objections not only went unpunished in the military, but was tolerated and even accommodated. Abu Hassan made a specific request to a Bedouin officer but was denied. He then complained to the officer's Jewish superior, "I told him directly I don't like Bedouins. I'm Christian and this officer is Muslim. I'm from the city and he's a Bedouin. He does not represent me." The superior then dealt with the soldier's request directly. Many soldiers echoed Abu Hassan's assessment that "nobody in the military is upset if the Bedouin is fighting the Druze or the Christian is fighting the Muslim or someone from one clan fights with someone from another clan—on the contrary, it makes them happy."

Beyond the ethnic labeling of units, recruitment centers, and benefits, authorities take advantage of disputes in Arab communities at a more ad-hoc level, encouraging parties to the conflict to enlist in the military in order to gain access to weapons and state protection. After the Shihab al-Din conflict in Nazareth between Muslims and Christians, especially the violence that erupted in 1999, many Christians were encouraged to enlist with the argument that the state is the only entity able to protect them from their Muslim neighbors.[31] Israeli historian Hillel Cohen even suggests that the number of Christian recruits since the conflict might exceed that of Bedouin recruits.[32] In addition to sectarian tensions, an inter-clan conflict in Kufur Minda, a so-called honor killing in 'Arrabi, intense election rivalries in Dayr Hanna and B'ayni, and similar conflicts in other villages have been followed by military recruitment of competing parties.[33] In the religiously mixed villages of Rami, Maghar, and Abu Snan, inter-communal tensions (which are also articulations of economic, electoral, and clan rivalries) take on much more violent proportions because of the involvement of soldiers and thus the presence of military arms. When one party to a conflict has soldiers among its members and thus access to weapons, this puts pressure on the opposing party to have members volunteer for the military so that it too can acquire weapons.

A Bedouin soldier told the story of a village where "a Bedouin man eloped with a Circassian girl, and the Circassians [a small Muslim minority who are conscripted to the military] attacked the Bedouin village with their weapons. So the people there then wanted to get employed [join the military] so they could fight the Circassians." According to a soldier whose father was killed in an "honor" dispute, he and his cousins joined the army because "our whole goal is to get a gun permit. We are all [Palestinian] patriots. But our father was killed. We know it is traitorous, but we need the guns."

Along with weapons, enlisted soldiers are also given a certain degree of impunity for their actions—impunity that exacerbates social cleavages.[34] In a riot in Maghar in 2005, in which Druze villagers attacked Christian homes and businesses, burning 152 cars and 122 buildings, off-duty Druze policemen, along with soldiers and ex-soldiers, were suspected of participating but were not punished.[35] The Druze police on duty were reportedly "apathetic" during the worst peaks of the violence, which they watched but failed to stop.[36] They reportedly ignored residents' pleas for help, and instead stood around "watching and eating baklava."[37] Yet in the end there was no official sanction for their behavior.

Similarly, in the longstanding and violent electoral conflict in Abu Snan, where military weaponry has been used, the police have been at best ineffectual. Local policemen are both party to the conflict and involved in the investigations—the authorities have not removed them from investigating the case although they are accused of some of the crimes.[38] This impunity and that of soldiers and policemen in other incidents give Palestinians the sense that the state wants Arabs—soldiers included—to fight with each other.

Cleavages among Palestinians today should be framed in the state-controlled contexts in which they are formed. The state and the military play a significant role in creating and re-creating the contours of these divisions. If being a soldier makes one *misudar*—organized or made—it also makes one *misudar* in another sense of the word—categorized.[39]

6

The Limits of Being a Good Arab

A VETERAN I MET BY THE NAME OF ISHMAEL served in the Border Guard, in the police force, in the military as a political analyst, and in the Foreign Service at the Israeli embassy in the United States.[1] He arrived on the Washington, D.C., campus where I taught courtesy of its University Students for Israel organization.[2] He came to speak of his military service and his love of Israel. He even boasted that his grandmother spoke Yiddish! But, Ishmael Khaldi is not Jewish.[3] He is the Israeli government's poster model for a category of identity it has long worked to create. Ishmael, Ish for short, is a "good Arab."[4]

"When you say Israel, the first thing that comes to mind is Jews fighting Arabs. It's unfortunately mostly true. But I'm not Jewish," he began. "I'm of the third generation of Bedouins whose fate is tied to the community who came to establish Israel." He described a history of Bedouin loyalty to the state and assistance to it from its very beginnings. His grandmother learned Yiddish from early Jewish "pioneers." He claimed that 60 percent of Bedouins in the north volunteer to serve in the Israeli military and many make "the ultimate sacrifice." In 2002 alone, nine Bedouin soldiers were killed in service with the Israeli military. Ish was particularly proud of his efforts to be even more loyal to the state than many Jews. When a group of Jewish pilots became refusniks and wouldn't serve in the Occupied Territories, Mr. Khaldi, together with a few other

Bedouin reservists, volunteered to serve extra weeks of reserve duty to compensate. At one key point in his lecture, Ishmael intoned, "Israel's fate is our fate, Israel's fate is our fate, Israel's fate is our fate."

The sympathetic, though not particularly well-informed, audience of Zionist students seemed unconvinced. They demanded answers to essential questions of identity they presumed Mr. Khaldi had glossed over. "How do you self-identify? Are you Bedouin first or Israeli?" "Does it bother you that your passport says 'Arab'?" "Do you identify with the Palestinian cause or state?" and "What is the legal status of Bedouins? Are they citizens?"[5] Like many other demonstrations of Palestinian citizens' loyalty to the Jewish state, Khaldi's talk that day, as eager as it was, was bedeviled by its underlying contradictions. Arab citizens in Israel are asked to be loyal not to a neutral state, but to another people, the Jewish collective.[6] The students prodded Ishmael to repeat his allegiance to the Jewish state again and again. In the end, they did not seem to buy it.

Some Arabs in Israel, Khaldi included, go to great lengths to conform to the state's requirements of its good Arabs. As non-Jews, however, they are structurally haunted by their Arabness, "lite" as it may be. As good an Arab as Khaldi might try to be, he cannot help it if his origins are from an unrecognized village—the very existence of which automatically places him in conflict with a state that puts Judaization above all else.

A Trojan Horse

Israeli governments historically exempted most Arab citizens from military service because their recruitment would "breach security."[7] Senior military and Ministry of Defense officials agreed that Muslim and Christian citizens were too unreliable and feared that their enlistment in the military "would amount to assisting a fifth column to penetrate its ranks."[8] Israeli governments worry that military service or even alternative national service for Arabs will raise their expectations for equality and "contribute to political irredentism."[9]

Although the Druze and Bedouins have been constructed as more trustworthy than other Arabs, the history of their recruitment in the military shows that their acceptance has been gradual and incomplete. There has always been a strong streak of distrust and concern that these special minorities could become an Arab "Trojan Horse" in the Israeli military.[10] The recruitment of Bedouins into the military is often advocated by state officials on the assumption that this will "discourage them from turning into Islamic radicals."[11] Similar statements to the effect that drafting Arabs can counter their otherwise sure path to political radicalization are commonplace in Israel. Palestinian journalist Hisham Naffa' points out that the statement of a high-ranking military officer that the recruitment of the Druze aims to prevent them from joining Hamas and from becoming terrorists implies a conception of the Arab as "a terrorist, perhaps currently dormant, but his 'terrorist-ness' could be activated at any moment!"[12] Suspect Arabness casts its shadow even on "good Arabs" serving in the military, not to mention the wider Arab population. As non-Jews and moreover as Arabs, even the few "good Arabs" cannot automatically be considered loyal in the way the state assumes Jewish citizens to be.

The persistent suspicion of Arab soldiers is manifest, for example, at the institutional level through the very process of enlisting. The military differentiates between the drafted soldier, who has the duty to serve regardless of his or her personal beliefs or political affiliations, and the Arab or "minority" soldier, who volunteers to enlist and must prove his (or on rare occasions, her) loyalty and trustworthiness by providing two recommendations, usually from current members of the military or veterans. This contrasts sharply with the difficulty Jewish citizens of Israel face in refusing service on ideological or political grounds: they are pressured, intimidated, and frequently accommodated with clerical or noncombat posts in order to prevent their outright refusal of military service.[13] Within a Jewish nationalist framework, their Jewishness labels them as automatically loyal, while Arabness—and Muslimness in particular—labels a citizen presumptively disloyal and not soldier material. A Jewish man who sought release from his yearly reserve duty received confirmation from the army that "a reserve soldier who converted to Islam would be dismissed from active reserve duty service" (although the release document he received "indicated that he was discharged under the mental clause").[14]

The drafted Druze do not need recommendations, but all Druze inductees are placed in Druze-only units for the first six weeks of training to undergo ideological indoctrination as Druze allies of the state.[15] Arab soldiers need to be trained, tested, and remolded in order to subdue their structurally suspicious status—a feat that by definition can have only limited success.

In addition to the added requirement of recommendations, Arab volunteers undergo rigorous "security" checks—they are "screened carefully."[16] A Druze policeman I interviewed who had seven years of police service (in addition to the three years of mandatory military service) reiterated what several others told me: "It is my impression that the security check [used Hebrew, *tahkir bithoni*] for minorities, including Druze, is more intense. This is at the initial stage. Later on, if you try and rise in the ranks, they dig around more and more. For Jewish soldiers, the check is only a formality on paper."

Some Arab applicants are rejected. One Christian man I interviewed was asked to identify himself and his family members in photographs of legal and peaceful political demonstrations before being turned down by the military as "incompatible." The very definition of compatibility with the military carries ethnic significance. Potential Arab volunteers are routinely disqualified if background security checks reveal that they have close relatives across the border (for example, in the West Bank or Gaza Strip, or Lebanon). And soldiers are forbidden from traveling to Arab countries.

They are also forbidden from speaking Arabic among themselves. Although Hebrew is officially the only language allowed, this rule is often selectively enforced, with Russian soldiers, for example, receiving unofficial permission to use their language.[17] One soldier noted: "This officer came shouting at me for speaking Arabic with my friends. Right around me were soldiers speaking Russian and Amharic, but it was only Arabic that bothered him."[18]

Position of Suspect

Historically, suspicion of Arab soldiers was behind their placement in separate units and under Jewish command. Almost all of the soldiers I interviewed essentially saw a glass ceiling for Arabs in the military. Many soldiers pointed out that the state does not trust Arabs with sensitive state secrets and decision-making power. Ahmad, a policeman with three decades of service, gave me the following account of his attempts to move up the hierarchy of command and the suspicion he was subject to even as a "special minority." It is worth quoting at length:

> Once they told it to me directly, "You are Muslim and the Shabak [secret service] doesn't like Muslims to be officers." After fourteen years of service they did not give me the chance to prove myself—even though all the Jewish policemen are sent for tests after three years. If I am a terrorist then jail me. Otherwise, if you are letting me stay in the police force, give me the chance to test my qualifications. . . .
>
> I went to the traffic accident division. And for this job too they had a question mark. They told me that I would be under scrutiny. They didn't say these things to Jewish officers of my rank. They said this because I was an Arab working in a Jewish area. I accepted the challenge. After three months I requested an evaluation and they told me "You are a good fit, and we are pleased with your work," and I got high grades, 10 out of 10. When I saw this, I asked for a promotion [from the rank of major]. . . . Many of the others who worked with me got promoted ahead of me, because they were Jews, but I stayed at the same rank.
>
> The situation was very sensitive in Jerusalem when there were a lot of suicide operations or martyr operations—write it anyway you like.[19] I was an Arab officer, with thirty or forty Jewish policemen under me. It was clear that there was a question mark on me. One day there was a bomb before I got to work. A fellow officer called me and asked me to send help from my unit to the police in the region where the bombing occurred. But I didn't have policemen that day in my unit; they were all out. I told him "I don't have any men today." He went to my boss and I heard how he spoke, what he said about me, over the radio. There is no trust. They didn't believe me.

Ahmad's sense of being constantly under question, under test, and denied promotion was echoed by many other soldier interviewees, from the most eager Zionists to the most reluctant Communist Party supporters. Despite their struggle to prove their loyalty, "minority" soldiers continue to come under suspicion and scrutiny, like the general Arab population.

Suspicion also informs the placement of Arab soldiers in particular units. A recently well-publicized appeal from an eighteen-year-old Muslim Arab commercial pilot to join the Israeli air force was rejected despite his high qualifications. According to his father, "a senior official at the

IDF's Personnel Directorate . . . explained . . . that the course is closed to the Arab sector for the moment."[20] The young man was directed to the paratroopers unit instead. His Jewish mentor admitted that the young man "is bound to face the question of where his loyalties lie."[21]

Many interviewees described an informal and daily level of mistrust in the military underlined by the general perception of them as unreliable mercenaries.[22] A Christian policeman, Jarir, said:

> When something happens, I start apologizing. Like when that guy from Abu Snan blew himself up at the train station in Nahariyya, I said things to the policemen with me, things that I don't want to say, so that they don't put me in the same category with him. . . . I would say things like: "Those Arabs, they don't know anything but violence [used Hebrew, *alimut*]." Or during the demonstrations in October [2000], they would ask me, "What's going on with the Arabs?" [Hebrew, *mah koreh 'im ha'aravim*]. Of course I have to say the things they want to hear.

When Lieutenant Colonel Omar al-Hayb was accused of spying for Hezbollah in 2002, his identity as a Bedouin was a central component of the case. At the time, the head of the military general command pointed out that this is "an isolated case, and must not be used to reach conclusions against all Bedouin in the country. The contribution of the Bedouin to protecting the security of Israel has been considerable and ongoing and has been proven since the establishment of the state until today."[23] The centrality of al-Hayb's inescapable Bedouin identity to the military and to the Israeli public becomes clear when compared to a situation in which an Ashkenazi Jew is accused of espionage: it would seem absurd if military spokespersons then urged the public not to generalize the soldier's betrayal to the entire Ashkenazi Jewish community.

Al-Hayb's defense attorney highlighted the years of military service and ranks of the defendant's clan members and the number of them killed during their military service.[24] Residents of Zarazir, al-Hayb's village, saw the accusation as "a state conspiracy and an attempt to muddy the name of all Bedouin."[25] "It's not him who's standing trial," said a relative in uniform, "the entire Bedouin sector is standing trial."[26] According to a relative, "they did him an injustice and they did an injustice to the entire village. I have a brother who's an officer, and this is very troublesome for the officers, because now they're being watched closely—and what's more, it's over a spy case. If it were about drugs, so what."[27] It is clear for all the involved parties that ethnic affiliation is paramount and that Bedouinness in this case is suspicious: Omar al-Hayb is not an Israeli soldier—he is a Bedouin, Arab, non-Jewish, Israeli soldier.

One veteran I interviewed who was absolved after being suspected of breaching security described the significance of ethnicity in his case:

> They came and took me in the middle of the night from the house like any other Arab. It didn't matter to them that I served in the military or not. Why did they accept me into the security system [used Hebrew, *ma'rekhet ha-bitaḥon*] in the first place? Once they even gave me a lie detector test while I was in uniform [Hebrew, *madim*]. To them I was an Arab just like any other.

These dynamics are highly visible in the example of Arabs in the military, but they are in no way exceptional. The military, like other state institutions, produces subjects it assumes are destined to be the source of threat and insecurity, who are then asked to fight these "inherent" characteristics. The state—whether through the educational, court, or health-delivery systems—attempts to produce subjects who are alarmed by their own existence: students reading about Arab enemies of the state in their history textbooks, court petitioners using state laws that exclude them by definition, and patients urged to use contraceptives that will lower their demographic threat to the state. "Good Arabs" and "bad Arabs" are perhaps better understood not as two separate categories—even good Arabs are always potentially bad in a Jewish state.

7

Broken Promises

> We say to each other, today you are a
> combatant, tomorrow you are an Arab
> [Hebrew, *ha-yom ata ḳravi, maḥar ata 'aravi*].
> *Hamadi, twenty, a soldier from*
> *an unrecognized village in the south*

KHALID SAWA'ID, a Bedouin who served for seven years in the Israeli military, lived on his ancestral land in the Galilee with his wife and children. His house and land became engulfed by the Jewish settlement of Makhmunim, which was trying to evict him and demolish his home (see Figure 5).[1] Back in 1988, Sawa'id applied to be admitted as a member of the settlement, promising to then sell them his land "so as not to harm the development of the lookout (settlement)."[2] He was rejected. The head of the committee of Makhmunim asserted that "despite all our friendship with Khalid, it would not be a natural situation if he lives with us."[3] Sawa'id even agreed to swap his property for land in the partly recognized Arab village of Kammani nearby, where his extended family lives, but "this too they rejected."[4] When asked about his military service he said: "I was stupid. I thought that if I serve I will receive my rights. I said, I will fight beside them and receive what I deserve, just like Jews receive. But this is not the reality. I am good for war, but not for living with."[5]

Arab soldiers are entitled to official benefits and they sometimes receive patronage benefits as well. But the Arabness of Arab soldiers haunts them and severely limits their rewards. The hopes of these soldiers for fuller citizenship in return for their service founders, again and again, on the Jewish/Arab dichotomy at the core of the idea of the Jewish state.

FIGURE 5   *Houses: Sawa'id's small house, on the lower right, is not allowed to connect to Makhmunim's electrical grid. Photograph by author.*

That good Arabs remain non-Jews in a state that continues to prioritize its Jewish character places a severe constraint on their ability to elevate their status.

Distorted Meritocracy

One particular area where this constraint was sensed by the men and women I interviewed was in promotions. According to many of them, ethnic considerations are responsible for the concentration of Arab soldiers in the lower ranks of the military and their limited promotions. Regardless of their varying levels of discontent or criticism of the security apparatus, none of the more than seventy soldiers, policemen, and Border Guards I interviewed between 2000 and 2005 believed there was full equality between Arabs and Jews in promotions. Even Hasan al-Hayb, the mayor of Zarazir and a former officer of the Bedouin Trackers in the Northern Command, told me: "The military is orderly. Any person who proves his capabilities, will advance. . . . There is discrimination among some of them and promotion is not 100 percent. . . . There isn't even one

Druze air force pilot." While the military seems to hold the promise of a meritocratic system for these men, in the end, ethnic considerations mar and distort it.

Samih, who had served five years in the army and three years in the Border Guard, believed "there is no Ashkenazi and Russian, and no Arab and Jew—in any case, you can't talk like that in the military. There are rules and it's not up to you to do as you like. A soldier is a soldier regardless of his background. In the end, we are all in the same trench." However, Samih noted that there were individuals within the military who did not follow these rules: "I have friends who were highly qualified and went to officer training but they were flunked because the [Jewish] officer in charge was right wing."

Another soldier, Butrus, claimed that

> even if one is employed in the military, he will still be perceived as an Arab. There was a Druze officer with me, and the [Jewish] soldiers got mad at him about something, and started cussing him: "Arab this and Arab that." Even if he is Druze, they still consider him an Arab in the end. . . . They even discriminate against Mizrahim who are Jewish, not to mention Arabs. Not all of them discriminate, but you can say more than half do. You can hear it in their voices and see it in their faces.

Asri Mazarib, the brother of Major Ashraf Mazarib of the Bedouin patrol unit who was killed in January 2002, told *Haaretz* that Ashraf was not accepted by Ofek, the "prestigious project aimed at cultivating company commanders" because "even though Ashraf was considered an excellent commander in his unit, as far as the IDF was concerned he always remained a Bedouin. . . . As a Bedouin you can't raise your head too high. If you climb too high, they'll smack you down again right away."[6] Even the widows of Arab soldiers are perceived as discriminated against. A recent *Haaretz* exposé accuses the military's Widows' Organization of blacklisting minority women members, not inviting them to events, and excluding them from receiving some benefits.[7]

I encountered a widespread sense that Arab soldiers were used as scapegoats for the selective enforcement of army rules. One policeman related the sense of being singled out: "I had a problem at work. A girl accused me of sexually harassing her during a search. It was a false accusation.

But Jewish colleagues had much worse problems, and they let it go. My problem they took to the press. Six months later I was found innocent but the damage had been done." Several recent cases involving Druze officers, including those of Colonel 'Atif Zahir, who was suspected of rape, Captain R., who killed a thirteen-year-old Palestinian girl in Gaza, and Colonel 'Imad Faras, former commander in the Giv'ati Brigade, who was indicted for conduct unbecoming an officer, all "reinforce the feeling among the Druze that they are . . . scapegoat[s] for a confused army and society."[8]

Taysir al-Hayb, who killed Tom Hurndall, a British International Solidarity Movement activist in Rafah, was "the first soldier to be tried for manslaughter since the outbreak of the [second] intifada and the first since the 1980s to be sent to jail for a lengthy term as a result of an intifada-related shooting incident."[9] According to a *Haaretz* report, "It is hard to find someone in [his village of] Wadi Hamam today who will not argue that Taysir 'was framed' or, according to the more popular version, 'The army chose him to show the world how much it values human life.'"[10]

While these cases can be seen as individual, isolated, and arbitrary, they can also be understood as systematic results of the state's power structure.[11] The attempt to co-opt or integrate Arabs into the military is structurally at odds with many of the state's Zionist goals, which give priority to Jews over Arabs both formally and informally.

Druze: Arabs After All

The policy of according special treatment to the Druze, making them allies of the state, and dividing them from other Arabs comes into conflict with the priority of Judaizing all Arab lands, including Druze lands, and with the prioritization of Jewish locales in municipal budget allocations.[12] It appears that when a contradiction arises, the Jewish priorities of the state take precedence. According to a Druze activist, "The policy of co-opting the Druze works in that most are no longer Arab, but we aren't Jews either. We are with the state. But the state is not with us."

Particularly troubling to the men I interviewed was the level of daily discrimination experienced by soldiers once out of uniform or once they had left the service, which they describe as comparable to the rest of the Arab population. A Druze "Arabist" (member of a unit trained to go undercover as Arab, to infiltrate Palestinian groups and areas) told an Israeli newspaper: "After three years in which you give everything you've got, they throw you to the dogs, like you were an Arab. They throw you out of work, they call you a dirty Arab, they don't care that you're a Druze. So what's the use of wasting your life?"[13]

According to another newspaper article, the Druze "have been pushed aside into a situation of neglect reserved for . . . Arabs in particular."[14] The dire economic state of Druze villages is comparable to that of Arab villages in which the men are not drafted. Druze lands have not been spared confiscation; according to the Israel Land Authority's 1988–89 records, Druze have suffered more land expropriation by the state per capita than other religious groups.[15]

The first declaration of the Druze Initiative Committee in 1972 included a call for an end to the conscription of Druze and an end to the expropriation of Druze land. In the past decade, land confiscation has been a central rallying cry for multiple conferences on ending the conscription of the Druze. In preparation for a November 2001 conference in Yarka, an article in the Arabic daily al-'Ittihad detailed the greatly diminished areas of land belonging to Druze villages in 2000 compared to 1948.[16] The movement to cancel mandatory Druze service has been gaining momentum in Israel and includes military officers, Likudniks, and other former supporters of conscription.

The Judaization of land was a breaking point for certain soldiers, as a resident of Bayt Jann related:

> Soldiers really felt discrimination when there were struggles over the Zubud land with the "protection of nature" folks.[17] They brought Druze Border Guards and lied to them that [Me'ir] Kahana [former parliament member and leader of the ultra-right Kach Party] was coming to the area. They play a lot of games and dirty tricks. The young men found themselves carrying weapons against their brothers and fathers, and were playing a role in the expropriation of their own land. At that point, the young men took off their uniforms and threw them away and went out to demonstrate and many of them resigned from their positions.[18]

Soldiers from Bayt Jann are reputed to have suffered proportionally more deaths and injuries than soldiers from any other single town in Israel, yet the majority of the village's land has been expropriated.

As a result of land confiscation for the benefit of neighboring Jewish settlements, residential land for Druze, like for all Arabs, has become inadequate for the size of the population, forcing residents "even" in places like Daliyat al-Karmil, with its famously loyal Druze population, to build homes deemed illegal by the state and hence subject to demolition.[19] At this level, Druze dissatisfaction with Israeli policy is said to be similar to that of other Arabs, Muslim and Christian alike.[20]

Good Arabs in Bad Houses

The co-optation of Bedouins is also incomplete. Generally, Arab unemployment rates are high, with Bedouin rates being the highest in the country. While, as I have pointed out, military service itself is sought as a form of employment and as a method of qualifying for additional security jobs, work opportunities for released "minority" soldiers remain meager. A March 2001 government report identified job placement as a major problem facing released Bedouin soldiers.[21] In the township of Kseifa, for example, young people claim that "more than half the demobilized soldiers . . . are unemployed."[22] These dire economic conditions led one soldier to provocatively call the largest township of Rahat a concentration camp (used Hebrew, *mahaneh hashmadah*).

The opportunity that military service supposedly provides for a fuller sense of membership and belonging to the Israeli collective is similarly circumscribed. One activist on behalf of unrecognized villages described to me how he felt his service in the Border Guard allowed him to speak assertively (Hebrew, *'im peh maleh*, literally "with a full mouth") and helped him win the ear of state officials in fighting for his village's recognition. This man hoped that his declaration that "I am a veteran and my brother gave his life in Lebanon" would be heard by the "listening ear" of state officials. This could potentially mean running water, electricity, health care, and schools for his village. But he believed his success was limited: "So far I think my military service helped me to a certain degree. I can clearly see the change in the behavior of officials as soon as I say, 'I just came back from reserve duty [used Hebrew, *milu'im*].' One official heard this and immediately gave me an invitation to a very important meeting. But I can't say for sure, since they haven't recognized our village yet!"

The major problems facing Arabs in Israel—including land confiscation, municipal underfunding, discriminatory zoning, home demolitions, and the refusal to recognize villages—are also faced by Arab soldiers. In a documentary aired on Israeli Channel 2, former soldier Bassam complains about the demolition of his family's home in the city of Shafa-'Amr while emphasizing that he is a disabled veteran from the war in Lebanon. He pleads: "I don't want the regime to forget me. . . . I was [important], and now I am not worth anything. Why?" At a memorial for fallen Bedouin soldiers, Bassam confronts a state official who was one of the signatories to the demolition orders on his house. The official responds: "I am for protecting the law. If I don't enforce the law, then I would be neglecting my job."[23] The rewards of military service for soldiers with Arab land are limited by no less than "the law."[24]

De-legalized homes slated for demolition are not only in unrecognized villages, but also within recognized villages and state-planned townships because of strangulating zoning and the withholding of building permits. Another soldier's family land lay on the outskirts of one of the state's planned Bedouin townships in the north.

> We are fifty meters from the village [official zoning] plan and we've tried to get electricity with much difficulty, running illegal lines to borrow electrical power from others. The cow stables near us have electricity. Consider us cows! . . . My father served eighteen years in the military and he lives in a shack and can't build a home. They demolished his home while he was at work. When they came to demolish the house, people in the village came out to plead with them and told them that he was away serving with the army. They [the authorities] said: "How is that relevant?"

Salim al-Atrash, then aged twenty-five, helped organize a demonstration in 2002 to protest demolition orders against "homes built illegally by former IDF soldiers." Al-Atrash told reporters: "This was my [military] discharge present. After discovering seven booby traps and sacrificing my spirit for the state, the state is destroying my home."[25] Mustafa, a retired soldier whose building—also in the Naqab—was demolished, similarly argued: "There was a big officer who was about to step on a mine, and I stopped him. He thanked me. But he didn't teach his daughter and son that it is because of me [used Hebrew, *bizkhuti*] that he is alive. I personally have saved maybe two hundred Jews from being blown up . . . but no one cares." While others protest home demolitions as human rights violations or as discrimination against Arab citizens, both Mustafa and Salim here attempt a different strategy: they argue that their specific individual services to the state and to Jews should entitle them to keep their homes.

Mustafa and Salim are likely encouraged by rumors of "special treatment" accorded to other individual soldiers whose homes were spared. In one unrecognized village in the Naqab twenty homes had been ordered demolished. I was told that one resident who retired after twenty years of military service asked that his case be separated from the other nineteen and the authorities "agreed on the condition that he won't publicize it." The case was reportedly still pending at the time of writing. In a separate case, one of my interviewees told me that his military service "personally helped me, they didn't demolish my home. They closed their eyes to the violation. But other people, it didn't work for them. One day the man is a president of the state, the next day they are demolishing his home."

The contradictions between co-opting Arabs and promoting Zionist goals are criticized by people from across the political spectrum, and not only from embittered veterans who have been personally victimized or from the nationalistically inclined. Salami Abu Ghanim, a "veteran enlistment activist" in the Naqab, who served as an adviser on Bedouin affairs to extreme rightist infrastructure minister Avigdor Lieberman and "founded the Organization of Negev Bedouin Heroes of Israel," declared: "It's hard to argue with the youth who don't want to sign up. . . . The youth [see] that the state doesn't help veterans. They die for the Jewish state, for the Jews, and the Jews treat them like lepers."[26] Ibrahim al-Hozayyil from Rahat, who recently enlisted his fifth son in the Desert Reconnaissance Battalion, told *Haaretz*, "Today's Bedouin youth knows that after he takes off his uniform, he'll go back to the world of discrimination from which the entire Bedouin community suffers. . . . It shouldn't be this way. . . . These kids should be given something, so they don't feel like suckers."[27]

At Best, Righteous Gentiles

In general, it appears that flying the Israeli flag above homes slotted for demolition in unrecognized villages and the decades of service of family members are not significant enough to prevent demolition. The goals of the Jewish state call for the removal of all Arabs living in unrecognized villages, just as they call for the confiscation of Arab lands, Druze and otherwise. Judaization policies target all Arabs—whatever their loyalties, military service, or political affiliations—and largely override any attempts to co-opt, Israelize, or integrate small groups within the Arab population. The occasional Israeli media outrage that Arab soldiers, loyal friends of Israel, are not being rewarded, elides this basic structural contradiction by characterizing such cases as matters of bureaucratic oversight, lack of agency coordination, or as Moshe Arens (former foreign minister and three times defense minister) puts it, a "non-policy" on the part of the state.[28] Yet, these cases are the result of the supremacy of one set of goals—of creating a homogenous nation-state of and for Jews and promoting their particular demographic, economic, linguistic, cultural, and political interests.[29] The individual Palestinian soldier may be able to achieve certain material and symbolic gains as long as these do not conflict with the ethnic goals of the state. In the end, the military, like all other state institutions, is a tool the dominant majority wields to preserve Jewish privilege.[30]

Sawa'id expressed his disappointment with the rewards for his military service by saying, "I was stupid. I thought that if I serve I will receive my rights." He of course is not stupid. All the soldiers I interviewed make choices, try various strategies, and take chances—in limited contexts. The state, presenting itself as a military democracy, after all explicitly promises improved conditions for them. One career soldier told me: "We don't trick ourselves; we all know the game. But sometimes one has no choice but to play it."

Serving in the military and trying to be "a good Arab" is never the same as being a Jew in Israel. Druze Sgt. Timor Abdullah was sent to prison for refusing to take part in the preparations for the evacuation of Jewish settlers from Gaza.[31] At a meeting of Jewish settler activists, Abdullah's father was thanked with a standing ovation from the crowd and presented with a framed certificate for his son, a certificate of "Righteous Gentile."[32] The best that Arabs can hope for in a Jewish state is this status of righteous gentile—or useful outsider.

8

Boys or Men?
Duped or "Made"?

> These guys are just traitor sons of bitches
> who think that joining the army and carry-
> ing a gun is going to make them into men.
> But they'll never be real men because they
> sell themselves for a very cheap price.
> What more do you need to know? They
> are the uneducated garbage of society, to
> be honest, and this is their naïve attempt
> at advancing. All young men want to build
> houses and get married and have children,
> but not this way, my son.
>
> *Shakir, a fifty-two-year-old store owner*
> *in Majd al-Krum in the Galilee*

PALESTINIAN SERVICE IN THE ISRAELI MILITARY is a frequent subject of discussion among Arabs—despite the small number of volunteers.
Popular debate on this topic is often articulated in terms of masculinity:
critics dismiss soldiers as immature adolescents and soldiers defend themselves as mature family providers. These gendered discussions are an important part of Palestinian concerns about citizenship and nationalism.[1]

Military, Masculinity, and Home

It is well known that for Jews in Israel, military service, masculinity, and identity are closely linked. Militaries the world over tend to

play a powerful role in the construction of both ethnic relations and patriarchal gender relations by manipulating notions of masculinity and femininity to serve military objectives.[2] In Israel, Jewish women are formally incorporated into the military but are relegated to the rear, where they perform feminized roles in service and administration. Men, on the other hand, are expected to occupy the military front, a masculine sphere of combat.[3] This gendered division shapes an Israeli masculinity that is highly militarized, one that clearly does not apply to Palestinians living inside Israel. The "holy quartet" of "Jewishness, masculinity, military service and collective membership" is actually defined against Palestinians and the so-called military melting pot clearly excludes them.[4]

Masculinity for Palestinian men is not linked to service in the military as it is for Jews.[5] For those living under military occupation in the West Bank and Gaza Strip, participation in *resistance* to the Israeli military—particularly as targets of its violence—signals heroism and manhood.[6] More generally, Palestinian masculinity centers on the ability to provide for and protect home and family.[7] Although Palestinians who serve in the Israeli military break with many social conventions by virtue of their service, my research suggests that support of home and family are central for them as well as their critics. They do not seek out combat glory within their communities—combat is in fact a liability there that they attempt to underplay or deny by focusing, instead, on how they support and provide for their families.[8]

Duped Soldier Boys

Many times during my research I encountered gendered criticism of Arab volunteers in the Israeli military that attributed a superficial, immature, pubescent masculinity to them.[9] Fuad, a member of the Communist Party seeking to dissuade men from enlisting, described one young man whom he failed to influence:

> He thinks that because he is in the army he can do whatever he wants. He is hiding behind the uniform and the weapon because of his weak personality. He wants to carry a gun to make himself powerful, to impose himself on

others. He is strutting around showing off his uniform and gun. But in reality, they don't place Arabs in combat units. They put them in the warehouse or the kitchen.

Given that Israeli authorities, as mentioned earlier, frequently reward Arab soldiers with impunity for offenses committed within their communities, it is not surprising that this soldier is perceived as "doing whatever he wants." Fuad went on to mock a former schoolmate of ours who enlisted soon after graduation: "Oh he's become a big man now, he's not the shy skinny boy you knew. In one year, he got himself a woman and a gun."

Soldiers are widely perceived as needing the military to bolster their weak masculinity. A therapist who has former soldiers among his clientele told me:

The uniform and the gun give young men a kind of elation. Their self-esteem is very low, and the word *soldier* gives them many things—power, grandeur, strength. It fulfils psychological needs. Now the man can go into the discotheque, which a regular Arab can't enter, without a problem, and he can talk to Jewish girls, who would not even look at him before. . . . But when they complete their service and return to being regular citizens, fear and weakness reemerge. Some of them develop phobias; if they see a car in the village with a West Bank license plate they run inside and hide because they are afraid that someone has come seeking revenge. When he was in Ramallah, the man made himself out to be Sylvester Stallone, carrying a gun and killing. Now that the gun is gone, the weakness comes back.

Men attributed with such masculinities are considered so weak and vulnerable that the Israeli authorities supposedly prey on them in an effort to gain young recruits and to divide and rule the Arab community. Palestinian soldiers are accused of "seducing" other young men into soldiering, under direction from Israeli authorities, by showing them their guns.[10] Soldiers are supposedly instructed to intervene in local conflicts—family feuds, wage disputes, and religious tensions—by suggesting to young men involved in the conflicts that getting a gun (by joining the military) will resolve such problems with ease.[11]

A pamphlet circulated by the Union of Communist Youth in the Galilee in 2000 condemned Arab soldiers and criticized young men who enlist as, among other things, thoughtless and vain. Hasan, one of the soldiers I interviewed, described himself as having in the past a shallow masculinity like the one described to me by the therapist and others. Although he completed three years of basic military service, he did so with some ambivalence and when I met him he was dodging summonses for reserve duty. He told me that "when people argue with me that being in the military is treason, I stop and think about it, and sometimes I think they are right." Hasan's ambivalence repositions his earlier eagerness to join the army as part of the shallow masculinity described by other critics of soldiering: "When I joined, I was young and saw myself in uniform as a foreign minister. I wanted to make an impression, and I would wear the suit knowing that a thousand eyes were on me. I was less than eighteen—I lied and joined underage at seventeen." His wife added that "when he enlisted he was really an adolescent. Quite simply he was immature. But it was a phase and he passed it. Now he realizes it was a mistake." Hasan responded, "You see, I sit here and listen to my wife talking about me this way. That's because I know she is right, and as a man I have to face it."

This type of criticism seems softer than accusations of treason or greed. It sometimes sounds like an apology, as in Myassar's comments: "Young men naturally like the army and police. They like the uniform, and the gun, and the exercises. They like to empty their energy. Soldiering involves a certain kind of machismo and masculinity that is normal for men that age." Yet Myassar was passionately against such behavior. Far from being an apology for the men who enlisted, this kind of explanation of their behavior has the effect of thoroughly dismissing them. Criticisms that identify these soldiers as "traitors" or as "greedy" give them credit for having made a political or economic decision, albeit a wrong one. The masculinity criticism conveniently writes off the soldiers entirely.

Describing soldiers as immature boys dismisses military service as a form of false or superficial masculinity—a masculinity that requires military props and cannot stand on its own. This masculinity is seen by many, not necessarily as alien or unnatural, but as part of a pubescent phase that should be quickly outgrown and transcended. Idealized Palestinian masculinity, in contrast, is not self-centered but focuses instead on mature and enduring commitments to the family.

Arab soldiering in the Israeli army is so commonly associated with immature masculinity that soldiers themselves often criticize and distance themselves from the shallow and weak desire for the masculinizing accoutrements of the military. I heard over and over from soldiers that "I was not seduced by the uniform and gun." Nihad, for example, emphasized that

I tried to avoid wearing my uniform in town. . . . A guy wearing a uniform and strutting around in the streets saying, "Everybody, look at me. I'm strong"—I don't like these external appearances. I don't need the uniform to feel like a man. . . . That guy just wanted to serve [in the military] so he'd have a gun to shoot [in the air] and show off during weddings. This is not what I was thinking about when I decided to serve.

Jamal, a policeman who enlisted in his mid-twenties, distanced himself from younger enrollees and their immature motivations:

You give somebody who is eighteen years old a uniform and authority, for example, to say "I'm taking you to the station and you can't do anything about it" and you give him a gun—this is what excites young men. For the young man, riding in a patrol jeep and turning on the siren, this for him is the best thing in the world. He thinks the army is a game. But I wasn't a naïve adolescent when I joined. I was in my late twenties and had a family to take care of.[12]

At the time, I couldn't help laughing with Jamal at the siren-sounding adolescents and nodding my head in recognition of his description of having "a family to take care of."

"Made" Family Men

Palestinians who serve in the Israeli military imagine a different masculinity for themselves—one that mimics the nationalist ideal and is constructed as centered on heterosexual marriage, the family, and its support. As mentioned earlier, when one joins the military, one becomes *misudar*, a made man who receives a regular paycheck, tax breaks, easier loans, educational grants, land discounts, and potentially improved public services. Soldiers argued that these benefits of service help make them better family providers. For example, Khalid told me: "I was able to raise my family from the lowest economic levels to a comfortable situation. You can't imagine how much better my children's lives are today compared to my childhood. This is all on account of the military."[13]

The monthly income alone (for career soldiers) is considered a dramatic financial improvement in some cases. Imm Mahmud described to me how her husband had joined the army twenty-five years earlier in the following terms:

> There was very high unemployment, and [my husband] Abu Mahmud would go for months without a single day's work. We found ourselves with eight children, and he was out of work, unable to keep a job for more than a few days. We couldn't find food for the children or soap to wash the clothes. His first wife poured kerosene on herself and burned herself up because she had to go around begging to feed the children. This is how bad the situation was. One day a man wearing a [military] uniform walked down our road, and I said to my sister sitting next to me, now there goes a real man. Only when he got closer did I realize that this was my husband—he had joined the army and was coming to surprise us. I ululated till my voice was hoarse. And our situation got much better from then on, thank God.[14]

As noted before, not all of the soldiers I interviewed came from poor backgrounds. The economic needs, desires, and ambitions they express are sometimes very basic, as in Abu Mahmud's case, but in other cases amount to middle-class aspirations.[15] Whereas some soldiers argued they were feeding and clothing hungry children, a few others argued they were buying necessary computers for them.[16]

Women Are Not Providers

If it is exceptional for Palestinian men to join the Israeli security system, it is even more exceptional for Palestinian women. But in contrast to the male soldiers I interviewed, who all pointed in one way or another to their role as family supporters, all three policewomen I interviewed saw their jobs as a burden on their families. Rania in fact complained that her service prevented her from supporting her family properly. When it comes to gender, Rania was far from a conformist; she vocally criticized and rebelled against traditional gender roles, as the people who sent me her way emphasized. Yet Rania did not explain her behavior as that of a family breadwinner—in fact, she emphasized the inconvenience of her job for her family:

> When I was younger, I wanted to be an airplane pilot or a dancer in a pop band. My father always encouraged my dreams, and he was very happy when I joined the police force. He was very proud of me, the whole family was very proud. My younger brother thinks his sister is Rocky. My husband, who initially encouraged me to apply, gave me what was essentially a lecture when I began the job—about priorities, and how the house and children come first. My in-laws did not exactly object, but I know they are unhappy about the long hours—and since I often depend on my mother-in-law to look after the children, they have the right to say this to me. I love my job; it's very rewarding and has a lot of room for advancement, but the only problem is the long hours and night shifts. And this makes me think of changing jobs. I always worry about where to put the children. I feel I'm not doing enough for them.

At no point did Rania mention her income or her contribution to supporting her family.

The homes of most of the men I visited featured a display of photographs in the formal living room, usually a portrait of the father or son in military or police uniform at the center top, surrounded by other images of the family, weddings, and graduations.[17] This standard portrait of the soldier in uniform was conspicuously absent from Rania's house. The photos in her living room were mostly of her wedding. Rania literally and figuratively framed her service in a way that departs dramatically from the explanations of male soldiers—provider masculinity was not available to her.

Another policewoman I interviewed, Reem, was recently married. Like Rania—and unlike most of the male interviewees—Reem described her work conditions as a burden on her marriage:

> On a given day they might tell us suddenly, "Go to Gaza [three hours away] for work," and then you have to tell your husband you're going and you don't know when you'll be back. It's difficult, but he is understanding. Is it really

worth it for me [used Hebrew, *shaveh li*]? My work bothers me and my husband. I would be prepared to go home at five and at the last minute they tell me, "No, you have to stay till eight." There is some conflict. If my husband wasn't so supportive, then it would be more difficult.

Reem expressed concern about continuing in her career once she had children and told me she would forgo promotions in the interest of her family:

There are new pressures today [after marriage]. How will my life be after I have children? But through my contacts with policewomen with children, I see that they somehow manage [used Hebrew, *mistadrot*]. But I don't want to advance in my position, because it means I'll be an officer and that means that twenty-four hours a day, my life will be work. It will destroy my personal life and the life of my home. Before I got married, I might have been prepared to do that, but not now. They've asked me several times about doing an officer's course but I've said no.

The third policewoman I interviewed had selected a desk job for the same reason Reem gave. She counseled her daughter against joining the police force because "it would be bad for her family."

Objections to and criticisms of Palestinian women who join any branch of the security apparatus in Israel are commonly voiced in different terms than those usually raised in relation to men. Instead of being labeled as immature, policewomen and women soldiers (though extremely rare) are more commonly cast as sexually immoral, even by their fellow male Arab soldiers and policemen. According to Reem,

As a woman in the police, you work in the middle of the night along with policemen, and for many people this is not acceptable. This is especially true if you go on patrol, and are not just a desk clerk or a detective. No one ever criticized me face to face, but the gossip about me reaches me indirectly. Arab policemen bothered me the most on the job. They thought, here's a girl who works at night and there's no one who asks about her. They eventually figured out that they would get nowhere and left me alone.

Many of the policemen and soldiers I interviewed were critical of women in the military. According to a senior policeman with over seven-

teen years of service, "I'm against girls joining the police. The conditions
are not appropriate for a Muslim or Arab girl. Policing and girls are two
separate worlds and they should stay that way. A girl who joins the police
force is carrying her divorce papers in her own hands. She's headed for a
downfall."[18]

A distant relative of mine by marriage who tried to put me in contact with a policewoman from his village told me that in addition to tens
of Arab policewomen, there was also one Arab girl from Wadi Hamam
who served in a combat unit in the military: "I swear our society is fall-
ing apart. The people in her village tried to make her family leave, and
they threw stones at them. But she didn't listen." According to an article
in *Haaretz*, this woman, named Amira al-Hayb, had served in a Border
Guard unit in the West Bank and thus "broke a deep-seated taboo . . .
and condemned her family to alienation and ostracism."[19] Her family
was subject to community harassment not because her two brothers enlisted in the army (according to *Haaretz*, 40 percent of the young men in
impoverished Wadi Hamam enlist), nor because her brother Taysir was
found guilty of killing the British ISM activist, but because an Arab woman served in a combat position.[20] Although widely criticized, women's
service in clerical positions in the police force appears to be less objection-
able, and indeed, the number of women in such posts rose considerably
during the period of my field research and was rumored to be nearly one
hundred by its end.

Providers Where Providing Is Tough

The male soldiers' narrative of providing for families is, to some extent, understood in Palestinian communities in Israel. This is not to say
that these communities accept service in the Israeli military—far from it.
But they sympathize with the economic predicament that it is supposedly
born of and with the masculine desires of men to provide for and support
families. Even the harshest critics readily agree that the economic situation
is difficult and that employment opportunities are extremely limited. That
men resort to soldiering to provide for their families is thus understand-
able if not acceptable. The soldiers' explanation has a limited sort of legitimacy, certainly more than the gun-toting pubescent scenario does.[21]

Of course, according to the local ideals of masculinity, to be poor and honorable is far better than to be "made" and a traitor. In this worldview, the poorest unemployed laborer can see himself as superior to an Arab general in the Israeli military. But self-described nationalists I interviewed recognized a problem in the incompatibility between providing for the family and being loyal to the nation. While the "family provider but traitor" framework had limited legitimacy, the "poor but honorable" prospect had limited appeal. On the one hand, Palestinian nationalism has idealized the peasant revolutionary, and many young Palestinians proudly wear pendants of Naji al-Ali's cartoon character Hanthala (a Palestinian refugee child in rags and bare feet).[22] But they don't necessarily want to become destitute refugees themselves. In fact, they also commonly see themselves as modernizing and as "bourgeois-in-the-making." Fuad, the Communist Party activist, explained that in the context of the housing crisis in Arab communities, arguing against soldiering and asking people to essentially give up the desire to have a house for their family is not easy.[23] In Israel, Palestinian commitments to the nation and commitments to the family are often at odds, rather than in harmony, with one another.

Masculinity and Other Forms of Israelization

Arab soldiers try to claim a masculinity that, to a great extent, mimics nationalist masculinity by focusing on their support for their families. Unlike Bolivian peasant conscripts or Mayan Guatemalan ones, for whom state-organized violence became "one of the most powerful public idioms of manhood," such violence is downplayed and hidden by Palestinian soldiers, who are cast as outsiders to the Jewish Israeli polity.[24] Those who do not mask the violence inherent in soldiering—symbolized by the image of the soldier turning on the siren and driving around in a jeep or strutting around in his uniform with his gun—are summarily dismissed by their fellow Palestinians. Not surprisingly, despite my probing, at no point during my interviews did soldiers openly describe to me their participation in fighting in the Israeli military. Although they might have done so in other contexts I did not access—for example, among other soldiers or in Jewish Israeli settings—within their communities, where my fieldwork took place, they framed their soldiering along the familiar lines of provider masculinity.[25]

These kinds of discussions around nationalism and masculinity are not confined to the specific and numerically marginal case of soldiers. A much larger concern about Israelization of Palestinians living in Israel is expressed in similar terms.[26] Young men's attempts to assimilate—wanting to get into the Jewish disco, to compete in the Hebrew Maccabiah sports competitions, or to work for the state environmental "protection" agency (notorious for harassing Arabs)—are also often considered symptomatic of an immature masculinity similar to that attributed to soldiers.[27] By characterizing young men who seek Israelization as pubescent, critics essentially point to their naïveté—their uncritical desire to join Jewish institutions and mimic cultural norms in a society that will, in the end, continue to exclude them.

Sa'id Ighbariyyi, who helped me mediate contacts with several soldiers, opined: "If the state really intended to Israelize us, two-thirds of us would have already been lost among them by now, dissolved into their society. But the state has never been interested in really Israelizing Arabs. It is not possible. It would mean the failure of the principle of a Jewish state."

Rather than articulating this criticism in political terms—which is common, as well—the gendered criticism of mere "boys" powerfully focuses on the individualism of the behavior at hand. In the face of a long history of exclusion of Arabs as a group, the assimilationist thinks he will make it in on his own. One young Arab man hangs an Israeli flag on his car, another tries to blend in by speaking only in Hebrew at the shopping mall, and another—an extreme example—decides to join the army. These attempts at assimilating are criticized not necessarily out of narrow nationalistic chauvinism—they are not threatening because they blur the boundaries of Arab and Jew. On the contrary, it is the continued rigidity of Israeliness as exclusively Jewish that makes these behaviors seem problematic and naïve.

The response of many of the criticized men is that theirs is a pragmatic masculinity, not formed by outdated notions of national taboos but, rather, aimed at advancing their families or themselves as current or future family providers. Underlying this argument is the notion that for Palestinians to "integrate," "develop," or gain their civil rights in Israel, they need to be pragmatic. This is not necessarily a rare notion among Palestinian citizens. That a sizable "Israeli Arab" camp preaches integration with Jewish Zionist parties illustrates the diverse strategies—often contradictory—that Palestinians use.

The Significance of Give and Take

The state plays a key role in setting the parameters for this game and for the debated masculinities.[28] If soldiers and aspiring assimilationists argue that Palestinians in Israel need to be pragmatic to improve their lot, then in order for this argument to be persuasive at all, they must in fact improve their lot. The two versions of masculinity attributed to soldiers—duped boys or made men—can be understood as two versions of relating to the Israeli state. The efficacy of each and its success are affected by state actions. Soldiering and assimilationism gain a currency among Palestinians in Israel based on the rewards that the state gives for such behaviors. The extreme example of the soldiers in this study and their provider narratives demonstrates that the state gives—land, income, and access—with one hand as a reward for certain behaviors. But it also takes away with the other hand, by continuing to enforce policies of racial discrimination, underlined by its conception as a Jewish state.[29] From the state's perspective, for Arabs to be Israelized is *emphatically* not to be Israeli.[30]

Many Palestinian soldiers I interviewed described hitting glass ceilings, being confined to ethnic units and subjected to constant suspicion, unable to escape from state Judaizing practices that exclude them from the common good. The competing descriptions of immature, pubescent masculinity and family-provider masculinity "stick" and are made culturally convincing by the success of the various strategies Palestinians pursue. That soldiering and other more minor assimilationist behaviors are widely criticized as the actions of duped boys indexes, at some level, their failure to gain the desired rewards—of successfully providing for families.[31] This situation is shaped by the state's reluctance to turn soldiering into a level playing field for Arabs and Jews and by its ongoing prioritization of its own Jewishness.

9

Blood in the Same Mud

THE MINORITY OF BLACKS IN SOUTH AFRICA who served in the armed forces under apartheid have been called "soldiers without politics."[1] This may be a provocative oversimplification, but their decisions to enlist certainly suggest a departure from the standard assumed ethnic, racial, national, or religious politics of soldiering. There are many cases from around the globe and from different times where soldiers similarly appear to be fighting in the wrong military, on the wrong side. These cases disrupt common, usually nationalistic, assumptions about why soldiers fight wars. From Kurds in the Turkish military fighting Kurdish rebels, Algerians fighting with the French against Algerian independence, or Indians serving in the colonial British Indian Army, these soldiers complicate tidy understandings of military conflict as occurring between two (or more) separate and bounded groups. They confuse this imagined order and suggest a more complex understanding of ethnic conflict.

In the case of the Israeli–Arab conflict, the story often told is that Jews and Arabs have hated each other from time immemorial, for centuries, always. Hence the military conflict of today.[2] The story I tell here is different. Palestinian citizens of Israel who volunteer to serve in the Israeli military frame their military service as an attempt—often failed—at upgrading their citizenship status in Israel. Those who are resentful or bitter are not so because of personal animosity or a clash of civilizations—but as a result of experiences of structural ethnic discrimination in the military. Ethnic conflict thus emerges as a *product* rather than simply a precursor of militarization.

It is by no means natural that Palestinians fight alongside other Palestinians, nor alongside Israeli Jews, or for that matter, fight at all. Why they fight is a product not of an essential identity they are born with, but of particular social, economic, and political conditions they encounter. Soldiers who appear to be on the wrong side of war, despite the radically different contexts, geographies, and histories they exist in, remind us of this fact and help tell a more complicated story normally hidden behind tales of patriotism and sacrifice.

Violence Work

This story includes the material rewards and punishments of soldiering. With soldiers on the wrong side, one is more likely to encounter references to the economic advantages or necessity of service, with militaries regarded as sources of work or land or as job training centers.[3] The possibility of acquiring a trade is said to have attracted many West African men to join the French colonial army in the late 1940s.[4] In a famous novel, Azzedine, an Algerian Harki who fought with the French during the Algerian war of independence, enters the army as he "would enter a factory," to fight against the poverty brought on by the French themselves.[5] One of the primary reasons poor men respond to the bi-annual recruitment calls in Bolivia, where the military fights other poor Bolivians, is the importance of the military completion document for "obtaining work in urban factories and businesses."[6]

If soldiering is a form of employment, for many soldiers it is employment in a context of poverty and need. Irishmen from "all parts of Ireland continued to join the British army even after partition."[7] Historian Keith Jeffery argues that "idle hands and empty stomachs . . . are a powerful antidote to patriotic idealism . . . and there were more of these in Dublin than in any other part of the country."[8] The areas that provided the most soldiers to the British Indian Army were areas where peasant dispossession was comparatively widespread.[9] This dispossession helped structure recruits' "predisposition towards military service."[10]

One Iraqi who joined the civil defense during the American occupation explains: "Should I sleep without dinner and not work with the Americans? No. I should work with the Americans and have dinner."[11] Food for work programs, or "beans with bullets," were used to recruit peasants for soldiering and intelligence work in Guatemala.[12] In these contexts, material forces outshine the simple ideological assumptions of nationalism, but they also shape the behavior of soldiers in more normalized contexts as well.

In the United States, military programs like JROTC (Junior Reserve Officer Training Corps) operate with an explicit goal of targeting populations "in 'less affluent large urban schools.'"[13] Public discourse often focuses on the benefits of military education for "at-risk" youth from these areas, and on the discipline and career opportunities provided to boys who would otherwise supposedly join gangs or girls who would succumb to unwed teen pregnancy.[14] Yet the fact remains that the United States Army is an all-volunteer army that fills its rank and file from lower socioeconomic classes. This process has been termed a "poverty draft."[15]

Recently, U.S. military recruiters have taken to crossing the border into poorer Mexico to find "green card soldiers" to boost the Latino numbers in the military from roughly 10 percent to as much as 22.[16] There are nearly 40,000 frontline troops who are noncitizen "green card soldiers." In 2002, President Bush signed an executive order granting fast-track citizenship to members of the military. Under this executive order, the normal five-year waiting period for green card holders to be able to apply for citizenship is abolished for soldiers, reducing the naturalization process to eight to ten months from the time of application until the oath of citizenship is administered. According to the Department of Homeland Security's U.S. Citizenship and Immigration Services (USCIS), as of February 2005 almost 16,000 active duty personnel have taken advantage of the executive order to gain citizenship.[17]

In the second U.S. war in Iraq, the first American casualty was a Latino noncitizen, a Guatemalan by the name of José Gutierrez.[18] The government has also granted "posthumous citizenship" to noncitizen soldiers killed during wartime. Guadalupe Denogean was given citizenship after being severely wounded in 2003 while serving in Iraq. He described his newly acquired citizenship in the following manner: "'It's kinda like borrowing a car and driving it all the time and all of a sudden you get the title.' And he has no loan to pay back either, he pointed out: 'I've already paid that.'"[19] This utilitarian language is a far cry from that of nationalist patriotism.

Many of the Palestinian soldiers I interviewed—particularly the men—highlighted the economic benefits of service in the Israeli military, such as improving one's ability to build a home, sustain a family, get rid of a tax debt, or get a water line for the village. It is these material rather than ideological goals that they most frequently cited in answering "Why do they do it?" Regardless of the ideological claims they made about their military service (or for that matter the patriotic claims of Israeli Jewish soldiers), material conditions and structural circumstances are significant factors that shape military service.

Choice: Degrees of Coercion

By highlighting these material circumstances, the imputation of choice in the query "Why do they do it?" becomes complicated. Although the system in 1970s South Africa under which blacks joined the military may be portrayed as voluntary, it is better understood "as an 'economic draft' in which unemployed blacks are forced, in a fashion, to volunteer."[20] In addition to economic forces, other forms of pressure are at play. In some cases, these amount to outright physical coercion. In the 1960s, military recruitment in Guatemala sometimes involved "being lassoed and tied up like cattle in the central square."[21] Recruitment in more remote areas of France's West African colonies during World War I has been described as "the largest, and the most inescapable 'man hunt' in the history of the region," reminiscent of slave raids of the past, though involving proportionately larger numbers.[22]

The threat of violence is also used to ensure adequate levels of recruitment. The threat not only of their own torture and death, but also that of their families, forced many Mayan men to commit monstrous acts for the Guatemalan military.[23] Lunn describes collective punishments in West Africa: "Crops and livestock were seized or destroyed, homes were indiscriminately put to the torch, and villagers—often irrespective of whether they were innocent bystanders, parents taken as hostages, or armed resisters—were killed or executed by soldiers."[24] A character in Ghosh's novel on Indian soldiers in the British Indian Army says: "all fear is not the same. . . . A man may fear the shadow of a gun just as much as the gun itself—and who is to say which is more real?"[25]

Such descriptions of military recruitment through the use of direct violence or threat of violence may appear extreme when compared to the circumstances under which Palestinian soldiers join the Israeli military. However, Palestinian recruitment falls on a continuum of coercion. French manhunts in West Africa may fall toward one end, but "fear of the shadow of the gun," "economic drafts," and "objective forces structuring recruits' predisposition" all fall along this continuum and significantly complicate the imagined voluntary choice to enlist out of patriotic idealism and a sense of national belonging. In Israel, Arabs volunteering for Jewish "mandatory" service, family leaders volunteering junior family members to enlist, and people choosing to perform duties to a state with military-contingent citizenship before asking for rights, all cast choice in a new light.[26]

Mix and Match Ethnicity

The various combinations of coercion, persuasion, pressure, and incentives demonstrate that military authorities strategize and deliberate over the acquisition of recruits as well as their management once enlisted. The strategies of managing soldiers from the "wrong side" generally build on the assumption that these soldiers are volatile and require special attention. Blacks in the South African forces were carefully selected based on which of them were easiest to manipulate and therefore could be efficiently used. This often involved the "the time-honored ploy of playing off one tribe, ethnic group, or nation against another."[27] This points to the military's role in the production of tribal, ethnic, and national identities. Such techniques might garner more attention in the case of soldiers on the "wrong side," but they are also implicit in militaries' management of all soldiers.[28]

Military authorities attempt to manage soldiers by specifying units' ethnic composition and leadership. During the First World War, soldiers in what became known as the Tirailleurs Sénégalais (Senegalese Scouts) served in segregated units, their companies were composed of what the French considered to be related races, and they were kept separate as much as possible from both French soldiers and civilians.[29] In contrast, in 1945–60, the French army decided it was in its best interest to include an ethnic mix among Africans in each regiment.[30] Interestingly, the U.S. military kept African Americans in segregated units until the end of the Korean War, but did not segregate Mexican Americans or Native Americans. Decisions such as these affect the contours of identity.

Authorities deliberate on the best location to place troops based on ethnicity. The military in Bolivia seemed to place conscripts outside of their home regions because it assumed they would be more likely to shoot "subversives" from another regional or ethnic background.[31] These divergent military strategies of separation and mixing are a visible feature of managing "wrong siders," but are also part of the production of soldiers on the so-called right side.

The naming of units is also part of the management of soldiers on the "wrong side." British military authorities in the late 1940s weighed different titles for brigades with the goal of avoiding anything that would "discourage men from Eire—who comprised half of all the recruits—from joining up," and "avoiding any title which would encourage political feeling within Regiments between men drawn from Ulster and those from Eire."[32] In Guatemala many task forces participating in deadly campaigns were given Mayan names to supposedly make Indians feel part of the nation.[33]

Another prominent technique to manage soldiers on the "wrong side" involves limiting them in rank. Lower standards for the recruitment of blacks to the South African Defence Force went along with higher standards for their promotion.[34] All officer positions in the U.S. military require security clearances—which in turn require citizenship. Therefore, noncitizen soldiers are concentrated almost exclusively in the enlisted ranks.

One of the major complaints of the Palestinian soldiers I interviewed in Israel revolved around their limited rank and promotions and confinement to special minority units. Appointments are commonly surrounded by "a mist of regulations"; beneath the manuals, regulations, and procedures is the murky shadow of "prejudice, distrust and suspicion."[35]

Placing Palestinians primarily in minorities units, keeping them out of the air force and intelligence, subjecting them to more intense background security checks, and forbidding them to use their native Arabic language are among the techniques the Israeli military wields to produce "minority" soldiers. Similarly, placing Jews in the units Arabs are kept out of, trusting them and minimizing their background checks, and instituting the use of Hebrew, are all part of the production of Israeli Jewish soldiers.

Lest it be obscured, many soldiers on the wrong side join and serve under conditions inferior to those of soldiers putatively on the right side. In the South African military, pensions and benefits "conformed to an overall ratio of 4:2:1, White:Colored and Indian:African."[36] West African subjects of France were forced to serve "under dramatically different terms from those that applied to French citizens," for longer periods and farther away from home.[37]

Perhaps death rates are the ultimate indicator of power dynamics in the military. Some historians argue that the mortality rate for the Tirailleurs Sénégalais was three times higher than that of French soldiers—the Tirailleurs were used primarily as "shock troops" and "many generals sought to spare French lives by sacrificing African ones."[38] The black mounted regiments known as the Buffalo Soldiers serving on the American Western frontier "consistently received some of the worst assignments the Army had to offer."[39] Many of the Palestinian soldiers in my study perceive their service as taking place under discriminatory conditions—confined to less prestigious units, dead-end posts, and dangerous locations.

Yet this unequal system often promises something of a better deal than what is available outside of the military. The army was one of the few institutions in colonized India that opened its doors to communities under colonial rule.[40] Racial discrimination was certainly not eliminated in the U.S. military, but it "surged ahead of civilian institutions in this regard."[41] According to an Arab American Marine, the corps has been a haven for fair treatment: "That's what I love about [it]. . . . Everybody sees your cammies and your rank, and that's how they deal with you."[42] It is this promise of meritocracy, even if limited by racial or ethnic categorizations, that is one of the attractions militaries hold for subjects of unequal systems. According to an Arab soldier I interviewed who complained of the ethnic limitations he faced within the Israeli military, "As bad as it is in there, I only wish we would be treated the same way outside the military."

Given the relative rigidity of militaries and their clear top-down authority structure, the military establishment's visions of ethnic, racial, and nationalist identities have a powerful impact on producing such identities. Many militaries actively construct notions of martial races—from the fighting Irish, to the fierce Gurkhas. After the Great Revolt in India, the British found new groups to be the *real* martial races. One military's warlike people is considered weak by another: Hausa-speaking peoples in Niger were considered poor soldiers by the French, but these same people were favored as soldiers in the British West Africa Frontier Force.[43] These "militarily expedient" constructs of warrior races often guided their use on the front lines.[44]

The Israeli military is no exception. Through its disciplinary practices, recruiting policies, and its naming and organization of units and duties, it attempts to construct not Palestinians but divided groups of Bedouins, Christians, Muslims, and Druze. And it attempts to assign different "natural" roles and allegiances to each, including for example, Bedouins as natural trackers and Druze as non-Arab enemies of other Arabs and natural warriors suited for the infantry, Muslims as most suspicious, and Christians as more modern, among others.[45] So the question is not only "Why do they do it?" or "Why do they fight on the wrong side?" or "What motivates the soldiers and what sorts of identities and loyalties do they *have*?" Rather, I would argue it is necessary to also ask important structural questions such as "How does the military produce sides of a conflict?" "How does it position various groups in terms of its own ideologies and practices?" and "How does it construct identities within its own ranks?"

The army in Guatemala tore apart existing "social relations to impose a new system of authority."[46] It appropriated Mayan customs and language to create sanctioned Mayans—supposedly docile, obedient soldiers who were "deprived of memory."[47] The military's assault on identity was so dramatic that Mayan youth departing with the Guatemalan military were said to "leave Indian but they don't come back Indian."[48] Similarly, in Bolivia, Indian identities are powerfully molded in the military, often producing complicit Latino ones—sometimes literally as when recruits use military registration as a way to change their Indian surnames to Spanish ones.[49]

Palestinian soldiers in the Israeli military also sometimes change their names to Hebrew ones (Isma'il goes by Ishmael, for example, and Yusif by Yosi). They are also required to perform historical amnesia by, for example, using official Zionist names of places that attempt to erase their recent Palestinian past. However, unlike subjugated groups in Guatemala and Bolivia, Palestinians in Israel are marked as "minorities" by the military and not really allowed to become Israeli, since that would require them to be Jewish. Palestinian soldiers in the Israeli military are daily taught the supremacy of Jewish symbols of the state; their role as "minorities" is to support those symbols even while not being able to fully claim them as their own.

Forced to choose between "with us" or "against us," a soldier in the Turkish military serving in the Emergency Rule Zone in the southeast described the military's role in forming his Kurdish identity for him. Some of his fellow soldiers cut off the ears of PKK (Kurdistan Workers Party) fighters and mailed them to their families: "If I objected, they would insult me, saying I was 'supporting the separatists.' And then it was probable that they might charge you with 'being a PKK member' and send you to the 'anti-terrorist unit' for interrogation. I became aware of my ethnic Kurdish origins during military service."[50] This is not altogether different from Maria Jansson's interview with a Bedouin soldier from the Naqab who told her: "I feel Arab Israeli. I was not really aware of this identity before the army. The army has put me in my place, where I belong. . . . To be put in our place is to show that you are not Jewish."[51]

Same-Sized Bullets

Many of the effects militaries have on those they discipline are not necessarily planned or intended. For example, how soldiers identify themselves seems to powerfully morph in relation to military casualty rates, in ways apparently unforeseen by military authorities. The 1987 film *Camp Thiaroye* narrates the history of African soldiers who served

France during World War II and were returned to a transit camp out-side Dakar. There, the military continued to subject them to a series of injustices, despite their extended and loyal service during the war. In a critical scene in the film, Corporal Diarra is in the mess line at the camp and looks with disgust at the inferior food ladled out to him. Diarra asks the camp cook why there was "no meat for us." The cook explains the diminishing portions allotted to different groups of soldiers: "Meat for whites is this much. Meat for mixed races, this much. Meat for natives, that much. As for infantry men [Tirailleurs], once a week, they can have a tiny bit of meat." Diarra retorts: "You idiot, during the war, were there bullets this size for whites, this size for mixed races, this size for natives, and tiny, tiny bullets for [combatants]? You idiot!" and he throws his food on the ground.[52] If fatality counts are considered, it was perhaps larger bullets rather than same-sized bullets that the likes of Corporal Diarra faced.

Veterans from French West Africa saw themselves as having served France "above and beyond the call of duty," and "as having been largely responsible for the Gaullist victory."[53] A bewildering number of veterans' groups thus became part of a struggle for political rights among African ex-soldiers and served as "an important lobby and forum for [their] polit-ical and economic grievances and aspirations."[54] Claims for military com-pensation were registered with the French authorities in the hundreds of thousands.[55] Veterans groups used the slogan "equal sacrifices = equal rights" just as urban Africans in the communes had demanded earlier in the century "equality in society as in the trenches before death."[56]

This emboldening of soldiers is captured in the film *Glory* (1989) about the American Civil War: a black Northern soldier states "colored soldiers stop a bullet just as good as a white one" before tearing up his payment papers that allotted him significantly lower pay than white sol-diers. Speaking on behalf of the 367,000 black troops returning from the First World War in Europe, W. E. B. DuBois proclaimed: "We return. We return from fighting. We return fighting. Make way for Democracy! We saved it in France, and by the Great Jehovah, we will save it in the United States of America."[57]

A similar strategy was used by an Arab American Marine who founded the Association of Patriotic Arab Americans in the Military shortly after September 11, 2001. Its members attempt to build on the fact that, as one of them put it, "Arab Americans in the military shed blood in the same mud that Americans did."[58] The Arab American Institute, with a wider membership, has a website featuring a list of Arab American contributions to the country. First in the long list are the military contributions of famous Arab Americans: "You talk about courage. . . . How about America's and the world's first jet ace? He was the Korean War hero, U.S. Air Force Col. James Jabara."[59] The website goes on to list other prominent American officers of Arab descent and vessels named after them. An entire museum in Washington, D.C., is dedicated to documenting and preserving "the contributions of Jewish Americans to the peace and freedom of the United States, educat[ing] the public concerning the courage, heroism and sacrifices made by Jewish Americans who served in the armed forces." An exhibit on Jewish participation in World War II notes that toward the end of the war a flurry of books appeared in the United States "making the case of Jewish participation" in the war with such titles as *Jews Fight Too!*, *Jewish Youth at War*, and a two-volume study, *American Jews in World War II*.[60]

Whether "shedding blood in the same mud" or "facing same-sized bullets," military participation in these contexts becomes a significant part of the making and unmaking of identities.[61] The unrecognized-villages activist whose service allows him supposedly to be more assertive, the group of fifty discharged soldiers using their service to protest orders that their homes be demolished, or organizers of the movement to end the Druze conscription who protest the expropriation of Druze lands despite their military service, are all prominent examples of minoritized soldiers who try to hold the state to its unfulfilled promises of reward.

The Dead

Given the symbolic value of shedding blood in the same mud—whether it be by Senegalese rescuing France, or brave African American units in Europe, or loyal Arab soldiers "saving Jewish lives"—the treatment of those who have given their lives becomes a focus of surviving soldiers' concern. What happens to those who have made the ultimate sacrifice in the face of "same-sized bullets"? Are their immolations recognized? The rites, funeral services, grave sites, and memorials to these fallen soldiers become a sort of measure of militaries' attitudes toward the subjugated. As a result, denials of a proper ceremony, for example, become major rallying points. Felix Longoria, a Mexican American private from Texas who died in combat during World War II, was denied chapel services in a local funeral home in 1949. According to notes taken by Longoria's supporters, the funeral home director, who was white, explained upon questioning that "'it doesn't make any difference' that Longoria was a veteran. . . . 'You know how the Latin people get drunk and lay around all the time.'"[62] A Mexican American veterans' advocacy group called the American GI Forum, then recently founded, took up the case. They organized a protest that drew the national media, and then-senator Lyndon Johnson offered to bury Longoria at Arlington National Cemetery. This incident "helped unify Latinos and bring national attention to the Mexican-American civil rights movement."[63] Though the Longoria affair was hardly the most severe instance of discrimination against Mexican Americans, it "became a flash point in Mexican-American history and ignited the activism of a whole range of interest groups."[64]

The bodies of Arabs who die while serving in the Israeli military similarly become a focus of weighty attention. Memorial parks and databases of the dead—all ethnically organized—demonstrate the Israeli military's awareness of the role of the dead in its management of minority soldiers. Military authorities try to establish a substantial presence at funerals and mark the dead as loyal to the state, using the corpse to mediate between themselves and the people.[65] But the etching on the tombstone of one Nayif Hayb who was killed in battle in Lebanon is in distorted, almost child-like and grammatically incorrect Arabic. As captured by Palestinian photographer Ahlam Shibli's lens, the grave and its etching function as stark illustrations of the ultimate inability of the state to properly address and recognize Arab soldiers and their families.[66]

The military wraps the bodies of dead Arab soldiers in Israeli flags. But even the ardently collaborative family of Yusif Jahaja covered the body of their deceased son with a blanket so as to conceal the flag.[67] The bodies of dead soldiers enter the argument between Palestinians and the Israeli state over citizenship. The military has faced great difficulty in finding Muslim imams willing to pray over the bodies of dead Muslim soldiers, though these imams are in effect government appointees on government-controlled salaries.[68]

Limits

If military service and war sacrifices become associated with demands for political and economic rights, it is striking how frequently this strategy has failed or yielded inferior results. During the Algerian war, a large number of Algerians served with the French forces colonizing their country. These Harki fighters placed their bets on the French, but wound up being, as one Harki put it, "the refuse of decolonization. Everyone preferred to pretend we didn't exist."[69] A 1960 Front de Libération Nationale (FLN) leaflet warns the Harki that "tomorrow [France] will abandon you, like it abandoned all those it used in Viet Nam, in Tunisia and in Morocco."[70] Indeed, the Harki were abandoned during France's abrupt withdrawal from Algeria. An infamous telegram issued by the minister of Algerian affairs forbade French army officers from assisting the Harkis and their families.[71] The result was tens of thousands of Harkis killed. In 2001, a group of former Harki filed a suit against one of the last surviving members of de Gaulle's cabinet for this abandonment as a "crime against humanity." The suit included the testimony of "a French army sergeant who recalled being ordered to disarm the Harkis, and later using his rifle-butt to beat them back as they tried desperately to climb aboard his departing truck. FLN fighters watched on."[72] Those who eventually made their way to France languished in camps and continue to feel unrecognized and neglected.

African soldier subjects of France were demobilized after World War II back to French West Africa, including those who wanted to remain in Europe. But the state did not take immediate responsibility for their care and, unlike French soldiers, they languished in camps awaiting shipment without back pay and were still subject to harsh military discipline.[73] In September and October 1944, 20,000 black African soldiers were abruptly withdrawn from the army "as part of the so-called 'whitening' of the Free French Forces." Without warning, African soldiers were "relieved of their front-line positions, their weapons, and the uniforms on their backs. They were sent to the south to wait for ships to take them back to Africa."[74] The active role played by colonial troops, including African ones, in the liberation of France was considered an embarrassment by de Gaulle, who tried to conceal their importance.[75] Subsequently, French authorities froze the military pensions of "indigenous" soldiers. It was not until 2002, forty-three years later, that a law for their restitution was passed, and not until 2006 that funds were allocated for payments.[76]

As long as subjugated soldiers are institutionally identified by their difference, equality with dominant soldiers in the trenches before death does not seem to go far beyond the battlefield. And it is often rigid state policies that insist on distinguishing minority soldiers from majority ones, not soldiers' behavior or sense of loyalty.

George Orwell wrote in Marrakesh when observing African soldiers recruited by the French: "There is one thought which every white man . . . thinks when he sees a black army marching past. 'How much longer can we go on kidding these people? How long before they turn their guns in the other direction?'"[77] In the Belgian-controlled Congo, eighteen mutinous black soldiers were executed in Boma in 1900. A photographer recorded a scene in which "condemned rebels were tied to stakes and a firing squad of loyal black troops has just fired a salvo. But in case the loyalists waver, the entire white male population of Boma is standing in a long row at right angles of both groups, each sun-helmeted white man with a rifle at the ready."[78]

It is the military's own view that it is tricking people, duping troops—whether they be African soldiers of colonial France or Arab soldiers in the Israeli military—that continues to underwrite the military's anxiety and the production of suspect loyalties. The fear that "they might turn their guns on us" arises in many cases from the underlying suspicion that "they" might have some cause to do so. As in the case of Palestinians in the Israeli military, mistrust, suspicion and the fear of what post-9/11 American journalists have called a "fifth column syndrome" are symptomatic of the common limits to the incorporation of men into the "wrong side" of war.[79]

During World War II, an American chief justice argued that "in time of war residents having ethnic affiliations with an invading enemy may be a greater source of danger than those of a different ancestry," though this suspicion was applied to Japanese Americans but not to German or Italian Americans.[80] Many U.S. officials have echoed Daniel Pipes' sentiment that "Muslim government employees in law enforcement, the military and the diplomatic corps need to be watched for connections to terrorism, as do Muslim chaplains in prisons and the armed forces."[81] In the days following the 9/11 attacks, a Gallup Poll reported that 58 percent of Americans supported "requiring Arabs, including those who are US citizens, to undergo special, more intensive security checks."[82] This resulted in, among other things, the black comedy of errors in which espionage charges were brought against the so-called spy ring at Guantanamo Bay including Muslim chaplain Captain James Yee, Air Force translator Ahmad al-Halabi, and others. All espionage charges against these Muslim soldiers were eventually dropped. But these incidents demonstrate the structurally suspicious nature of particular identifications and categorizations, rather than actions or deeds. Arab soldiers in the Israeli military are subject to suspicion regardless of their individual behavior.

Another apparently common method of designating soldiers from the other side as suspect and dangerous is through their construction as sexual threats to dominant women. African colonial troops sent to occupy the Rhineland became known in Germany as "the black shame," with sensational accusations of numerous sexual assaults against German women.[83] These charges echoed so powerfully in the British and American press, despite repeated and documented refutations, that France transferred black African soldiers to the Levant.[84] Female nurses were expelled from Senegalese hospitals "to spare them the undue attentions of the men" and "'marraines de guerre,' . . . were warned of the African 'contempt for women.'"[85]

Black American soldiers returning from service in Europe in World War I were rumored to have "interracial contact" with French women and accused of attacks on them. Returning black soldiers were seen as beast-like rapists, and many were lynched between 1918 and 1919.[86] These racial sexual fears of suspect soldiers are dramatically illustrated in Julie Otsuka's novel on the Japanese American internment. The father in the novel voices white American fears: "I crept into your house while you were away and sullied your wife. . . . I touched your daughters . . . I pulled out the nails from your white picket fence and sold them to the enemy to melt down and make into bullets."[87]

Fears of Arabs in the Israeli military are occasionally sexualized as well. Palestinian men in general are in fact often characterized as menacing threats to Jewish women in Israel.[88] A number of soldiers mentioned their military service afforded them increased access to "Jewish discos," which other Arab men cannot enter, and thus to dating Jewish women. However, they complained that this access is only partial, with just as many stories of denied entry and rejections by Jewish women who "won't look at an Arab, even if he is a soldier." Within the military, a few high-profile cases in which Palestinian men have been accused of sexually harassing Jewish women seem to garner disproportionate media attention. In one such case, Colonel 'Atif Zahir was found guilty in 2005 of indecent sexual acts and illegal intercourse with his eighteen-year-old Jewish secretary. The judges in the case reprimanded him by quoting David Ben Gurion: "every Hebrew mother knows that she has put the fate of her child in the hands of worthy commanders."[89] The mention of *Hebrew* mothers functions to remind Zaher that he is a non-Jew in a Jewish state attacking a Jewish woman, thus intensifying the unacceptability of his offense.

Soldiers "from the wrong side" are identified as such literally in instances of mistaken identity. Navajo soldiers complained many times of almost being killed by friendly fire incidents during World War II and of being captured and interrogated by other Americans. William McCabe recounts one such incident: "All of a sudden I heard somebody say, 'Halt,' and I kept walking. 'Hey you! Halt, or I'm gonna shoot!' . . . There was a big rifle all cocked and ready to shoot. I'm just from my outfit, I was coming here to get something to eat. And he said 'I think you're a Jap. Just come with me.'"[90] Such incidents of being mistaken for the enemy were so common that Navajo soldiers had to have a white soldier tethered to them in order to "vouch for their GI status," and basically were assigned bodyguards to protect them against their fellow soldiers.[91]

Despite their hope that military service makes those from the wrong side more equal, being identified with the "other" continues to haunt them. The commonly heard refrain that in the U.S. Army "we are all green" depicts the military uniform—the symbol of military membership—as unifying all those who wear it. However, uniforms are notorious for failing to be the weighty symbols of unity they are promised to be. Soldiers in uniform often continue to be identified by skin color, creed, or ethnicity. During the racial clashes of 1917 in the United States, military uniforms provided little protection to African Americans, some of whom were stopped at railroad stations and stripped of their uniforms, while others were lynched in uniform.[92]

During the events of October 2000 in Israel, uniformed Arab policemen were attacked by angry Jewish Israelis in Acre and Tiberias. In January 2002, a hitchhiking Druze soldier in uniform was picked up by an Israeli Jewish driver, who immediately detected the soldier's strong Arabic accent when he spoke Hebrew. Fearing that he might be "an Arab terrorist disguised as an Israeli soldier," the driver took him to the nearest police station. "Good thing they didn't shoot him," one of the soldiers I interviewed told me. "I've served in the army for seventeen years, but people can still tell I'm an Arab, even in uniform. Sometimes, I'm on duty patrolling in the central bus station and I can see the foreigners [that is, Israeli Jews] looking at me suspiciously. They are probably thinking, 'What if he is from the West Bank but is in disguise?'"[93] Uniforms—and military service—do not go far in blurring the fundamental policy of defining citizens in Israel as either Jewish or Arab.[94]

Underlying these "failures" of uniforms to eliminate mistrust is often an essential contradiction in government policies. Navajos were subjects of concerted efforts to eradicate their language and then were expected to turn around and use that same language to create a secret military code and to serve as military "code talkers." The recent belated official recognition of the Navajo code talkers is notably silent on "just how despised this invaluable language was before May 1942."[95]

For the Tirailleurs Sénégalais, soldiers were expected to fight and die "in defense of a nation-state of which they are not fully a part."[96] Similarly, in the South African military, the very existence of black units was incompatible with the government's aim of delineating black African "homelands" separate from "white" South Africa.[97] This contradiction was sarcastically described by Chief Gatsha Buthelezi of Kwa-Zulu: "They expect us to be 'patriotic foreigners'"—a concept not so distant from "righteous gentiles" in Israel.[98] Palestinians are constantly defined in terms of their non-Jewish minority status in a state "of and for the Jews." And not unlike the U.S. government's treatment of the Navajo, the Israeli state displaces Bedouins, for example, from their lands, expropriates their livestock, and supposedly "modernizes" them, yet wants to use their connection to their land, their experiences shepherding livestock, and their denigrated so-called traditional lifestyle as the basis for their service in the military as trackers.

Rebels

Such basic contradictions in government policies or practices can at certain points erupt in soldier protest, ranging in magnitude from throwing food on the ground to desertion, from the establishment of veterans associations to armed mutinies. The tensions among the lure of joining the powerful, and the economic and physical pressures to serve on the one hand, and the often disproportionate hardships and risks of service, and the rejection, suspicion, and categorization as potentially dangerous within the military on the other hand, can rupture at certain junctures. Rebellions might be as minor, "covert and subtle" as black South African soldiers complaining about the quality of food or reporting sick.[99] Or they might involve religious conversions, such as black U.S. Marines converting to Islam during the Gulf War as "a way to dissent from U.S. Policy" and racism in the military.[100] Or they might take individually violent forms such as the hundreds of "fragging" incidents, the killing of an officer or NCO by his soldiers with a grenade or other fragmentation device, during the American war in Vietnam.[101]

Resistance can also take more collective organized forms. In 1944 at the barracks in Thiaroye, African ex-POWs refused to obey orders and briefly held a French general hostage. The immediate cause of this protest was "the failure of the French authorities to provide them with back pay and demobilized premiums" though even these were inferior to what European French soldiers received.[102] Delays in repatriation caused not only the rebellion at Thiaroye, but some fifteen other recorded incidents involving ex-POWs and recently discharged African soldiers.[103]

These examples remind us that soldiers are not without agency. Even in strict, authoritarian, hierarchical, and all-encompassing military systems, certain fissures of protest are cracked open. Soldiers make the best of the limits militaries impose on them.[104]

Blaise Diagne, an ambitious Senegalese politician, headed a French military recruiting mission to Senegal in 1918 that included a large group of highly decorated African officers paraded before Senegalese audiences to demonstrate the enhanced status military service can bring.[105] Diagne was attracted to "the egalitarian precepts of French republicanism" and strove to recruit colonized Africans into the French military by "explicitly linking the performance of military duty with the acquisition of civic rights."[106] He essentially strove for "increasing egalitarianism in an inherently inegalitarian order." This gave rise to exaggerated expectations, which were eventually frustrated and became "a source of disillusionment."[107]

There have not been any large-scale mutinies among Arab soldiers in Israel, though frustrated expectations and reasserted promises underlie the rises and falls in the (overall low) levels of Arab enlistment. Arab critiques of the Israeli military "underscore how [it] is basically a Jewish army and how non-Jews can only be granted secondary status within it."[108]

Battling Chance

A great number of soldiers I interviewed claimed to be motivated by a search for equality—or at least improved status—implicitly or explicitly promised to them in return for their military service. Some held on to this optimism after their experiences of service, but the narratives of the majority seem to follow that of so many other soldiers on "the wrong side." Some benefits and individually arranged rewards were obtained, but disappointments abounded as did unfulfilled promises and persistent, fundamental contradictions. A few men I interviewed have gone AWOL, others have not renewed their contracts, and yet others trudge along since "I have only a few years till retirement; I can't start from zero now." An enthusiastic minority continues to hope to "prove myself through service," buying the Israeli citizenship logic of "we have to give to the state before we can take." It is the opportunity for equality—theoretically possible yet apparently unattainable, frequently promised yet repeatedly denied—that undergirds Palestinian persistence in playing Israeli games, in the military and beyond. Palestinians in Israel have been described as separated from Jews by a barrier akin to a glass wall—invisible to outsiders but nonetheless solid and unyielding.[109] Military service does not seem to bring that wall down—it cuts through the military as it does through the rest of society.

The experiences of Palestinian soldiers in the Israeli military, and the diverse examples briefly put together here, illustrate that the dual "sides" of a conflict are not natural, preexisting, and ahistorical. When asking why someone is on the wrong side of a war, one has to inquire how those "sides" came to be in the first place. And the answer often is militarization and war itself.[110] Stories of endemic Arab animosity to Jews, and the assumption that Arabs naturally hate Jews (or vice versa) and therefore fight against them, become less tenable. Seen in this light, binaries that at first feel satisfying, even commonsensical (us / them, loyal / traitor, mercenary / patriotic soldier, resistance / acquiescence, good Arab / bad Arab), are no longer so. They become more problematic and much more messy, complicated, and embattled. Arab soldiers can be understood as marginal individuals who accommodate the state in order to give themselves literally a fighting chance. Yet military authorities frequently continue to define them by their otherness, unable to give up on associating them with the enemy. After all, this sustained image of a menacing enemy is the raison d'être for such a large military in the first place.

It has been noted that states attempt to mask "power relations under the guise of public interest."[111] But in Israel, that "public interest" has to date been marked as Jewish. The various minority categories the state insists on, of Bedouins, Druze, Christians, and Muslims, are in the end seen "in terms of deviance from the desired profile" of Jewishness.[112] The position of non-Jews (and women) in the military and in Israel more generally is always "subordinate to those men epitomizing the holy quartet of ideals."[113] Palestinians, soldiers and otherwise, must constantly acquiesce to the Jewish majority and play by stacked rules in a game they are destined not to win. They are asked to salute the Israeli flag with the Jewish symbol of the star of David—together with the ghost image of the bulldozer and the tank that "deserve to be on [it]."[114]

In the documentary film *Power*, Saqir, from an unrecognized village, is filmed at his swearing-in ceremony. He takes an oath, in Hebrew of course, to "be loyal to the state of Israel, to obey all orders, and even to sacrifice my life to protect the homeland and the liberty of Israel." He stands near the Jewish religious site of the Wailing Wall and under ruffling flags with stars of David to sing the Israeli national anthem "Ha-Tikvah"

(The Hope): "Our hope is not yet lost, the hope of two thousand years, to be a free people in our land, the land of Zion and Jerusalem." (See Figure 6.) He is thus made to perform his own marginalization. Even the mayor of Mashhad village, a loyal member of the Zionist Labor Party, admits that "Ha-Tikvah" does not stir any feelings of belonging in him.[115] The anthem describes a longing for Zion, at the heart of which lies the *nefesh yehudi*, Jewish soul. It excludes Palestinians, who must nonetheless sing it and somehow endeavor to be stirred by it, though clearly not on their own behalf.

Emile Habiby's fictional character Saeed the luckless pessoptimist survives by becoming a collaborator with the Israelis. Habiby's narrative teaches readers "to love, hate, ridicule, despise but eventually appreciate [Saeed] for his resilience."[116] If Palestinian soldiers, and Palestinians in Israel more generally, resemble at some level the pessoptimist, their behaviors are sometimes despicable, sometimes lovable, and certainly resilient. During the war against Lebanon in 2006, Hezbollah katyushas landed

"Our hope is not yet lost,

FIGURE 6 *Saqir (center) sings "Ha-Tikvah" and is sworn in at the Wailing Wall. From the film* Power *(2006), directed by Ayelet Bechar.*

in some Arab areas in northern Israel. Friends of Palestinian historian Sherene Seikaly wrote to her from around the world "commenting on the irony and absurdity of our location. . . . We were stuck on the wrong side, they noted. But the position of Palestinians in Israel, Sherene asserts, "is not the *wrong side*, but a central core of this long arduous struggle."[117]

Afterword

Unsettling Methods

I CONDUCTED TEN MONTHS of what turned out to be challenging and profoundly humbling fieldwork from 2000 to 2005, and interviewed seventy-two Arab men and three Arab women who had served in various branches of the Israeli security apparatus, the military, the Border Guard, and the police force. They served for periods ranging from eight months to twenty-three years, many of them in more than one branch.

I attempted to interview soldiers from a variety of religious, economic, educational, and regional backgrounds. This group of men and women included Muslims, Christians, and Bedouins (I also interviewed eleven Druze soldiers). The majority of interviewees (59) identified themselves economically as lower- or lower-middle class, whereas the rest claimed middle-class status. Only two had a postsecondary education prior to enlistment (none had a Bachelor's degree). Most hailed from three major regions where Palestinians live in Israel (the Galilee, the Triangle, and the Naqab), in Arab villages (recognized and unrecognized) or towns in Israel, and four lived in mixed Arab-Jewish cities. Several were defined by the state as "present absentees" (refugees expelled from their homes but who remained within the borders of Israel).

Military Versus Police

Although I sometimes identify individual interviewees by branch of service, I often use the term *soldiers* to refer to what were, in fact, policemen, Border Guards, and members of the military of varying rank. Distinctions are sometimes made between these forces, particularly between the police and the military. It is typically argued that the police handle criminal and civil cases that are distinct from military duties, especially the duties of units stationed in the West Bank and Gaza engaged in or supporting combat. As one of my interviewees put it, there is sometimes a perception that police work is "cleaner." The state has increased "community policing" since 2000 and tried to portray its duties as protecting the Arab community and promoting its welfare. I have chosen, however, not to focus on these differences for a number of reasons.

First, many of the men I interviewed had served in more than one branch, often serving in the military and then in the Border Guard or police. Second, policemen explained that whether they were detailed to traffic duty in Tel Aviv or criminal investigations in Nazareth, their duties extended well beyond these areas in "emergency" situations—from a nearby bomb scare to the so-called disengagement from Gaza. According to one of the soldiers I interviewed: "Because there is a national struggle, there is no [distinction between] police and military. Their 'function' [used Hebrew, *tafkid*] is one." Third, the policemen I interviewed described an implicit requirement of serving several years in the Jerusalem area, where the criminal-political divide is further blurred. According to a retired policeman: "The police belonged to the military in the West Bank. They would use us for night arrests. They used us to suppress the intifada. We would give out tickets randomly. I sensed the injustice. I had unbearable headaches at night." Another policeman described standing guard while Israeli workers demolished a house in East Jerusalem: "It didn't help to object. Our commanding officer said, 'I agree with you, this is very difficult, but they have a court order [used Hebrew, *tsav mishpat*] and we are here to enforce the law.'"

A fourth reason I do not focus on distinctions between various security branches is that a sought-after package of benefits accrues to those who serve in any of the three branches. Perhaps most significantly, I found that to a large extent, questions of citizenship, nationalism, loyalty, and gender cut across these divides. Indeed, in my interviews with non-soldiers, the terms police, military, and Border Guard were often used interchangeably. One of the policewomen I interviewed told me: "When I joined the police my father was happy because he had wanted me to join the military, and it's the same 'system' [used Hebrew, *ma'rekhet*]."

Although my focus was on voluntary military service, I also interviewed several Druze.[1] Equally as important as interviewing soldiers was fieldwork and interviews with non-soldiers. This included soldiers' relatives and neighbors as well as other members of the community: politicians and political activists, Druze army resisters, human rights lawyers, therapists, school administrators, journalists, and also many people who were not particularly invested in the issue of soldiering.

Sampling Challenges

It would be difficult to study a "representative" sample of soldiers because statistical data on the group as a whole are classified and unavailable to the public. Moreover, it is extremely difficult to secure soldier participation. Identifying volunteer soldiers, Border Guards, and policemen was easy because they were generally infamous in their communities; getting them to agree to be interviewed was more difficult. For each soldier, I had to employ a mediator, or sometimes multiple mediators, before I could establish any contact. I urged mediators to assure the potential interviewee that I was conducting an academic study and would guarantee his or her anonymity. Several soldiers wanted reassurance that I had no connections to any newspapers or broadcast media. Others told me they did not give a damn what others thought and that I could "print my name in bright red." One soldier acted offended when I told him I guaranteed his anonymity—"I have nothing to hide"—while another told me at the end of the interview "Keep what you have seen secret."

Mediators played a substantial role in my research. In order to cast a wide net in finding soldiers to interview, I tried to work a diverse set of connections. I was put in touch with soldiers by a variety of interlocutors—from the construction worker fixing a leak in my parents' roof who did a lot of work in a village widely known for its high rates of military service, to my cousin's husband in a more distant city who was an activist in

Communist Party politics, to my former classmate, now an attorney, who put me in touch with his clients and their soldier relatives in the Naqab, to an Association of Forty activist who took me to soldiers in unrecognized villages—and by snowballing from one soldier to his friend.[2] This last method was often unplanned and indeed it surprised me when on several occasions soldiers told me: "You have to talk to my friend X. It will be good for him too—he'll feel good about getting things off his chest."

Some mediations failed, with soldiers refusing to be interviewed. On a few occasions, soldiers did not show up at our agreed upon meeting places or times, perhaps due to a last minute change of heart. Several men said they agreed to be interviewed in principle, but that I needed to get permission from their commanding officers—which amounted to "no," given that these officers almost never took my calls or returned my messages. At other times, soldiers called me to cancel appointments after having agreed to be interviewed. One retired soldier from Zarazir called after a suicide bombing in the Nahariyya train station to tell me, "I have nothing to do with politics. I've served more than twenty years and I've never allowed myself to get involved in politics. I don't want to answer any political questions."

Even when I did manage to secure interviews, many of them were strained. These tensions were a product of the highly sensitive nature of the subject. On the one hand, soldiers were wary of discussing their politics because of the risk that this might expose them to in relation to the state. The fear of being deemed disloyal by the ever-suspecting authorities seemed to lie behind, for example, the Zarazir man's decision to cancel our interview. When, during my introductory remarks, I explained to soldiers that they may, of course, choose not to answer particular questions I pose to them, some of them misinterpreted this. They responded that they would indeed be unable to answer questions about military secrets and classified information. The fear that I could, after all, be an Israeli spy was evident in one soldier's joking caution to another: "Watch what you say; this will all reach Sharon." Another soldier asked me: "What will you do if they force you to answer 'who said this?'?" Palestinian fear of the ubiquitous state's questioning also led soldiers to give me some of the juiciest information after the interview had officially ended, I had packed my notebook, and was getting ready to leave, or after interviewees asked me to "turn off your tape recorder" or "don't write this down."[3] Indeed, after taping my first four interviews I subsequently only took written notes because the tape recorder seemed too intrusive.[4]

There was also an opposite source of mistrust in my fieldwork—resulting not from the lurking state, but from a wide Palestinian consensus that serving in the Israeli military is fundamentally wrong. The soldiers' varying conceptions of politics, which they usually assumed (often rightly so) were at odds with my own, emerged as an abiding dynamic in my research. Once, I upset a soldier by scowling when he described "pressuring" a suspect to confess. He almost ended the interview, but instead talked at length about how he saw his role in enforcing the law. One mediator jokingly reassured a nervous interviewee that "she's from America and America loves Israel. No harm will come to you."

While soldiers were generally infamous and soldiering widely considered immoral and traitorous, somehow a few soldiers—a minority within this minority—were considered "good men" by their neighbors and co-villagers despite their jobs. One mediator was highly critical of service in the Israeli police:

> The police are a tool in the hands of the authorities that it uses to reach its goals. The authorities see us as an enemy body. So they use the police against us. The police don't perform their duties—fighting drugs, organizing traffic, and the rest. As a teacher when I see a child in school that has been abused, I should be able to notify the police, but I can't. We have to find alternative solutions. To us, the police kill, shoot; it's frightening, not something to protect us.

Yet this same mediator introduced me to two policemen: "They are okay. They never hurt anyone and their social relationships are good. You can't judge an entire group the same way."

A Woman Researcher and a Masculine Military

My gender was probably a factor in reducing interviewee mistrust, or at least fear of me. I was often not taken very seriously. Many interviewees assumed I was a student rather than a professor—despite my attempt to use my education to gain access by introducing myself as *Doctor* Rhoda Kanaaneh.

From the very beginning of my fieldwork, notions of the soldiers' masculinity played a central role. Sawsan and her husband, Kamal, were two of the many people who helped me to arrange interviews with soldiers, and they were present during parts of some of my initial meetings. Sawsan asked me after one of these introductory visits, "Kamal and I were wondering why you were so serious and unsmiling at those people's houses—I thought it was because you were trying to say, 'Look, just because I'm a woman doesn't mean you can fool with me.' You were demanding that they respect you, weren't you?"

Although my facial expression probably betrayed my nervousness and discomfort at asking the difficult questions at the heart of my research, Sawsan's assessment of the gendering of these dynamics also makes sense. Indeed, many people who acted as intermediaries to help arrange interviews with soldiers—some of them soldiers or former soldiers themselves—expressed their concern about my contact with such men, especially the younger ones. "Don't go to the interview alone. Make sure to have someone else around," I was told, and "I will stay with you so they behave properly." Although I dismissed the notion that the soldiers I interviewed posed a direct threat to me, the imputation that they possessed an immature masculinity that is somehow improper filtered into my work and turned into a central theme.

My gender was also significant to those few interviewees whom I contacted through very circuitous mediation and as a result knew very little about my personal background. For those interviewees, the fact that I was a woman researcher from America, even though I was Arab, seemed to feed their perception of me as less informed about and less directly embroiled in the controversies surrounding soldiering. Although I conducted all my interviews in Arabic, one soldier who was very briefly introduced to me by another, insisted on answering all my Arabic questions in Hebrew and in a condescending tone at that. He assumed I knew very little on the subject and that as an American and an academic I could understand Hebrew better than Arabic (though the opposite was true).

Although my other interviews were conducted in Arabic, most speakers (soldiers and non-soldiers alike) sprinkled Hebrew words or Arabized Hebrew terms throughout their statements. When quoting them in this book, I note whenever such language switches occur—they often suggest

certain political genealogies of power. Although these language changes—
or the use of what Anton Shammas calls Arabebrew—merit a research
project on its own, they bear a quick mention here.[5] Like most Palestinian citizens of Israel, soldiers switch from Arabic to Hebrew for many
military terms such as "reserve service," "security," "recruiting," "uniform,"
and "discharged." They also use Hebrew terms when discussing interactions with the state, such as "court order," "system," "state worker," "position," "law-breakers," and "benefits," reflecting the Jewish character of the
state and the dominance of Hebrew in it. That they use Hebrew words for
"college degree" and "club" reflects a wider dominance of the Jewish majority. Shammas argues that rather than understand this as bilingualism in
the sense of a discourse of equal partners, it is "a case of a monologically
sealed-off language, namely Hebrew, imposing itself on the language of
the Palestinian 'Other'" and is produced in a context of highly asym-
metrical relations of power.[6] Hebrew thus operates as a Jewish language
rather than an Israeli one.[7] My interviewees sometimes used Hebrew eth-
nicized state terminology such as "the Bedouin area," "the Arabic sector"
and "good past" that denotes a Jewish Israeli vision of Arab loyalty.

Locations

During my fieldwork, I was based at my family's home in the Palestinian village of 'Arrabi in the Galilee. In addition to interviewing soldiers, I also interviewed other members of the community about service
in the security apparatus and discussed my research widely with relatives,
friends, and acquaintances. In essence I was interviewing and speaking
with people who had strongly opposing views of military service—and
strongly critical views of each other. I interviewed a mother of a soldier
who was killed in an accident in the military—she prominently displayed
a glass case with his automatic weapon and a menorah in her living room
and wept during the interview. I also interviewed a fellow villager who
said he spits on the grave of the son, "may God not forgive him." I was
placed in the awkward position of maintaining relationships, some more
intimate than others, with both groups. I was witness to frequent diatribes
on opposing sides, some of which I sympathized with more than others,
while trying to maintain an open mind to what the diatribes foreclosed.

This difficulty is more than simply a conflict between the pragmatics of data collection and my moral judgment. On the one hand, I was accustomed to dismissing the soldiers as, at best, bearers of a false consciousness, as victimized, exploited, or duped by the state, and I was skeptical of their "excuses" for joining the security forces. This attitude is captured in exaggerated form by a lawyer acquaintance who told me: "If you look at the kind of people who go to the military, you will see they are not aware, not educated, some of them don't even know how to read or write. They go out of ignorance."

On the other hand, these marginalized soldiers continue to be integrated into Palestinian communities at a certain level—and this encouraged me to try to understand their agency and the complexity of their motivations. Moreover, the stereotype that they hailed mostly from disadvantaged or vulnerable backgrounds—poor families, unrecognized villages, religious minorities—raised the possibility that soldiering for them was a sort of "weapon of the weak."[8] I alternated between seeing their behavior as self-interested with no ideological pretense and seeing them as potentially irreverent boundary-pushers challenging narrow nationalist orthodoxies. This tension, I hope, breeds a textured and multilayered analysis, not unlike the position of these men (and the few women) in their communities.

These contradictions aside, my fieldwork called into question the common solidarity assumptions of anthropological methods. Pamela Ballinger writes of how the traditional anthropological expectation of "empathetic rapport" with informants became particularly problematic during her fieldwork "where individuals or groups may in different moments or contexts have been both victimized and victimizer . . . [and] may variously inhabit either the (relative) margins or centers of power."[9] As scholars increasingly recognize, many identities, actions, loyalties, and nationalisms lack fixity. The terms "studying up" and "studying down" failed to capture my sense of positionality vis-à-vis the soldiers; these men are able to exercise considerable power and physical force, yet they do so under terms that marginalize them by definition—in the name of the Jewish state. The soldiers were "above me" in that they were able, nay required, to use force against other Palestinians, and were given relative impunity when they bullied or beat up their neighbors. Yet they were "below" me in other ways, including their position in the Palestinian community as morally questionable, and in terms of their educational and economic backgrounds. One soldier tried to equalize our status by reminding me "you're American; you're just as bad as we are."

Standard manuals on ethnographic methods offer the following caution to help ensure "an open flow of communication: avoid offering opinions or making judgments about what the interviewee says, despite having strong feelings on the topic."[10] This was frequently not possible in my research, first, because interviewees often asked me about my own opinions and turned my questions to them back on me: "Well, what do *you* think about Arabs serving?"[11] I answered these questions cautiously, trying simultaneously not to lie about my own politics, not to cause the interview to come to an abrupt end, to communicate my sympathy with some if not all of their reasons for serving, and to convey my interest in their honest opinions. I explained that they were right to ask me such questions since this research was part of a larger concern that Arabs in Israel are forced to deal with, as the state requires demonstrations of loyalty and cooperation with Zionist policies and institutions, and because equal rights are often presented to us as conditional on military service. Moreover, I tried to convey my goal of representing their opinions accurately by explaining that if I knew all about the pros and cons of military service, I would not have to interview them.

Over time, my standard introductory "little ethics speech" expanded to include these explanations.[12] However, our presentation of ourselves to others we study is a process subject to divergent interpretations and rarely a completed act.[13] Researchers do not necessarily have "adequate insight for a perfect presentation of [their] identit[ies]; it is always a matter of greater or lesser misrepresentation."[14]

All parties to these ethnographic or "research bargaining" encounters probably recognized an element of "insincerity" and mistrust in them.[15] It was a far cry from the idealized "mutual exchange of experiences whereby . . . we laughed together, cried together, got angry together."[16] In large part, underlying these complex relations was the violence implicit in soldierly duties. Not surprisingly, few interviewees were willing to openly discuss acts of violence or harm, or actions that they regretted or made them uncomfortable. Some of the soldiers were reluctant and some outright unwilling to discuss basics such as the units they were assigned to and the duties they had to perform, a reluctance I interpret as an evasion of culpability for their units' actions.[17]

Tests

The soldiers I interviewed repeatedly tested my sympathies and political limits. I telephoned one Arab official in the Tel Aviv headquarters to request a copy of the released soldiers' benefits bulletin. He surprised me by asking:

"You could serve in the police, right? Is there any reason you couldn't serve?"

Me: "What do you mean?"

Him: "Because, you know, we're always looking for educated women like you. You could really serve your community by working in the area of family violence. There's no reason you couldn't serve, right?"

I interpreted this as some kind of test of whether I could be trusted with, or was deserving of, the material I was requesting.

Me: "I'm not sure I understand your question. I am a citizen of the state and technically, yes, I could apply to join the police force."

Despite a dozen phone calls over several months, this gentleman in the end informed me that the material I was requesting was classified (although I later found it was available on the Ministry of Defense's website) and could not be given to me.

A less calculated test was presented to me by the family of 'Omar Sawa'id, a Bedouin soldier who was captured by Hezbollah in southern Lebanon in 2000 and remained missing for almost four years. I interviewed members of the family about their attitudes toward military service after their son's disappearance—especially since they had another son serving in the military. The emotionally beleaguered mother explained how she just wanted to know whether her son was dead or alive, many people were helping in a letter writing campaign to pressure authorities to reach a deal concerning her son, and by the way, would I be willing to help out? This was not a cause to which I would typically devote my time.

I did not necessarily want to be part of a campaign to pressure Hezbollah to accede to Israeli demands. But I also felt sorry for this mother who had initially objected to her son's enlistment. "I'll see what I can do" was the answer I blurted out at the time, but was haunted by the prospect of her contacting me to make good on this vague promise.

In addition to the problem of handling interviewees questioning me about my opinions, it was also difficult to maintain neutrality because neutrality can "easily become complicity."[18] It is clear that researchers "cannot extricate themselves from unequal relationships and should be careful about writing texts that attempt to stand outside the world of struggle, contest, and competition."[19] Traditionally, anthropologists have not claimed neutrality but have seen themselves as giving voice to the voiceless and to advocating on behalf of the marginalized, an "ethical-political overlay that precludes many critical areas of study."[20]

According to the American Anthropological Association's principles of professional responsibility, "anthropologists' paramount responsibility is to those they study. When there is a conflict of interest, these individuals must come first. Anthropologists must do everything in their power to protect the physical, social, and psychological welfare and to honor the dignity and privacy of those studied."[21] However, later commissions of the association pose the following complex questions:

> Who determines what is in the best interests of the people studied? Most communities will not be of one mind as to what is in their best interests, and it seems paternalistic, if not presumptuous, to expect an anthropological researcher to make that judgment for someone else. . . . Do all groups studied by anthropologists deserve efforts to promote the group's general welfare? It would seem not (i.e., hate groups, terrorists, drug cartels, etc.).[22]

Rather than attempt to categorize the soldiers in my study as either worthy or unworthy of my advocacy—and I did wind up to my surprise liking some of them and disliking others for reasons I cannot entirely explain—it seems prudent to question anthropology's naïve "ethical political overlay."[23]

Anthropology implicitly relates "proximity" to knowing where researchers "ought to move as close as possible to a 'native' point of view."[24] In my case, I never attempted to follow the guideline of attempting to become "fully integrated into the group" and never tried to immerse my-self in military bases or posts.[25] I half-consciously never tried to master military terminology—and deliberately avoided the ideologically loaded Zionist names of places, people, and events that are entrenched in Israeli military discourse. On only one occasion, due to the zealousness of one of my mediators, did I get official permission, almost accidentally, to visit a military recruiting center for Bedouins.

It might be fruitful for researchers to resist the impulse to always bridge the gulf between researcher and the people she studies.[26] Overall, I tried to maintain a distance from the research. Most of my interviews were relatively short and did not involve extensive socialization with in-terviewees as they did in previous projects. Rather than trying to gain knowledge by breaking down barriers as is common in anthropology, I was interested in exploring the nature, dimensions, and source of those barriers as they stood.

Moments of "bridging" were often disturbing to me and jolted me into reexamining my position. Once during a visit to the Bedouin cen-tral command office in Bir al-Sabi', I asked one of my interviewees if he knew of any written sources on Bedouins serving in the military. That afternoon, he gave me a book on the topic published by the Ministry of Defense. I later noticed that the book had been signed by the com-manding officer, with whom I had briefly spoken: "With friendship and recognition, on the occasion of your visit to the Naqab, and wishing you success in all that you do." I wondered what the commander thought he was wishing me success in, and how he had been able to muster this image of "friendship and recognition" from what I saw as my short, de-tached, "strictly business" interaction with him.

Conducting field research is "always risky, personally, emotionally, ideologically, and politically, just because we never know for sure just what results our work will have."[27] I've had the frightening experience of seeing previous work of mine—that explicitly aimed to humanize Pales-tinians—used to dehumanize them.[28] When I submitted an article from this research to a journal, a peer reviewer warned the editors that

> [due to] the way the issue is treated and the fact that it is compared to other experiences it is "normalized." . . . Although the author express[es] his/her

disapproval of the phenomenon, it is indirectly humanized and thereby legitimated. Despite the fact that I know [this] is an academic journal and should not be influenced by political considerations, I just wanted to point out this issue for your consideration.

This study certainly does not seek to legitimate Palestinian service in the Israeli military. It does, however, aim to undo (hopefully more successfully than the article the reviewer read) precisely the assumptions that underpin the reviewer's comments—common but problematic assumptions about politically marginal "treasonous" behavior.

In addition to my interviews I also draw on, among other things, a wide array of newspaper articles. These include articles published in the Arabic press in Israel, such as *al-'Ittihad*, the only Arabic daily, run by the Communist-led Democratic Front for Peace and Equality; the Arabs48 website, associated with the National Democratic Assembly Party; the more tabloid-esque *al-Sinnara*; and others. I also use pieces from the Israeli Jewish press, ranging from *Haaretz*, which brands itself as more left leaning and intellectual, to the more rightist and populist *Yedioth*. These articles together with secondary sources complement my own fieldwork by providing discussions of soldiering beyond the specific context of my interviews.

Reference Matter

Acknowledgments

MANY PEOPLE AND INSTITUTIONS are to be thanked for helping make this book possible. Research was supported by a Richard Carley Hunt Writing Fellowship from the Wenner Gren Foundation for Anthropological Research, a Palestinian American Research Center fellowship, and an American University Faculty Research Award. Various stages of writing were also made possible by a Faculty Fellowship at New York University's Center for the Study of Gender and Sexuality, a Jean Monnet Fellowship at the Robert Schuman Center for Advanced Studies of the European University Institute, and appointments as a visiting scholar at Columbia University's departments of Anthropology and Middle East Languages and Civilizations, and NYU's Department of Social and Cultural Analysis and the Department of Middle East and Islamic Studies.

I am indebted to many individuals—relatives, friends, acquaintances, friends of friends, and especially my parents' network of colleagues—who assisted in mediating with soldiers to encourage them to agree to participate in this study. Although they must remain anonymous here, for this key role I am extremely grateful. The soldiers themselves, though we disagree on many things, must be thanked for their willingness to meet with me and for their time and energy.

As this project has gone through various stages and drafts, it has benefited from the feedback and suggestions of many wise people. Long discussions with Salim Tamari and Amitav Ghosh planted the seeds of a number of ideas in this book. Rashid Khalidi shepherded the manuscript over several obstacles. Lila Abu-Lughod, Deborah Bernstein, Ayse Caglar, Geraldine Chatelard, Carolyn Dinshaw, Salman El-Bedour, Samera

Esmair, Lesley Gill, Lisa Hajjar, Frances Hasso, Amal Jamal, Zachary Lockman, Altha McDermott-Brown, Annelies Moors, Isis Nussair, Jennifer Olmsted, Fatmeh Qassem, Shira Robinson, Rina Rosenberg, Sherene Seikaly, Ahlam Shibli, Ella Shohat, Rebecca Stein, Rebecca Torstrick, Brett Williams, and Elia Zureik have all read various portions and incarnations of the manuscript and offered important comments. Virginia Dominguez and Julie Peteet kindly read the entire manuscript twice over, proposing significant and detailed changes. Elaine Combs-Schilling and Roger Lancaster continue to faithfully play the role of devoted advisors, tirelessly reading, commenting, rereading, answering questions both profound and silly, all in an intimidatingly timely fashion and well beyond the call of duty. Their contributions and encouragement were vital. Kate Wahl has been a dedicated editor and has thoughtfully nurtured this project.

Many people suggested sources, answered questions, and/or sent materials that were key in shaping this book: I thank Bashir Abu-Manneh, 'Issam Abu-Rayya, Anwar 'Afifi, Lori Allen, Neta Bar, Moustafa Bayoumi, Ayelet Bechar, Shiko Behar, Jonathan Cook, Leena Dallasheh, Amal Eqeiq, Stephen Gasteyer, Lesley Gill, Linda Green, Ibitisam Ibrahim, Hassan Jabareen, Lamese Kanaaneh, Areen Khalil, Fadia Khoury, Dolores Koenig, John Loughlin, David Lublin, Lucy Mair, Hisham Naffa', Sabiyha Prince, Mohammad Qaraqra, John Richardson, Rina Rosenberg, Aseel Sawalha, Cathy Schneider, Irene Shigaki, Banna Shougri-Badarne, Kenda Stewart, Nimer Sultaney, and Hadas Tagari. Saleh Kanaaneh and Zainab Khatib were particularly devoted collectors of articles from the Arabic press in Israel.

I thank all the then graduate students in my seminar on minorities and the military in spring 2003 for helping me digest materials for my final chapter. Special thanks to Mysara Abu Hashem for the sources he assembled for his research paper on Arab American soldiers, Katherine Altom for sources on Filipino soldiers in the U.S. military, Susie McFadden-Resper for sources on African American soldiers, and Katy Van Every for sources on the Navajo code talkers. I have been the lucky recipient of research assistance from Yodit Fitigu, Ananta Khatri, Devin Molina, Russell Smith, Shannon Telenko, and especially Mysara Abu Hashem, as well as editorial assistance from Katie Moore.

Finally, I thank my family. My parents, Hatim and Dolores Ka-naaneh, were basically by my side physically during much of the research, intellectually through all the sometimes weekly twists and turns of the project, and emotionally throughout. My husband, Seth Tapper, was my first and last sounding board for ideas small and large, and an indispens-able daily support from the first passing mention of the subject to the final delivery of the manuscript to the Press. I'm also thankful for the en-couragement, friendship, and advice of Sana Odeh and Peter Mitchell.

Notes

Chapter 1

Earlier versions of a portion of the material in this chapter, as well as in Chapter 2, appeared in "Embattled Identities: Palestinian Soldiers in the Israeli Military," *Journal of Palestine Studies* 32, no. 3 (Spring 2003): 5–20.

1. Batya Gur, "Dancing in the Dark," *Haaretz*, February 8, 2002, Week's End.

2. A group of Israeli intellectuals and politicians filed a petition with the Israeli High Court demanding that the state allow them to be listed as "Israelis" on their identification cards. In response, the state prosecutor's office argued such an option "does not reflect, is not suitable and undermines the very principles under which the State of Israel was created." See Yuval Yoaz, "State Refuses to Register 'Israeli' Nationality," *Haaretz*, www.haaretz.com/hasen/objects/pages/PrintArticleEn.jhtml?itemNo=429149 (accessed February 14, 2008).

3. By law, all Israeli citizens are subject to conscription. It is the minister of defense who has complete discretion to grant an exemption to individual citizens or classes of citizens.

4. Part of Tel Aviv University is built on the remains and ruins of the village of Sheikh Muwannis. See Mark Levine, "Nationalism, Religion and Urban Politics in Israel: Struggles Over Modernity and Identity in 'Global' Jaffa," in *Mixed Towns, Trapped Communities: Historical Narratives, Spatial Dynamics, Gender Relations and Cultural Encounters in Palestinian-Israeli Towns*, eds. Daniel Monterescu and Dan Rabinowitz (Hampshire, England: Ashgate, 2007), 298.

5. Ibid., 288, 299.

6. The derogatory term in Israel is *'avodat 'aravim*.

7. With inferior prenatal health care, it could be argued that this process begins before birth.

8. See Raif Zureik's commentary on Palestinians asked to support "the rule of law, a law that in many cases was specially adapted in order to hurt me." Raif Zureik, "The Unbearable Lightness of Enlightenment," *Adalah's Review (Politics, Identity and Law)* 1 (Fall 1999): 7.

9. Amal Eqeiq, "Louder than the Blue I.D.: Palestinian Hip-Hop in Israel," paper presented at the Middle East Studies Association Conference, Boston, November 2006.

10. Shira Robinson, "Occupied Citizens in a Liberal State: Palestinians under Military Rule and the Colonial Formation of Israeli Society, 1948–1966," Ph.D. diss. (Stanford University, 2005), 92.

11. See www.adalah.org/eng/october2000.php for more on the October 2000 events and the state's failure to adequately respond.

12. Salma Khadra Jayyusi, introduction to *The Secret Life of Saaed the Ill-Fated Pessoptimist*, by Emile Habiby (Columbia, LA: Readers International, 1989), xv.

13. Despite their critical importance, these soldiers have thus far not been adequately studied by scholars, Israeli Jewish, Palestinian, or other. There are the exceptions: a 2003 MA thesis by a Swedish researcher and a photography project. See Maria Jansson, "Bedouin Soldiers—Loyal 'Israelis'? A Study on Loyalty and Identification among a Minority Group in a Nation Building Process," MA thesis (Gothenburg University, Sweden, 2004); and Adam Szymczyk, ed., *Ahlam Shibli Trackers* (Cologne: Kunsthalle Basel, 2007). Lisa Hajjar's work addresses Druze soldiers who are conscripted but not other Palestinians, who volunteer. See Lisa Hajjar, "Speaking the Conflict, Or How the Druze Became Bilingual: A Study of Druze Translators in the Israeli Military Courts in the West Bank and Gaza," *Ethnic and Racial Studies* 23, no. 2 (2000): 299–328; Lisa Hajjar, *Courting Conflict: The Israeli Military Court System in the West Bank and Gaza* (Berkeley: University of California Press, 2005).

Particularly absent is scholarship on the perspectives of Palestinians under occupation on Arab soldiers in the Israeli military. See Nasser Abufarha, "The Making of a Human Bomb: State Expansion and Modes of Resistance in Palestine," Ph.D. diss. (University of Wisconsin, Madison, 2006). This overall neglect in the literature is partly due to what can be described as methodological nationalism, the fact that many scholars operate from within a nationalist paradigm. See Ayse Caglar, "Outline of a Transregional and Transdisciplinary Research Agenda Centered on Turkey," unpublished paper (Free University of Berlin, May 2001), 12; Beshara Doumani, *Rediscovering Palestine: Merchants and Peasants in Jabal Nablus, 1700–1900* (Berkeley: University of California Press, 1995), 7; Ted Swedenburg, "The Palestinian Peasant as National Signifier," *Anthropological Quarterly* 63, no. 1 (1990): 18–30. The Palestinian nationalist paradigm precludes a focus on such "traitors" whose voices are absented from the collective in an active reconstruction of unity. See Lila Abu-Lughod and Ahmad Sa'di, "Introduction: The Claims of Memory," in *Nakba: Palestine, 1948, and the Claims of Memory*, eds. Ahmad Sa'di and Lila Abu-Lughod (New York: Columbia University Press, 2007), 8; and Ted Swedenburg, "Occupational Hazards: Palestine Ethnography," *Cultural Anthropology* 4, no. 3 (1989): 269. The Zionist paradigm sees them as "accommodationists" too peripheral to study and they do not fit in the exoticizing "camel and tent" areas of interest. See Aseel Sawalha, "Anthropology Faces a Crisis after Orientalism," *Al-Adab* 51 (November–December 2003): 18.

14. For more on the inclusion of soldiers and policemen in the same group, see the Afterword.

15. An estimated 3,000 or so Palestinian citizens of Israel are currently serving in the Israeli military and Border Guard and several thousand others serve in the police force. In the absence of official statistics, these estimates are based on those of officers and soldiers I interviewed. This number does not include Druze men, who are drafted.

16. Ilan Pappe, *The Making of the Arab-Israeli Conflict 1947–1951* (London: I. B. Tauris, 1994); Nira Yuval-Davis, "Front and Rear: The Sexual Division of Labour in the Israeli Army," in *Women, State and Ideology: Studies from Africa and Asia*, ed. Haleh Afshar (Albany: State University of New York Press, 1987), 190.

17. Sara Helman, "Militarism and the Construction of Community," *Journal of Political and Military Sociology* 25, 2 (1997): 305–32; Sara Helman, "Citizenship, Regime, Identity and Peace Protest in Israel," in *Military, State, and Society in Israel: Theoretical and Comparative Perspectives*, eds. Daniel Maman, Eyal Ben-Ari, and Zeev Rosenhek (New Brunswick, NJ: Transaction, 2001), 295–318.

18. David Ben Gurion quoted in Alon Peled, *A Question of Loyalty: Military Manpower Policy in Multiethnic States* (Ithaca, NY: Cornell University Press, 1998), 128; Meira Weiss, *Chosen Body: The Politics of the Body in Israeli Society* (Stanford, CA: Stanford University Press, 2002), 44.

19. Danny Kaplan, "The Military as a Second Bar Mitzvah: Combat Service as Initiation to Zionist Masculinity," in *Imagined Masculinities: Male Identity and Culture in the Modern Middle East*, eds. Mai Ghoussoub and Emma Sinclair-Webb (London: Saqi Books, 2000), 138; Myron Aronoff, *Israeli Visions and Divisions: Cultural Change and Political Conflict* (New Brunswick, NJ: Transaction, 1989), 132.

20. Edna Lomsky-Feder and Eyal Ben-Ari, "From 'The People in Uniform' to 'Different Uniforms for the People': Professionalism, Diversity and the Israeli Defense Forces," in *Managing Diversity in the Armed Forces: Experiences from Nine Countries*, eds. Josep Soaters and Jan van der Meulen (Tilburg, Netherlands: Tilburg University Press, 1999), 162.

21. Yuval-Davis, "Front and Rear," 201.

22. Cynthia Enloe, *Ethnic Soldiers: State Security in Divided Societies* (Athens: University of Georgia Press, 1980), 15.

23. This exemption does not apply to Druze males, who have been conscripted in the army since 1956. See Hajjar, "Speaking the Conflict"; Kais Firro, "Reshaping Druze Particularism in Israel," *Journal of Palestine Studies* 30, no. 3 (2001): 40–53; Oren Yiftachel and Michaly Segal, "Jews and Druze in Israel: State Control and Ethnic Resistance," *Ethnic and Racial Studies* 21, no. 3 (1998): 476–506. See Chapter 5 for more on the Druze.

24. Sara Helman, "Militarism and the Construction of the Life-World of Israeli Males: The Case of the Reserves System," in *The Military and Militarism in Israeli*

Society, eds. Edna Lomsky-Feder and Eyal Ben-Ari (Albany: State University of New York Press, 1999), 211.

25. Hassan Jabareen, "Towards a Critical Palestinian Minority Approach: Citizenship, Nationalism, and Feminism in Israeli Law," *Plilm* 9, no. 53 (2000).

26. Lomsky-Feder and Ben-Ari, "People in Uniform," 163; Helman, "Citizenship, Regime, Identity," 303; Hajjar, "Speaking the Conflict," 304; Peled, *Question of Loyalty*, 139.

27. See Alina Korn, "Crime and Legal Control," *British Journal of Criminology* 40, no. 4 (2000): 574–94, for more on the criminalization of Arabs in Israel.

28. There are some rare cases of Palestinian soldiers who have become Jews; they left their communities, formally converted to Judaism, often becoming Orthodox, and married Jewish women. They were not included in this study, but would make interesting subjects of a study on their own.

Chapter 2

1. "Amazon.com: Birthing the Nation: Strategies of Palestinian Women in Israel (California Series in Public Anthropology, 2): Books: Rhoda Ann Kanaaneh," Amazon, www.amazon.com/birthing-nation-strategies-palestinian-anthropology/dp/0520229444/ref=pd_bbs_sr_1/002-3310311-4626435?ie=UTF8&s=books&qid=1179874930&sr=8-1 (accessed May 11, 2007). As Samera Esmair explains, "for Israel, Palestine, if granted any reality, is an entity that can be located in the future next to Israel, in the West Bank and Gaza, and not one that existed on the very land of Israel before its establishment"—nor of course, one that currently exists within Israel today. Samera Esmair, "Memories of Conquest: Witnessing Death in Tantura," in *Nakba: Palestine, 1948, and the Claims of Memory*, eds. Ahmad Sa'di and Lila Abu Lughod (New York: Columbia University Press, 2007), 236–66. I was reminded of this "terminological paradigm" when my use of the term Palestinian to refer to the descendents of Palestinians in this book generated, after a highly favorable peer review process, "intense discussion" among the faculty board members of a major university press. They took its very use as evidence of my unexplained adoption of a "Palestinian nationalist perspective." On "terminological paradigm," see Ella Shohat, *Taboo Memories, Diasporic Voices* (Durham, NC: Duke University Press, 2006), 353.

2. Firro, "Reshaping Druze Particularism," 40–41.

3. Ibid., 41; Sabri Jiryis, *The Arabs in Israel* (New York: Monthly Review Press, 1976), 197; Hillel Cohen, *Good Arabs: The Israeli Security Services and the Israeli Arabs* (Jerusalem: Ivrit Hebrew Publishing House, 2006), 43.

4. Firro, "Reshaping Druze Particularism," 40.

5. Avirama Golan, "Where the 'Alliance of Blood' Has Led," *Haaretz*, February 17, 2005, www.haaretz.com/hasen/objects/pages/PrintArticleEn.jhtml?itemNo=541263 (accessed January 28, 2006).

6. Lisa Hajjar, "Israel's Interventions among the Druze," *Middle East Report* 26, no. 3 (1996): 3; Laila Parsons, *The Druze between Palestine and Israel, 1947–1949* (New York: St. Martin's Press, 2000).

7. Note the plural "minorities" in the preferred Hebrew term (*bne mi'utim*), literally sons of minorities—rather than a single Arab minority. See Cohen, *Good Arabs*, 204, 196; Ilan Pappe, *The Ethnic Cleansing of Palestine* (Oxford: One World Publications, 2006), 188.

8. Hajjar, "Israel's Interventions," 3.

9. Cohen, *Good Arabs*, 163, 192.

10. Ibid., 188.

11. Not only were incentives, weapons licenses, and so on, offered, but the police detained the refusniks, opened criminal files against them, and released them only after they agreed to enlist. See Cohen, *Good Arabs*, 188–89.

12. Ian Lustick, *Arabs in the Jewish State: Israel's Control of a National Minority* (Austin: University of Texas Press, 1980), 133.

13. Hajjar, *Courting Conflict*, 135.

14. Hajjar, "Speaking the Conflict," 323n7. It is important to note that there have been Druze exceptions and resistance to the Druzification policy all along, including, for example, the vigorous resistance to Zionist forces in Yanuh in 1948, conscientious objectors to military conscription or less confrontational draft evaders, the Arab Druze Initiative Committee, legal battles waged to register nationality as Arab rather than Druze, reclaiming the joint Muslim-Druze holiday of Eid al-Fitir, and so on. See Laila Parsons, "The Druze and the Birth of Israel" in *The War for Palestine: Rewriting the History of 1948*, eds. Eugene L. Rogan and Avi Shlaim (Cambridge, UK: Cambridge University Press, 2001), 66. Such forms of resistance illustrate that the state's segmentation policy has always been contested to some degree.

15. Lustick, *Arabs in the Jewish State*, 211.

16. Hajjar, "Israel's Interventions," 4.

17. Emile Tuma, *The Path of Struggle of the Arab Masses in Israel* (Acre: Dar Abu Salma Press, 1982), 208.

18. Jack Khoury and Fadi Eyadat, "An Intifada in the Carmel," *Haaretz*, www.haaretz.com/hasen/spages/782043.html (accessed November 1, 2006).

19. Hajjar, "Israel's Interventions," 3; Hajjar, *Courting Conflict*, 140. Ahmad Sa'di argues that Israeli policy after all did not lead to the emergence of a new category of identity different from the two existing categories of Jews and Palestinians. Rather, Druze identity became a "half identity" as Druze were "treated as Arabs in some respects and as non-Arabs in others." Ahmad Sa'di, "The Incorporation of the Palestinian Minority by the Israeli State, 1948–1970: On the Nature, Transformation, and Constraints of Collaboration," *Social Text* 75, vol. 21, no. 2 (2003): 92.

20. It goes without saying that the category "Bedouins" includes diverse groups,

with divisions along tribal lines as well as regional (north–south, Galilee–Naqab) divisions. Within each tribe there are divisions between Bedouin "nobles," incorporated peasants, and "slaves." Longina Jakubowska, "Resisting 'Ethnicity': The Israeli State and Bedouin Identity," in *The Paths to Domination, Resistance, and Terror*, eds. Carolyn Nordstrom and JoAnn Martin (Berkeley: University of California Press, 1992), 87.

21. Clinton Bailey, "Lieberman and the Bedouin," *Haaretz*, February 24, 2002, 5; Rohen Shamir, "Suspended in Space: Bedouins under the Law of Israel," *Law and Society Review* 30, no. 2 (1996): 231, 237; The Hajj, Smadar Lavie, and Forest Rouse, "Notes on the Fantastic Journey of The Hajj, His Anthropologist, and Her American Passport," *American Ethnologist* 20, no. 2 (1993): 375. Amahl Bishara convincingly argues that Palestinians more generally are often characterized in Zionist texts as nomadic and thus unentitled to land. See Amahl Bishara, "Examining Sentiments about the Claims to Jerusalem and Its Houses," *Social Text* 75, no. 21 (2003): 141–62.

22. For example, starting in the 1948 war, a unit in the Palmach (acronym for "strike companies," a major part of the Jewish forces at the time) consisting of forty members of the al-Hayb family, with a Jewish commander formerly of the French Foreign Legion, was given the tribal title "Pal-Hayb." See Ya'cov Havakook, *Footprints in the Sand: The Bedouin Trackers in the IDF* (Tel Aviv: Israeli Ministry of Defense, 1998), 127.

23. Ghazi Falah, "How Israel Controls the Bedouin in Israel," *Journal of Palestine Studies*, Special Issue: The Palestinians in Israel and the Occupied Territories, 14, no. 2 (1985): 37–38.

24. Jakubowska, "Resisting 'Ethnicity,'" 85. The state also emphasized Bedouin internal fragmentation and required the Bedouin to register by tribe, with nineteen officially recognized tribes. Elisabeth Marteu, "Some Reflections on How Bedouin Women of the Negev Relate to Politics: Between Political Marginalisation and Social Mobilisation," *Bulletin du Centre de Recherche Français de Jérsualem*, 16 (2005): 273.

According to a study by Salman El-Bedour on the development of ethnic identity among Bedouin-Arab adolescents, "73 per cent of [participants] stated that the term 'Israeli' was not an appropriate definition of their identity, and 44.9 per cent stated that the term 'Palestinian' was." Salman Elbedour, "Who Are the Bedouins of the Negev? Are They Israelis or Palestinians or Both? Ethnicity and Ethnic Identity among Bedouin-Arab Adolescents in Israel," unpublished paper, Howard University.

25. Falah, "How Israel Controls the Bedouin," 41.

26. Ghazi Falah, "Israeli State Policy toward Bedouin Sedentarization in the Negev," *Journal of Palestine Studies* 18, no. 2 (1989): 78.

27. Ibid., 86.

28. Table 2, Local Councils and Municipalities by Socio-Economic Index, Ranking and cluster Membership in "Characterization and Classification of Local Authorities by the Socio-Economic Level of the Population 2003," www.cbs.gov.il/www/publications/local_authorities2003/pdf/t02.pdf (accessed May 8, 2008).

29. This system also transforms Bedouins from citizen claimants of rights to the land to law-breaking criminal defendants whose collective rights to land are diffused into numerous individual cases. Leena Dallasheh, "The Bedouins in the Naqab: The Citizens Israel Would Rather Forget?" unpublished paper written for New York University course on the Anthropology of Citizenship and Displacement, New York, (December 25, 2006), 7, 20.

Palestinian villages destroyed during the 1948 war have been memorialized in special books well analyzed by Susan Slyomovics and Rochelle Davis among others. See Susan Slyomovics, *The Object of Memory: Arab and Jew Narrate the Palestinian Village* (Philadelphia: University of Pennsylvania Press, 1998); Rochelle Davis, "The Attar of History: Palestinian Narratives of Life before 1948," Ph.D. diss. (University of Michigan, 2002); and Rochelle Davis, "Mapping the Past, Re-creating the Homeland: Memories of Village Places in Pre-1948 Palestine," in *Nakba: Palestine, 1948, and the Claims of Memory*, eds. Ahmad Sa'di and Lila Abu-Lughod (New York: Columbia University Press, 2007). Unrecognized villages are increasingly being documented in books with a similar set of common themes to serve as "dossiers of evidence," often with Israeli governmental documents that prove the existence of the villages in question. See Davis, "Mapping the Past," 58. There is a need for a study of these new books as well as the forms of "inhabitation" and cultural property claims used by residents. See Bishara, "Examining Sentiments," 158. These villages were de-legalized by the Planning and Construction Law of 1965, which left the unrecognized villages out of the planning schemes and forbade any construction there. See Dallasheh, "Bedouins in the Naqab," 6. Like many other Palestinians, the residents were forcibly removed from their lands, in this case to the closed Seyag area, and the lands they were forcibly "absented" from were confiscated under the Absentee Property Law of 1950.

Many among the Bedouin have in fact been relocated by the state multiple times. For example, the 'Azazma tribe was evicted a first time after 1948 from its original location and resettled in the areas of Jabal al-Qarn, Halusa, and Wadi al-Na'im, in the western and northern Naqab desert. In 1956, the Military Administration evacuated them from Jabal al-Qarn and Halusa, and concentrated them in Wadi al-Na'im. And in 1990, the Israel Land Administration demanded their evacuation from the latter area, on the grounds that they were "occupying state lands." These multiple dislocations also convolute the land claims involved. See Human Rights Association, *By All Means Possible: A Report on the Destruction by the State of Crops of Bedouin Citizens in the Naqab (Negev) by Means of Aerial Spraying with Chemicals* (Arab Association for Human Rights, 2004), www.arabhra.org/HraAdmin/UserImages/Files/CropDestructionReportEnglish.pdf (accessed February 14, 2008). For an analysis of repeated dislocations in Lebanon, see Aseel Sawalha, "'Healing the Wounds of the War': Placing the War-Displaced in Postwar Beirut," in *Wounded Cities: Destruction and Reconstruction in a Globalized World*, eds. Jane Schneider and Ida Susser (New

York: Berg Publishers, 2003); Nuri El-Okbi, *Waiting for Justice: The Story of the Elokbi Tribe in Israel* (np, 2004).

30. Human Rights Association, *By All Means Possible*; Rhoda Kanaaneh, *Birthing the Nation: Strategies of Palestinian Women in Israel* (Berkeley: University of California Press, 2002); and Longina Jakubowska, "Finding Ways to Make a Living: Employment among Negev Bedouin," *Nomadic Peoples* 4, no. 2 (2000): 94–105.

31. For example, the Southern District Police Force published on its website a report claiming that "the Arab Bedouin society in the Naqab overall is criminal by its very nature." See Human Rights Association, "On the Margins: Annual Review of Human Rights Violations of the Arab Palestinian Minority in Israel 2005," www.arabhra.org/HRA/SecondaryArticles/SecondaryArticlePage.aspx?SecondaryArticle=1339 (accessed February 14, 2008), 16–17. See Korn, "Crime and Legal Control," on the criminalization of the Arab presence in Israel. Also see Martin Woollacott, "War Comes Home: Israel's Killing of Its Own—Eight Israeli Arabs—Changes Everything," *The Guardian*, www.guardian.co.uk/Columnists/Column/0,5673,377059,00.html (accessed February 8, 2006); Dallasheh, "Bedouins in the Naqab," 7; and Hana Hamdan, "Individual Settlement in the Naqab: The Exclusion of the Arab Minority," *Adalah Newsletter* 10 (February 2005). This is the case even though Bedouins are approximately a quarter of the Naqab's population but live on only 2 per cent of its land. See Human Rights Association, "On the Margins," 16. The Public Lands Expulsion of Intruders Law, first enacted in 1981, permits the expulsion of "illegal" inhabitants from what is defined as state land. A 2005 amendment to the law allows for speedier expulsions and concentrates greater power in the hands of the supra-governmental Israel Land Administration. See Dallasheh, "Bedouins in the Naqab," 9–10.

32. Salim Tamari, "Factionalism and Class Formation in Recent Palestinian History," in *Studies in the Economic and Social History of Palestine in the Nineteenth and Twentieth Centuries*, ed. Roger Owen (London: Macmillan, 1982), 186; Laurence Louer, *To Be an Arab in Israel* (New York: Columbia University Press, 2007).

33. Robinson, "Occupied Citizens," 148.

34. Ibid., 183. They famously tried to assist right-wing Geula Cohen, then member of the Jewish underground, to hide from the British Mandatory authorities. Rebecca Luna Stein, *Itineraries in Conflict: The Political Life of Tourism in Israel and the Middle East* (Durham, NC: Duke University Press, forthcoming): chap. 5, note 8.

35. Ibid., chap. 5, p. 6.

36. Ronny Shaked, "Abu Gosh: Hummus and Coexistence," *Ynetnews*, www.ynetnews.com/Ext/Comp/ArticleLayout/CdaArticlePrintPreview/1,2506,L-3308173,00.html (accessed September 27, 2006).

37. Stein, *Itineraries*, chap. 5, p. 4. In the long run, Israeli governments did little to reward the legacy of village loyalty and failed to develop a local economy to replace the agricultural one they decimated through massive land expropriation. Ibid., 7.

38. James C. Scott, *Seeing Like a State: How Certain Schemes to Improve the Human Condition Have Failed* (New Haven, CT: Yale University Press, 1998), 83.

39. This influence can be both "positive," as in soldiers wanting to agree with me by identifying as Palestinian, and "negatively," as in soldiers provocatively disagreeing with me by identifying as non-Arab.

40. The Green Line is the pre-1967 border of Israel that now separates Israel "proper" from the Occupied Territories of the West Bank.

41. Cohen, *Good Arabs*, and Robinson, "Occupied Citizens" describe a number of similar cases involving spying in exchange for being allowed to remain inside Israel or for residency—including cases in which state promises were broken after the security-related services were rendered. There are also many other examples of Palestinians fighting against the Jewish forces in 1948, and later collaborating with them or serving in the Israeli military. See Cohen, *Good Arabs*, for more. A contingent of five hundred Druze in the Arab Liberation Army deserted in April 1948 and joined the Jewish forces. Pappe, *Ethnic Cleansing*, 114.

42. Amitav Ghosh, "India's Untold War of Independence," *New Yorker* (June 23–30, 1997): 116. Anthropologist Iris Jean-Klein similarly emphasizes the "duplexity" of human subjects whereby they address two—or for that matter, more—"discrete interests, problems, or projects *at once*." See Iris Jean-Klein, "Domestic Nationalism and Resistance: The Two Faces of Everyday Activism in Palestine during the Intifada," *Cultural Anthropology* 16, no. 1 (1992): 92. And Rashid Khalidi writes of a Palestinian "tapestry of loyalties." See Rashid Khalidi, *Palestinian Identity: The Construction of Modern National Consciousness* (New York: Columbia University Press, 1997), 87.

43. Ghosh, "India's Untold War," 116.

44. Seeds of Peace, *A Tribute: Memories of Our Friend Asel Asleh, 1983–2000* (2000), 24.

45. The October 2000 events are not entirely unique in terms of the killing of Palestinian citizens by security forces. According to a report by the Mossawa Advocacy Center for Arab Citizens of Israel in 2004, sixteen more incidents occurred after October 2000 in which Palestinian citizens were killed by security forces. Quoted in Amalia Sa'ar and Taghreed Yahya-Younis, "Masculinity in Crisis: The Case of Palestinians in Israel," *British Journal of Middle East Studies* 35, no. 5 (2006).

46. Isis Nusair, "Gendered Politics of Location: Generational Intersections," in *Women and the Politics of Military Confrontation*, eds. Nahla Abdo and Ronit Lentin (New York: Berghahn Books, 2002), 98.

47. During the subsequent Or Commission investigations, the chief of police of the Sakhnin region (who is Jewish) became the prime suspect in the killing of the two men in Sakhnin. He was also under investigation at the same time for setting fire to his own police station in an attempt to suppress evidence, and was suspected of having started the rumor implicating an Arab policeman.

48. Jonathan Cook, *Blood and Religion: The Unmasking of the Jewish and Democratic State* (Ann Arbor, MI: Pluto, 2006), 67.

49. Soraya Sarhaddi Nelson, "Is 'Capt. R.' a War Criminal or a Scapegoat?" *Honolulu Advertiser*, December 26, 2004, A21.

50. 'Arrabi's population was about 15,000.

51. See for example, Aliza Arbeli, "Bedouin Soldiers Hold Protest against Home-Razing Orders," *Haaretz*, January 18, 2002, 3; Moshe Arens, "Criminal Negligence," *Haaretz*, January 15, 2002, 5; Clinton Bailey, "Lieberman and the Bedouin," 5; Amos Harel, "Stemming the Tide: Bedouin No Longer Flock to Join the Army," *Haaretz*, June 14, 2001, 1–2; "Gag on Names of Bedouin Soldiers," *Haaretz*, June 21, 2001, News in Brief; and Ori Nir, "Alienation Rife in Once Quiet Community," *Haaretz*, May 29, 2001, 5.

52. Jewish settlement towns in Israel prohibit Arab residents from buying land and homes there, despite a recent Supreme Court ruling allowing them to do so. See Association for Civil Rights in Israel, www.acri.org.il/english-acri/engine/story.asp?id=177 for details of the landmark Katzir case.

53. Liberal Jewish soldiers often use a similar justification for their service in the Occupied Territories.

54. Jiryis, *The Arabs in Israel*, 168.

55. A similar example from the press is that of the notorious Captain R. (who killed a thirteen-year-old girl), who pointed to photos of himself setting some caged pigeons free before bulldozers leveled a home in Rafah, and another of "him sitting with a handful of Palestinian children while one of his subordinates handed out chocolate bars." Nelson, "Is 'Capt. R.' a War Criminal or a Scapegoat?"

56. Hassan Jabareen, "On the Oppression of Identities in the Name of Civil Equality," *Adalah's Review (Politics, Identity and Law)* 1 (1999): 27.

57. Slyomovics, *The Object of Memory*, 45–53; *500 Dunam on the Moon*.

58. Lena Meari, "The Roles of Palestinian Peasant Women, 1930–1960: Al-Birweh Village as a Model," paper presented at Middle East Studies Association annual meeting, Boston (November 2006), 19.

59. Hatim Kanaaneh, A *Doctor in Galilee: the Story and Struggle of a Palestinian in Israel* (London: Pluto, 2008), 51.

60. Salim Tamari, "Building Other People's Homes: The Palestinian Peasant's Household and Work in Israel," *Journal of Palestine Studies* 1, no. 41 (Autumn 1981): 31–66; Tobias Kelly, *Law, Violence and Sovereignty among West Bank Palestinians* (Cambridge, UK: Cambridge University Press, 2006), 54–79.

61. Nadim Rouhana, *Palestinian Citizens in an Ethnic Jewish State* (New Haven, CT: Yale University Press, 1997), 122.

62. Givat-Haviva: Jewish Arab Center for Peace, *Attitudes of the Arabs to the State of Israel* (2001).

63. As'ad Ghanem, *The Palestinian Arab Minority in Israel, 1948–2000: A Political Study* (Albany: State University of New York Press, 2001), 37.

64. B'Tselem, *Collaborators in the Occupied Territories: Human Rights Abuses and Violations* (Jerusalem: B'Tselem, 1994), 9.

65. Ibid.

66. This follows from seriously questioning nationalism's conception of itself and undoing its image as "a unitary and internally unconflicted ideal that represents the authentic core of personhood in all circumstances superior to or even excluding all other identities, sentiments, interests, loyalties, and aspirations." Zachary Lockman, "Arab Workers and Arab Nationalism in Palestine; A View from Below," in *Rethinking Nationalism in the Arab Middle East*, eds. James Jankowski and Israel Gershoni (New York: Columbia University Press, 1997), 254.

67. Orna Sasson-Levy, "Constructing Identities at the Margins: Masculinities and Citizenship in the Israeli Army," paper presented at the Joint Princeton-Columbia Graduate Student Workshop: National Identity and Public Policy in Comparative Perspective, Princeton, NJ (September 29–October 1, 2000).

68. Edna Lomsky-Feder and Tamar Rappoport, "'Homebred Masculinity' Resists the Local Model of Manhood: Russian-Jewish Immigrants Confront Israeli Masculinity," unpublished paper (2001); Danny Kaplan and Eyal Ben-Ari, "Brothers and Others in Arms: Managing Gay Identity in Combat Units of the Israeli Army," *Journal of Contemporary Ethnography* 29, no. 4 (2000): 396–432.

Chapter 3

1. "The Jewish Collectivity and National Reproduction in Israel," in *Khamsin, Special Issue on Women in the Middle East* (London: Zed Books, 1987), 64.

2. Nadim Rouhana and Nimer Sultany, "Redrawing the Boundaries of Citizenship: Israel's New Hegemony," *Journal of Palestine Studies* 33, no. 1 (2003): 14.

3. Danny Rabinowitz, "Rights before Service," *Haaretz*, www.haaretz.com/hasen/pages/ShArt.jhtml?itemNo=517521 (accessed September 29, 2006).

4. Shahar Ilan, "The Undocumented: Fifth in a Series—Bedouin Trackers: Israeli Enough for the IDF, but Not for an ID Card," *Haaretz*, www.haaretz.com/hasen/objects/pages/PrintArticleEn.jhtml?itemNo=772444 (accessed October 10, 2006).

5. Havakook, *Footprints in the Sand*, 14.

6. The association has tried to use the courts, lobbied ministers, and appealed to the press. Its strategies include arguing that there are just a few of these stateless people (and thus implicitly they do not pose a numerical challenge to the state's Jewish majority), that they are stateless due only to "bureaucratic failures and irregularities," that past official commitments were made to grant individuals permanent residency but remain unfulfilled, and that some of these people have never lived elsewhere and have no affinity to any other country. See Ilan, "The Undocumented."

7. Ibid.

8. On "martial citizenship," see Francine D'Amico, "Citizen-Soldier? Class, Race, Gender, Sexuality and the US Military," in *States of Conflict: Gender, Violence, and Resistance*, eds. Susie Jacobs, Ruth Jacobson, and Jennifer Marchbank (London: Zed Books, 2000), 105. I am indebted to Banna Shougri-Badarneh for providing me with Association for Civil Rights in Israel documentation and other background information on stateless Bedouins.

9. "Israel Strips Citizenship from Arab Suspect," *New York Times*, September 10, 2002 (late edition—final), A10. There have been numerous threats to revoke the citizenship of Arabs. For example, Zevulun Hammer, then minister of the interior, threatened in 1990 to revoke the citizenship of Arabs who crossed a red line and opposed Jewish immigration to Israel. Areej Sabbagh-Khouri, "Palestinian Predicaments: Jewish Immigration and Refugee Repatriation," in *Blue ID: Palestinians in Israel Revisited*, eds. Rhoda Kanaaneh and Isis Nusair (Albany: State University of New York Press, forthcoming).

10. "UN Human Rights Committee—Information Sheet #3," Adalah, www.adalah.org/eng/intladvocacy/unhrc_03_fam_uni.pdf (accessed February 14, 2008).

11. Mazal Mualem, "Interior Minister Poraz Grants Citizenship to Ten Non-Jewish Soldiers," *Haaretz*, May 5, 2004, www.haaretz.com/hasen/objects/pages/PrintArticle En.jhtml?itemNo=290230 (accessed November 14, 2006).

12. Global Jewish Agenda, "Interior Minister to Foreign Minister: Soldiers Who Are Not Halachically Jewish to be Granted Israeli Citizenship," www.jafi.org.il/agenda /2001/english/wk4–12/2.asp (accessed November 14, 2006).

13. This easing is formally restricted to non-Arab non-Jews. Initially, the Ministry of Justice objected that Palestinian undocumented children might take advantage of some of these reforms intended for the children of foreign undocumented labor migrants. Adriana Kemp, "Managing Migration, Reprioritizing National Citizenship: Undocumented Migrant Workers' Children and Policy Reforms in Israel," *Theoretical Inquiries in Law* 8, no. 2 (2007): 684. This was hardly the intention of their architect, then interior minister Avraham Poraz: in stark contrast to his lenient policies on non-Arab non-Jews, he was a strong advocate of "one of the gravest steps limiting the boundaries of citizenship for Arab citizens," the Nationality and Entry into Israel Law, passed on July 31, 2003, which aims to reduce the number of Palestinians from the West Bank and Gaza who become naturalized following marriage to an Israeli (usually Arab) citizen. See Rouhana and Sultany, "Redrawing," 13.

14. Moshe Arens, "The Wages of a Non-Policy," *Jerusalem Post*, April 10, 1998.

15. Andy Bickford, "Disposable, Deployable, Forgettable: Race, Class and Health in the US Military," paper presented at the American University Department of Anthropology, Washington, D.C. (January 6, 2004), 7. See Chapter 9 for more on this.

16. Nira Yuval-Davis, "Front and Rear."

17. Ibid., 86.

18. Nurit Stadler and Eyal Ben-Ari, "Other-Worldly Soldiers? Ultra-Orthodox Views of Military Service in Contemporary Israel," *Israeli Affairs* 9, no. 4 (2003): 17–48.

19. This arrangement is also the result of the ability of religious political parties to extract concessions in exchange for entering government coalitions. See Gershon Shafir and Yoav Peled, *Being Israeli: The Dynamics of Multiple Citizenship* (Cambridge, UK: Cambridge University Press, 2002), 146. However, this tipping power is only part of the story. The ultra-Orthodox are the bearers of Jewish tradition who symbolize the ethno-national principle of Jewish historical continuity, the source of the Jewish claim to Israel, and thus the legitimacy of the Zionist project. See ibid., 137, 149.

20. Ibid., 147, 149.

21. High Court of Justice (HCJ) 200/83, Watad v. Minister of Finance, Supr. Ct. Rep. 35 (3) 113. Also see Jabareen, "Towards a Critical Palestinian Minority Approach," 23n37.

22. Ibid.

23. Ibid.

24. Helman, "Citizenship, Regime, Identity," 303.

25. HCJ 3267/97, Rubenstein et al. v. Minister of Defense, Supr. Ct. Rep. 52(5) 481.

26. Jabareen, "Towards a Critical Palestinian Minority Approach," 30.

27. "News Update: Jewish and Palestinian Academics Testify Before the Or Commission," Adalah, www.adalah.org/eng/pressreleases2002.php (accessed April 20, 2007).

28. Ameer Makhoul in Julia Kernochan and Rina Rosenberg, "A Critique of Equal Duties, Equal Rights," *Adalah's Review* 1 (1999): 29. This logic also falsely implies that "the government has been awaiting anxiously to grant Palestinians their long-denied rights. . . . The smooth road of Equal Duties, which leads to Equal Rights, has been there all along, somehow overlooked by Arab citizens." See ibid.

29. Human Rights Association, "On the Margins."

30. Ibid.

31. Ibid.

32. Shafir and Peled, *Being Israeli*, 126.

33. Jabareen, "Towards a Critical Palestinian Minority Approach," 38. The Ivri Committee commissioned by former defense minister Shaul Mofaz recommended national service for Arabs as "a first step towards military service for the minority." See Human Rights Association, "On the Margins." Parliament members Naomi Hazan and Zahava Galon drafted a bill for alternative national service for all those whose conscience prevents them from doing conventional military service. See Moshe Negbi, "Not Activist, But Phlegmatic," *Haaretz*, February 24, 2002, 5. Many more proposals for alternative service duties for Arabs have emerged over the years.

34. Hadas Tagari, "Petition 9173/96" (Association of Civil Rights in Israel, 1996).

35. Ibid., 3.

36. Ibid., 8.

37. Jabareen, "Towards a Critical Palestinian Minority Approach," 36n57.

38. Sasson-Levy, "Constructing Identities at the Margins."

39. HCJ 4541/94, Alice Miller v. Minister of Defense, Supr. Ct. Rep. 49(4) 94.

40. Jabareen, "Towards a Critical Palestinian Minority Approach," 12.

41. The Arab political parties as well as the National Committee of Arab Mayors have strongly condemned them.

42. Aiman Odeh, "Serving Which Nationality and Which Nationalism Exactly?!" *al-'Ittihad*, January 14, 2004, 2–4.

43. Jabareen in ibid.

44. Ministry of Defense, *Bulletin for Released Soldiers 2001/2002: The Fund for Absorbing Released Soldiers and the Unit for Guidance of Released Soldiers* (Holon: Mieri Press, 2001), 5.

45. Havakook, *Footprints in the Sand*, 137.

46. While almost all of the interviews in this study were conducted in Arabic, interviewees often used some Hebrew words. I indicate when such a language switch occurs because, as I argue in the Afterword, it is often linked to a particular genealogy of power.

Chapter 4

1. For example, an article discussing the impact of a soldier's death in Ein Mahel on the number of volunteers from the village quoted varying opinions: the newspaper received information about an increase in the number of volunteers, the mayor of the village claimed there was a decrease, and a Likud activist from the village reported there was no change in the number. See Amneh Abu Ras, "The Number of Those Who Serve in the Military from Ein Mahel Has Increased," *Al-Sinnara*, February 18, 2005. Statements by military authorities do suggest, however, a link between enlistment rates and benefits.

2. See Ghazi Falah, "Israeli 'Judaization' Policy in Galilee and Its Impact on Local Arab Urbanization," *Political Geography Quarterly* 8, no. 3 (1989): 229–53; and Oren Yiftachel, "The Dark Side of Modernism: Planning as Control of an Ethnic Minority," in *Postmodern Cities and Spaces*, eds. Sophie Watson and Katherine Gibson (Cambridge, UK: Basil Blackwell, 1995), 216–42.

3. Roee Nahmias, "GDP Per Capita of Arab Israelis Third of That of Jews," *Ynetnews*, www.ynetnews.com/articles/0,7340,L-3354260,00.html.

4. See Falah, "Israeli 'Judaization' Policy"; Yiftachel, "Dark Side"; Noah Lewin-Epstein and Moshe Semyonov, *The Arab Minority in Israel's Economy: Patterns of Ethnic Inequality* (Boulder, CO: Westview, 1993); Human Rights Watch, "Second Class: Discrimination against Palestinian Arab Children in Israel's Schools," www.hrw.org/reports/2001/israel2/ (accessed December 16, 2004); and Zeev Rosenhek, "The Exclusionary Logic of the Welfare State: Palestinian Citizens in the Israeli Welfare State," *International Sociology* 14, no. 2 (1999): 195–215.

5. Sharif used the Hebrew term *mitun* which literally means slow down, referring to the unemployment period.

6. While this is generally true, I did find a small minority of volunteers who had completed some postsecondary education prior to applying to the military / police force.

7. Released soldiers and their families had exclusive access to the products and discounted prices at the Shekem department store, a state-owned enterprise under direction of the Ministry of Defense. However, the company was privatized in 1994–95.

8. Initially Arab soldiers were recruited for regular service or as "civilian IDF workers" with regular salaries. This changed in 1986 when a ceremony for enlisting trackers to *mandatory* rather than regular service took place. See Havakook, *Footprints in the Sand*, 114. With this shift, Bedouins and other Arabs could no longer join the military directly as regulars, but had to first "volunteer" for three years of mandatory service with more meager stipends, just as Jewish soldiers do.

9. Ministry of Defense, *Bulletin for Released Soldiers*, 7.

10. Ibid., 23–24; "Frequently Asked Questions," Ministry of Defense, www.hachvana.mod.gov.il/pages/general/FAQ.asp?UN=9&HD=12 (accessed July 31, 2003). During the years 1970–96 an increased child allowance was paid for the third and every subsequent child to families in which one member was a released soldier. See National Insurance Institute of Israel, "Quarterly Statistics," www.btl.gov.il/english/rivon_E/htm/en_rivon_3_061.htm (accessed November 14, 2006).

Jewish immigrants and ultra-Orthodox Jews were eligible for the higher allowance even if they did not have a released soldier in the family. See Alisa Lewin and Haya Stier, "Who Benefits the Most? The Unequal Allocation of Transfers in the Israeli Welfare State," *Social Science Quarterly* 83, no. 2 (June 2002): 493. The benefit clearly discriminated against Arab families, the majority of which had three or more children but did not have a member who had served in the military (and were not new immigrants or ultra-Orthodox). In 1993 the Rabin government decided to equalize child allowances and this benefit was phased out by 1997. See Shafir and Peled, *Being Israeli*, 290; and Rosenhek, "Exclusionary Logic." In 2002, the Sharon government passed an emergency budget in which it attempted to reintroduce this disparity: families with no released soldiers would suffer a 20 percent cut in their child payments. See "News Update: Adalah Challenges Attorney General's Claim That Discriminatory Cuts in Child Allowances Are Legitimate and Proportional," Adalah, www.adalah.org/eng/pressreleases/pr.php?file=03_03_10 (accessed February 14, 2008).

11. Although a court ruled in 2003 that a job can only require military service if that service is related to performing the job, this ruling is certainly not reflected in standard employment practices in Israel. See Ruth Sinai, "Court: IDF Service Not Necessary to Get Job," *Haaretz*, June 16, 2003, 2.

12. Ministry of Defense, *Bulletin for Released Soldiers*, 41, 50.

13. Ibid., 29.

14. Ibid., 28.

15. Ibid., 34.

16. Tamara Traubmann, "Court Rules Haifa University Must Halt Housing Advantages for IDF Veterans," *Haaretz*, www.haaretz.com/hasen/objects/pages/PrintArticleEn.jhtml?itemNo=752686 (accessed August 21, 2006); Human Rights Association, "On the Margins," 60.

17. For example, at many universities, applicants for medicine and dentistry must be at least twenty-one years old. Tel Aviv University "introduced a new enrollment condition specifying that those wanting to study social work, nursing or naturopathy must be at least twenty years old," while at Haifa University "prospective students for courses in biology, mathematics, physics, and computer science must be at least nineteen years old." See Human Rights Association, "On the Margins," 57; Nimer Sultany, "Palestinian Arabs in Israeli Universities," on Arab48, July 15, 2002 (Arabic); "News Update: Adalah Asks Tel Aviv University to Cancel Discriminatory Application Policy," Adalah, www.adalah.org/eng/pressreleases2003.php (accessed October 19, 2006).

18. Human Rights Association, "On the Margins," 57.

19. "A Peak in the Voluntary Recruitment of Minorities in the IDF," www1.idf.il/dover/site/mainpage.asp?sl=HE&id=7&docid=49095.HE (accessed October 2, 2006).

20. This practice of leasing land previously expropriated by the state back to Palestinians was also used by the military governor as early as 1951 as a form of reward to collaborators and informers. A small class of collaborators—including informants, *mukhtars*, local council and regional leaders—was thus leased larger-than-normal tracts of land in order to demonstrate to the Palestinian community that collaboration with the state is rewarded. See Cohen, *Good Arabs*, 40.

The strategy is also not unique to Israel. British colonial authorities used the distribution of plots of land in the Punjab to reward Indian officers who served in the British Indian Army, and Guatemalan authorities gave the lands of people who were considered "uncooperative" with the army to those who collaborated with it. See Mustapha Kamal Pasha, *Colonial Political Economy: Recruitment and Underdevelopment in the Punjab* (Oxford: Oxford University Press, 1998), 240; and Jennifer Schirmer, *The Guatemalan Military Project: A Violence Called Democracy* (Philadelphia: University of Pennsylvania Press, 1998), 72.

21. "Supreme Court Petitions: Land Rights," Adalah, www.adalah.org/eng/legaladvocacyland.php (accessed February 14, 2008); Human Rights Association, "Discrimination against Arabs on the Basis of Military Service," in *Weekly Review of the Arabic Press in Israel*, 195 (November 5–12, 2004), www.arabhra.org/publications/wrap/wraphome2004.htm (accessed January 18, 2005); "News," Ministry of Defense, www.hachvana.mod.gov.il/pages/news/news.asp?UN=9&HD=14 (accessed July 31, 2003).

22. Housing assistance is increased beyond what non-serving families are entitled to by 1 percent per month of mandatory service for each parent—up to a 60 percent

increase if both parents have served. See Ministry of Housing, "Ministry of Housing," www.moch.gov.il/NR/rdonlyres/0F7E9446–CBA8–411C-858A-FB40F89D0F1F/5347 /2–1–4.pdf (accessed March, 2004).

23. Lesley Gill, "Creating Citizens, Making Men: The Military and Masculinity in Bolivia," *Cultural Anthropology* 12, no. 4 (1997): 537.

24. Havakook, *Footprints in the Sand*, 42.

25. Ministry of Defense, *Bulletin for Released Soldiers*, 15.

26. A documentary film by Ayelet Bechar follows eighteen-year-old Saqir (pronounced Sagir in the local Bedouin dialect), who hails from an unrecognized village, as he is about to join the military:

> Everyone thinks I'm joining the army to kill people! But the military is not like that. It's something else altogether. The army makes a man out of you. It's enough that if I go to government places, I say to them 'I served,' they look at me differently. An Arab in uniform is respected in this country. But when he takes it off, that's it, you stay an Arab, an Arab Bedouin. So I'm doing this and requesting my rights, making my rights. First of all, I'm going to ask for electricity. This is the most important thing.

Saqir's younger sister suffers from a disease requiring her to daily use a respiratory device that normally requires electricity. Saqir's mother, who objects to his joining the military, says, "In our village, they look at someone who was in the army in a different way [that is, critically]. But this is in his head. He says 'until the end [she uses the Hebrew term *'ad hasof*], I will continue to fight until I bring electricity.'" *Power*, dir. Ayelet Bechar.

27. Joesph Algazy, "In Israel Too," *Le Monde Diplomatique*, http://mondediplo.com/ 1997/09/israel (accessed December 16, 2004); Human Rights Association, "Land and Planning," www.arabhra.org/factsheets/factsheet2.htm (accessed December 16, 2004).

28. For example, Bedouins in the south serving in the military were paid a salary suggested by their "volunteering" shaykh, and missing wages and certificates of release were handled through these leaders as well. Havakook, *Footprints in the Sand*, 74, 38. The first Druze unit included thirty men, many of them recruited by Salih Khnayfis, who was appointed as a member of the parliament. Parsons, *Druze*, 103. In order to win favor with the authorities, collaborating Arab leaders are encouraged to compete with each other in offering men to the military. Particularly notable has been competition between Bedouins in the Naqab and those in the Galilee—the latter having historically higher rates of military service. A 2006 official military report feeds this ongoing competition by noting that for the first time the absolute numbers of new Bedouin recruits from the Naqab (78 during that cycle) exceeded the number of those recruited from the Galilee (69). This state division between north and south is not surprising given that during the period of the Military Government, the authorities "cultivated the internal fragmentation of the Bedouin" by requiring them to register according to their tribal affiliation. See Lustick, *Arabs in the Jewish State*, 135.

Arab leaders who recruited soldiers enjoyed relationships of patronage with key Jewish recruiters. The village of Arab al-Hayb had built a small monument to honor one of
their primary recruiters and patrons, Raḥav'am Ze'evi. Ze'evi was "the founder of the
extreme rightist Moledet party whose core ideology is the transfer (ethnic cleansing)
of the Palestinians from the occupied territories and the encouragement of Palestinian
citizens of Israel to accept 'voluntary' transfer." See Rouhana and Sultany, "Redrawing," 14. Around the time of his death, the monument was neglected and destroyed,
demonstrating an ambivalent relationship to Ze'evi's legacy. While searching for its
remains, I asked some people for directions, but they denied its existence. However, a
little boy on a bicycle took me there. A man in a car whom I asked on the side of the
road told me, "He helped the village a lot, and opened the road to it, but during weddings with kids playing, its traces were lost." His companion in the car added: "When
they widened the road, it became difficult to keep the monument and it is no longer
there." When I said I had heard it was burned down, they admitted, "Yes, there was
once an attempt but rocks don't burn."

29. Sa'di, "Incorporation of the Palestinian Minority," 80.

30. Hillel Cohen documents this with regard to collaborators who were given influence to foster relationships of patronage with other Arabs. See Cohen, *Good Arabs*,
chap. 1.

31. A policeman from 'Ayn Rafa told me, "There isn't a guy in my village that I
haven't cleared two or three tickets for." Another policeman, from Jatt, told me, "We
protect the security of the village and if there is a problem we try to solve it quietly with
a *sulḥa* [traditional reconciliation]. Before we open a criminal file [Hebrew, *tik plili*],
before it reaches the police up above. So far I've never given anyone from the village a
ticket, even though I can."

Far from being embarrassing, connections to Jewish intermediaries are the subject of
boasting by collaborating figures. In his memoirs, the famous "government man" Sayf
al-Din Zo'bi, who was appointed to the first Knesset, boasts about his personal relationships with Jewish Israeli officials—documented by numerous photos of handshakes
and visits—that helped him "solve problems" for fellow Arabs. Sayf al-Din Zo'bi, *Eye
Witness: Memoirs* (Shafa-'Amr: al-Mashriq, 1987), 51. In Nizar Hassan's documentary
Istiqlal, the mayor of the village of Mashhad boasts about the relationships he has built
with Jewish Israeli officials and claims that undoubtedly this has helped him garner
special financial support for his village. *Istiqlal*, dir. Nizar Hassan, 1994.

32. Sa'di, "Incorporation of the Palestinian Minority," 80.

33. "Ze'ev Hartman, Consultant to the Mayor of Mashhad: 'I Will Try to Enlist All
the Young Men in the Village of Mashhad and One Day, an Arab Will Be the Commander in Chief,'" *Kul al-'Arab*, February 8, 2002.

34. The Arabic term used here was *yiblashū fina*.

35. The Arabic term used here was *yḥammil allah jmīli*.

36. The Green Patrol is a paramilitary unit with extensive powers, established by Ariel Sharon to fight "so-called Bedouin infiltration into national Jewish land. . . . It mobilizes for special operations to pull down Bedouin tents, seize flocks, and destroy crops planted without the appropriate permit." See Regional Council for the Unrecognized Villages in the Negev and the Arab Association for Human Rights, "The Unrecognized Villages in the Negev: Submission to the UN Committee on Economic, Social and Cultural Rights," (2003), 22.

37. Falah, "How Israel Controls the Bedouin," 44. For example, the 1959 Black Goat Law to prevent "dangerous overgrazing" allows for the confiscation of herds. According to Havakook, this commander "found himself answering requests of shaykhs and trackers to intervene with this authority or that" and became very influential. Havakook, *Footprints in the Sand*, 111.

38. Ori Nir, "Bedouin Teens Reject Army, Not Wanting To Be 'Suckers,'" *Haaretz*, www.haaretzdaily.com/hasen/pages/ShArt.jhtml?itemNo=115747&contrassID=2&sub ContrassID=1&sbSubContrassID=0&listSrc=Y (accessed October 1, 2002).

39. According to a Druze veteran interviewed by *Haaretz*, social status in the Druze community is often derived from military rank, and even "the women—they stand in line at the store in accordance with their husbands' rank." See Anshel Pfeffer, "Double Vision," *Haaretz*, www.haaretz.com/hasen/objects/pages/PrintArticleEn .jhtml?itemNo=909583 (accessed October 7, 2007).

40. According to the son: "The irony is that at the same time that my father's name is mentioned in the Martyrs of Israel building with his picture, the Ministry of Defense did not recognize him as a martyr of war and has deprived us of those rights." See Husam Harb, "For Twenty Years the Ministry of Defense Deprives the Ilias Family from Maghar of Benefits after the Death of the Father Who Served in the Border Guard," *Kul al-'Arab*, February 8, 2002.

41. Ibid.

42. The Arabic term used was *mitkhūzqīn*.

Chapter 5

1. He used the Arabic term *fatanū finā*.

2. Peled, *Question of Loyalty*, 147.

3. Havakook, *Footprints in the Sand*, 69, 110, 114.

4. Ibid., 114.

5. Peled, *Question of Loyalty*, 138.

6. Jansson, "Bedouin Soldiers."

7. Quoted in ibid., 31.

8. Havakook, *Footprints in the Sand*, 65, 96, 157, 207.

9. Ibid., 223.

10. Cohen, *Good Arabs*, 188.

11. Lomsky-Feder and Ben-Ari, "People in Uniform," 173.

12. Amos Harel, "IDF to End Forced Druze Separation," *Haaretz*, November 20, 2001, 1.

13. Rouhana, *Palestinian Citizens*, 230.

14. This differentiation between Bedouin, Druze, and other Arabs remains shallow and is sometimes collapsed into a general Arab category or simply confused. For example, non-Bedouin Arabs are usually directed into the Bedouin units, and some have been given the benefit of the Bedouin educational military track. Ali, a Bedouin soldier, explained to me that the system even allows "a lot of Arab fallahīn [meaning farmers, that is, non-Bedouins] to register as Bedouins, to make it easier for themselves" in the military.

15. Havakook, *Footprints in the Sand*, 113.

16. Ibid., 82.

17. Ibid., 198. The state often put words into the mouths of its collaborators. The conscription of Druze, for example, was presented not as a state-initiated project, but as a fulfillment of a request from the Druze community itself.

18. Ibid., 122.

19. Ibid.

20. Ibid., 205.

21. Ibid., 224, 140, 122.

22. Ibid., 198.

23. Jawad said that Mizrahi Jews *māklīn hawā zaynā*, literally meaning "they eat air like we do."

24. According to a former Druze officer, Amin: "If there are problems in Nablus or Gaza, they take the Druze there. Because the more victims there are, the more identification the Druze have with the state and the more animosity to other Arabs." According to the *Haaretz* newspaper, "The harsh policing jobs that were given to the Druze pushed them into the twilight zone between the Jews, who try hard to boast of their purity of arms, and the Palestinians [in the West Bank and Gaza], for whom the friction with the Druze has given rise to . . . a focused hatred of the group." See Golan, "Alliance of Blood." The Druze officer, Amin, objected that: "The whole Druze population is 80,000, and half of them are female. If you remove the children, the elderly, the religious people, and teachers and workers—what is left is a small minority. The issue becomes one of some 2,000 Druze soldiers. Why is every murderous act blamed on them?" At a conference in the village of Yarka, Druze academics and intellectuals argued that "the occupation has destroyed our youth, and, in effect, our entire ethnic community." See Golan, "Alliance of Blood." During the first intifada, Israeli media coverage fostered "an image of Druze as vicious lackeys of the State." See Hajjar, *Courting Conflict*, 140. This violent image of the Druze conveniently deflects attention from Jewish military brutality, and illustrates the incomplete integration of the Druze.

25. He used the Arabic term *būz midfa'*.

26. "Discrimination in Life and Death," editorial, *Haaretz*, December 15, 2004.

27. Samir described this exam as difficult and key to success in the officer's course.

28. These are in fact not exclusive to Bedouins.

29. Daniel Ben Simon, "A Community on Trial," *Haaretz*, www.haaretz.com/hasen/objects/pages/PrintArticleEn.jhtml?itemNo=712637 (accessed May 8, 2006).

30. Susan Slyomovics, "The Rape of Qula, a Destroyed Palestinian Village," in *Nakba: Palestine, 1948, and the Claims of Memory*, eds. Ahmad Sa'di and Lila Abu Lughod (New York: Columbia University Press, 2007), 42.

31. Ahmad Ashqar, *Self Destruction, the Nazareth Example: Conflict in Shhab EdDin Theater* (Ramallah: Al Mashriq, 2000), 96. This conflict centered on competing plans for a plot of land in Nazareth near the Church of the Annunciation, whereby the Likud government gave conflicting promises to the Vatican and the Islamicists. The ensuing violence in April 1999 resulted in some thirty injuries. See Jonathan Cook, "The Holy War Israel Wants," *The Electronic Intifada*, www.jkcook.net/Articles1/0023.htm (accessed October 5, 2007); Jonathan Cook, "Divide and Destroy," *Al Ahram Weekly* issue 645, http://jkcook.net/Articles1/0022.htm (accessed October 5, 2007); and Yosef Jabareen, "The Right to the City: The Case of the Shihab el-Din Crisis in Nazareth," in Suhad Bishara and Hana Hamdan, eds., *Makan: Adalah's Journal for Land Planning and Justice, Volume 1: The Right to the City and New Ways of Understanding Space* (Shafa-'Amr: Adalah—The Legal Center for Arab Minority Rights in Israel, 2006).

32. Cook, *Blood and Religion*, 210.

33. For more on state use of clans or "hamulas," see for example, Talal Asad, "Anthropological Texts and Ideological Problems: An Analysis of Cohen on Arab Villages in Israel," *Economy and Society* 4, no. 3 (1975); Kanaaneh, *Birthing the Nation*, 122–29; and Taghreed Yahya-Younis, "Between 'Normativity' and 'Violation': Women's Political Loyalty in Municipal Elections in Palestinian-Arab Society in Israel," in *Blue ID: Palestinians in Israel Revisited*, Rhoda Kanaaneh and Isis Nusair, eds. (Albany: State University of New York Press, forthcoming). The term "honor killing" refers to the murder, usually of a female relative, who is suspected of sexual improprieties that supposedly dishonor the entire family. In a case in 'Arrabi, a bomb was thrown at a woman and the husband with whom she had eloped (she survived and the husband was killed). The husband's relatives threatened to avenge his death, and some of the woman's relatives joined the military in order to arm themselves in case of a revenge attack. Nahla Abdo argues that the state uses "honor killings" to divide and rule the Palestinian population. See Nahla Abdo, "Honour Killing, Patriarchy, and the State: Women in Israel," in *Violence in the Name of Honour: Theoretical and Political Challenges*, eds. Shahrzad Mojab and Nahla Abdo (Istanbul: Istanbul Bilgi University Press, 2004).

34. Lesley Gill, *The School of the Americas: Military Training and Political Violence in the Americas* (Durham, NC: Duke University Press, 2004), 16. Human Rights Watch has

argued that the "Israeli authorities' failure to bring perpetrators to justice fosters a culture of impunity." See Human Rights Watch, "World Report 2006—Israel / Occupied Palestinian Territories (OPT)—January," www.unhcr.org/cgi-bin/texis/vtx/rsd/rsddocview .html?tbl=RSDCOI&id=43cfaea22 (accessed October 9, 2007).

35. "Attorney Rabi' Jahshan Prepares to Submit a Suit to Compensate the Residents of Maghar for the Damage to Their Property," *Kul al-'Arab*, February 25, 2005.

36. Amram Mitzna, "There Was a Pogrom in Maghar," *Haaretz*, February 16, 2005, editorial page; Nazir Majali, "Like in the Third World," *Haaretz*, February 15, 2005, editorial page.

37. "Attorney Rabi' Jahshan." According to the lawyer representing the Christian families in a suit against the police, "There are hundreds of witnesses, from all three religions, who have testimony that is not in the police's favor." Nayif Zaydan, "Yesterday I Went to Maghar to Record the Latest Pictures and Visit the Villages' Schools and Car Cemetery," *Panorama*, February 25, 2005, 37.

38. "The Parliamentary Committee on the Interior Studies the Acts of Violence in Abu Snan," *al-'Ittihad*, February 17, 2005, 5.

39. I thank Hisham Naffa' for pointing out this double meaning.

Chapter 6

1. The Arabic version of his Hebrew name is Isma'il.

2. Lecture by Ishmael Khaldi, "An Arab Muslim in an Israeli World," March 16, 2004, American University, Ward Room 104, Washington, D.C.

3. Isma'il was going by the Hebrew name Ishmael. Some Arab soldiers change their names to Hebrew ones. For example, the well known Abd-al-Majid Khader (1920–1971) of the village of Na'ura, a commanding officer of the Bedouin unit, changed his name to 'Amos Yarkoni—a name chosen for him by Jewish leaders. When such name changes allow for moments of passing, they serve to "reinscribe hegemonic categories and boundaries." See Carol Bardenstein, "Cross/Cast: Passing in Israeli and Palestinian Cinema" in *Palestine, Israel, and the Politics of Popular Culture*, Rebecca Stein and Ted Swedenburg, eds., 99–125 (Durham, NC: Duke University Press, 2005).

4. Firro, "Reshaping Druze Particularism," 40. The fact that Ishmael is a poster model is driven home on his website, www.ishmaelkhaldi.com (accessed May 12, 2008).

5. Similarly, a published interview with Khaldi includes the following questions: "Minorities in other societies often complain about systematic discrimination. How would you describe the Bedouin experience in Israel? What is the relationship like with the wider Arab community? How does your experience as an IDF soldier, and later as an Israeli policeman, colour your relations with the Palestinians and Arab Israelis who support them? How do you feel about, say, Israeli Arab Member of Knesset Azmi Bishara's frequent exhortations in support of Palestinian violence?" See Nadav Shlezinger, "Israeli Bedouins: Ishmael Khaldi Discusses Israel's Bedouin Minority," electronic docu-

ment (accessed October 6, 2006). Rafik Halabi, a well-known Druze television corre-
spondent who describes himself as an Israeli patriot, says that when speaking to Israeli
Jewish audiences "the one question that inevitably comes up is: 'Who are you, Rafik
Halabi? A Druze? An Israeli? A Palestinian? An Arab? Or perhaps a Zionist?'" Quoted
in Virginia Dominguez, *People as Subject, People as Object: Selfhood and Peoplehood in
Contemporary Israel* (Madison: University of Wisconsin Press, 1989), 159.

6. Jabareen, "Oppression of Identities," 27.

7. Peled, *Question of Loyalty*, 147. This exemption is often presented as humanistic;
the state does not want Arabs to face dilemmas of conscience in military service. However, even this packaging of exemption figures Arabs as inherently sympathetic to the
enemies of the state.

8. Ibid., 137–38.

9. Ibid., 140–41.

10. Ibid.

11. Harel, "Stemming the Tide."

12. Hisham Naffa', "The Dirty Military Mirror," *al-'Ittihad*, August 25, 1997.

13. Helman notes that Israeli peace activists in fact use their prior military service
as a means to legitimate their dissidence since that service is "perceived as a prerequisite
for political opposition." See Helman, "Militarism and the Construction of Community," 8; and Helman, "Militarism and the Construction of the Life-World of Israeli
Males," 209.

14. Oz Shelach, *Picnic Grounds: A Novel in Fragments* (San Francisco: City Light
Books, 2003), 31–32.

15. Hajjar, *Courting Conflict*, 142.

16. Yaacov Bar-Natan, "Arabs in the IDF: Is Conscription of Christians and Moslems to the Israeli Army a Realistic Proposition?" *Spectrum: Israel Labour Movement
Monthly* 6, no. 1 (1988): 23.

17. Lomsky-Feder and Ben-Ari, "People in Uniform," 169.

18. Russian soldiers, unlike Arabs, receive "unofficial permission," for example, to
"maintain a 'local' culture in the units" by being concentrated in certain units and
allowed to speak Russian between themselves, to read Russian language books and
newspapers, and watch Russian TV programs. Ibid.

19. As mentioned in Chapter 2, many Arabs use the term "martyr" to describe any
Palestinian killed in the Israeli–Palestinian conflict.

20. Yossi Yehoshua, "Arab Muslim Wants to Join IAF," *Ynetnews*, www.ynetnews
.com/home/1,7340,3083,00.html (accessed January 26, 2006).

21. Ibid.

22. According to a Ministry of Defense book on Bedouin soldiers, "not every Bedouin that enlisted to IDF service did so because he saw himself or defined himself as
'Zionist,' or because he understood the military as 'a realization of the renewed Zionist

project in the young Israeli state'; most of them or all Bedouins that volunteered to the military did so out of personal considerations, considerations of benefit and necessity." See Havakook, *Footprints in the Sand*, 46. Although this is deemed "not a criticism," within the framework of the Jewish state, Bedouin service fundamentally cannot be figured as patriotic, but is necessarily considered mercenary and thus more suspect.

23. "Extension of Arrest of Lieutenant Colonel 'Omar al-Hayb Accused of Spying for 'Hezbollah," *al-'Ittihad*, December 25, 2002, 4.

24. Amos Harel, Jalal Bana, and Baruch Kra, "Bedouin Officer Says He's Innocent of Spying for Hezbollah, Drug Dealing," *Haaretz*, October 25, 2002.

25. Daniel Ben Simon, "Community on Trial."

26. Ibid.

27. Ibid.

Chapter 7

1. Although settling and claiming Palestinian lands in the West Bank and Gaza are more widely known, settling and claiming Arab lands for Jews inside Israel is part of the same Israeli demographic priority. In fact, the Settlement Department of the Jewish Agency intentionally does not distinguish between the West Bank and Gaza and Israel "proper," but rather categorizes areas only according to the number of Jews living in them. See Reinhard Wiemer, "Zionism and the Arabs after the Establishment of the State of Israel," in *Palestinians Over the Green Line*, ed. Alexander Scholch (London: Ithaca, 1983), 51–52.

2. Ja'far Farah, "The Other Side of Judaizing the Galilee," *Zavonı–Karmiel*, May 14, 1993, 16.

3. Ibid. A similar answer was given in the landmark Katzir case, in which the Jewish town rejected the request of the Arab Qa'dan family to build a home because it "would be difficult for them to integrate socially." See Association for Civil Rights in Israel, www.acri.org.il/english-acri/engine/story.asp?id=177. The Jewish residents of Makhmunim expressed the fear that the Sawa'id family would reproduce rapidly, become a larger minority, and take control of the settlement. Farah, "Judaizing the Galilee," 16.

4. Ibid., 17.

5. Ibid. When I visited the Sawa'id family in 2004, the entrance to the gated barbwire-encircled settlement read in Hebrew "Makhmunim: Dreams That Come True." It would be more accurate if it stated "Makhmunim: Jewish Dreams That Come True."

6. Avihai Becker, "Unsweet Revenge," *Haaretz*, January 19, 2002, magazine section.

7. Guy Leshem, "IDF Widows' Organization Blacklisted Minority Members," *Haaretz*, www.haaretz.com/hasen/objects/pages/PrintArticleEn.jhtml?itemNo=843940 (accessed April 10, 2007). In April 2006, Andy As'ad from 'Isifya was nominated by the "IDF widows and orphans organization" to make history by being the first Druze widow to pass the torch to the president of the country at a Memorial Day ceremony—only to

have the Ministry of Defense cancel her role, according to As'ad, for "political reasons." Hanan Greenberg, "Who Doesn't Want the Druze Widow in the Memorial Ceremony?" *Ynetnews*, www.ynet.co.il/articles/0,3740,L-3240614,00.html (accessed April 18, 2006).

8. Golan, "Alliance of Blood." Similarly, in an article titled "Is 'Capt. R' a War Criminal or a Scapegoat?" the defense lawyers argued they would not allow their client to be "portrayed as a 'bloodthirsty monster' or to be railroaded by a military intent on avoiding uncomfortable revelations about its culture or its practices." See Nelson, "Capt. R." Note that at the time, the full name of Captain R. was not made public.

9. Aryeh Dayan, "Who Put Taysir el-Heyb in Charge?" *Haaretz*, www.haaretz .com/hasen/objects/pages/PrintArticleEn.jhtml?itemNo=618220 (accessed September 5, 2005).

10. The *Haaretz* article continues: "'If it had been a Jewish soldier' says Mahmoud Wahib, Taysir's uncle, 'he wouldn't even have gotten a one-year sentence.'" Taysir was "sentenced to eight years in prison for killing Tom Hurndall, a young Briton active in the International Solidarity Movement (ISM) who was shot in the head in Rafah when he tried to keep Palestinian children away from an IDF post along the Philadelphi route commanded by el-Heyb." See Dayan, "Taysir el-Heyb."

Palestinian soldiers' perceptions that Israeli Jews fail to appreciate them surfaced repeatedly. They found expression, for example, during the 2005 so-called disengagement from Gaza. At the time, rumors circulated in the Israeli press of a Jewish religious ruling permitting settlers to shoot at non-Jewish soldiers during settlement evacuations. Ronny Sofer, "'Fire Back If Needed': New Edict Allows Bedouin (IDF) Soldiers to Kill Settlers Who Attack Them," *Yedioth*, March 3, 2005, www.ynetnews.com/ articles/0,7340,L-3053327,00.html (accessed March 15, 2005). Israeli media noted the concern of Druze and Bedouin soldiers who questioned then minister of defense Shaul Mofaz on the military's response to this incitement against them. Hanan Greenberg "Can Druze Soldiers be Shot?" *Yedioth*, March 1, 2005, www.ynetnews.com/Ext/Comp/ ArticleLayout/CdaArticlePrintPreview/1,2506,L-3052594,00.html (accessed September 28, 2006). A Bedouin shaykh allegedly issued an Islamic ruling allowing Bedouin soldiers who took part in the evacuation to "protect themselves" and shoot at anyone who tried to harm them. Nir Hason, "Fatwa Allows Bedouin Soldiers to Return Fire in Evacuation," *Haaretz*, www.haaretz.com/hasen/pages/ShArt.jhtml?itemNo=547219&c ontrassID=1&subContrassID=7&sbSubContrassID=0&listSrc=Y (accessed September 28, 2006).

11. The analysis by Palestinian journalist Hisham Naffa' of an incident in which two Jewish officers from an elite unit beat a Bedouin soldier is relevant here. Rather than see the case as a random aberration or as an exception to military rules, Naffa' argues that Israeli racist policies against Arabs in the Occupied Territories "will necessarily and directly cause the same behavior in relationship to Arabs here." Naffa', "Dirty Military Mirror."

12. Cohen argues that this is true for collaborators as well: "The will to reward collaborators did not hold before the more basic Zionist desire, to transfer the majority of land for Jewish settlement." See Cohen, *Good Arabs*, 47.

13. Ada Ushpiz, "Doves among the Druze," *Haaretz*, www.haaretz.com/hasen/objects/pages/PrintArticleEn.jhtml?itemNo=401368 (accessed February 14, 2008).

14. Golan, "Alliance of Blood."

15. Oren Yiftachel, "State Policies, Land Control and an Ethnic Minority: The Arabs in the Galilee Region, Israel," *Environment and Planning D: Society and Space* 9 (1991): 340.

16. Ghalib Sayf, "Land and Military Recruitment," *al-'Ittihad*, November 23, 2001, 11.

17. Zubud is an area of land near the village of Bayt Jann that the state tried to confiscate from its Druze owners, to turn into a nature preserve.

18. These soldiers were punished for not completing their full period of service. In addition to accounts of such direct resistance, a resident of Yanuh mentioned the use of the mental clause to avoid conscription: "In our village alone there are eighty crazy men, including doctors and engineers."

19. Ushpiz, "Doves among the Druze."

20. Oren Yiftachel and Hubert Law Yone, "Regional Policy and Minority Attitudes in Israel," *Environment and Planning A* 26, no. 4 (1993): 387–403.

21. Harel, "Stemming the Tide."

22. Ada Ushpiz, "Tents of Mourning: Soul-Searching in the Bedouin Towns of Rahat and Kseifa Following the Death of Their Soldiers in Rafah This Week," *Haaretz*, December 17, 2004, B6.

23. *Tuba and Migdal*, dir. Gil Karni, 1998. In the Naqab alone some 113 Arab homes were demolished in 2002, 132 in 2003, and 150 in 2004. See Human Rights Association, "On the Margins," 27–28.

24. Judaizing goals of the state trump its attempts at co-opting Palestinians. This order of priorities is clearly crystallized in the attempt (though unsuccessful) by then agriculture minister Rafael Eitan to intensify the policy of Bedouin displacement in the Naqab, by advocating the disbandment of the army's Bedouin unit, so as to disarm its soldiers lest they raise their weapons in anticipated defense. Negbi, "Not Activist."

25. Arbeli, "Bedouin Soldiers Hold Protest."

26. Nir, "Bedouin Teens Reject Army."

27. Ibid. *Haaretz* spelled the name as Ibrahim al-Huzeil. Nir, "Bedouin Teens Reject Army." The Israeli military itself blames recent declines in the number of Bedouin recruits on insufficient rewards. While no statistics on the overall number of Arabs in the military are available, the Ministry of Defense stated to the press that 390 Bedouins joined the military in 2006, down 20 percent from 490 in 2005, which itself was down 10 percent from 2004. However, other statements by military representatives discuss the

rise of recruitment rates. See "Decline in the Percentage of Arab Bedouin Recruitment in the Military by 20% from Last Year," Arabs48, www.arabs48.com/display.x?cid=19% sid=57&id=44330 (accessed April 10, 2007). Similarly, As'ad As'ad, long-time Likudnik and supporter of Druze military service, was reported as saying that "Druze young men are like the nigger (*kushi*) that has done what was required of him, and is now dismissed." Hisham Naffa', "Maghar, the Responsibility of All of Us, and Not Only in Slogans," *al-'Ittihad*, February 18, 2005, 5.

28. Arens, "The Wages of a Non-Policy."

29. Sami Smooha, "Ethnic Democracy: Israel as an Archetype," *Israel Studies* 2, no. 2 (1997): 199–200.

30. Amal Jamal, "Ethnic Nationalism, Native Peoples and Civic Equality: On Collective Rights in Israel," paper presented at the Conference on the Legal and Socio-Economic Status of Arab Citizens in Israel, New York University (April 3, 2003), 4.

31. "IDF Reserve Soldiers and Officers Say No to Disengagement," *Arutz Sheva: Israel National News*, www.israelnn.com/news.php3?id=84374 (accessed September 29, 2006).

32. Ibid. There is in fact a government-recognized category of "righteous gentile," defined as a resident of Israel recognized by the Yad Vashem Memorial Authority. As of 1995, the National Insurance Institute pays a benefit to them by law. See National Insurance Institute of Israel, "Quarterly Statistics," www.btl.gov.il/english/rivon_E/htm/ en_rivon_1_13.htm (accessed November 14, 2006).

Chapter 8

Portions of this chapter appeared in the article "Boys or Men? Duped or 'Made'? Palestinian Soldiers in the Israeli Military," *American Ethnologist* 32, no. 2 (May 2005): 260–75.

1. Much work on nationalism and gender has focused on the manipulation of women and their identities in nation-state formation by both colonial or ruling elites and nationalists resisting them. To mention just a few: Lila Abu-Lughod, ed., *Remaking Women: Feminism and Modernity in the Middle East* (Princeton, NJ: Princeton University Press, 1998); Leila Ahmed, *Women and Gender in Islam: Historical Roots of a Modern Debate* (New Haven, CT: Yale University Press, 1992); Begoña Aretxaga, *Shattering Silence: Women, Nationalism, and Political Subjectivity in Northern Ireland* (Princeton, NJ: Princeton University Press, 1997); Partha Chatterjee, *The Nation and Its Fragments: Colonial and Postcolonial Histories* (Princeton, NJ: Princeton University Press, 1993); Victoria DeGrazia, *How Fascism Ruled Women: Italy, 1922–1945* (Berkeley: University of California Press, 1992); Ellen Fleischmann, *The Nation and Its "New" Women: The Palestinian Women's Movement, 1920–1948* (Berkeley: University of California Press, 2003); and Caren Kaplan, Norma Alarcon, and Minoo Moallem, eds., *Between Woman and Nation: Nationalisms, Transnational Feminisms, and the State* (Durham, NC: Duke University Press, 1999).

Much less attention, however, has been directed to the relationship between masculinity and nation-states—although the phrase "nationalism and gender" constantly alludes to it—and even less to the masculinities of nondominant men. Exceptions include: Mai Ghoussoub and Emma Sinclair-Webb, eds., *Imagined Masculinities: Male Identity and Culture in the Modern Middle East* (London: Saqi Books, 2000); Michael Herzfeld, *The Poetics of Manhood* (Princeton, NJ: Princeton University Press, 1988); Joseph Massad, "Conceiving the Masculine: Gender and Palestinian Nationalism," *Middle East Journal* 49, no. 3 (1995): 467–83; and Mrinalini Sinha, *The "Manly Englishman" and the "Effeminate Bengali" in the Late Nineteenth Century* (Manchester: Manchester University Press, 1995). As a whole, the field of gender and nationalism is disproportionately focused on women. Indeed *gender* is commonly used to refer to women: "no women, no gender." See Matthew Gutmann, "Trafficking in Men: The Anthropology of Masculinity," *Annual Review of Anthropology* 26 (1997): 385–409. Furthermore, Joane Nagel argues that the field "fails to examine systematically what is uniquely masculine in a structural, cultural or social sense, about such clearly gendered activities and institutions as crime, nationalism, politics or violence." See Joane Nagel, "Masculinity and Nationalism: Gender and Sexuality in the Making of Nations," *Ethnic and Racial Studies* 21, no. 2 (1998): 244. My project, thus, contributes to this body of scholarship by pointing to the role of the state and colonial powers in setting the parameters for contests over the masculinities of both dominant and nondominant men. Not unlike Joseph Massad, who suggests that Palestinian nationalist masculinity is "a new type of masculinity" that has "little to do with 'tradition,'" I suggest that the agency of Palestinian men in Israel, both inside and outside the military, is better understood within strict limits set by the Israeli state. See Massad, "Conceiving the Masculine," 467.

2. Enloe, *Ethnic Soldiers*.

3. Yuval-Davis, "Front and Rear," 188. For more on gender, militarization, and the constructions of the homefront, see Catherine Lutz, *Homefront: A Military City and the American 20th Century* (Boston: Beacon, 2001). According to Danny Kaplan and Eyal Ben-Ari, the Israeli military is "the central cultural site for the construction of a hegemonic masculinity among many social groups." See Kaplan and Ben-Ari, "Brothers and Others," 401. Indeed, the term *masculitary culture* was coined to refer to this "hegemonic masculine military culture" (see ibid., 398), which prepares "young [Jewish] men to sacrifice themselves for the nation-state." See Eyal Ben-Ari with Galeet Dardashti, "Tests of Soldierhood, Trials of Manhood: Military Service and Male Ideals in Israel," in *Military, State, and Society in Israel: Theoretical and Comparative Perspectives*, eds. Daniel Maman, Eyal Ben-Ari, and Zeev Rosenhek (New Brunswick, NJ: Transaction, 2001), 260.

Orna Sasson-Levy points out, however, that "the connection between masculinity, the military and the state is not unified. . . . Soldiers in varied military roles construct different conceptions of masculinity and citizenship, both of which are constituted through an ongoing dialogue of imitation or rejection of the hegemonic masculinity of the combat soldier." See Sasson-Levy, "Constructing Identities at the Margins," 4. For example, Sasson-Levy points to soldiers with blue-collar jobs for whom combat masculinity is unavailable. They are allowed entrance into the state, although this entrance is "by no means equal." Ibid., 16.

4. Lomsky-Feder and Ben-Ari, "People in Uniform," 162. To date, social science research on the Israeli military has largely neglected the subject of how the culture of Israeli masculinity defines itself in opposition to Palestinians. It has also neglected Palestinian masculinity and, for that matter, Palestinian soldiers.

5. In contrast to what scholars have described for Israeli Jewish masculinity, Julie Peteet argues that "historically, Palestinians did not directly conflate war-making activities with manhood. Indeed, under the Ottomans, Palestinian peasants tried to escape military conscription, finding little honor or future in the military. Masculine honor was more associated with one's cleverness in evading conscription." See Julie Peteet, "Icons and Militants: Mothering in the Danger Zone," *Signs* 23, no. 1 (1997): 107. Areen Hawari found that during the Military Administration period (1948–1966), Palestinian masculinity was "linked to the patient endurance of pain and physical suffering that men withstood." See Areen Hawari, "Men under the Military Regime," *Adalah's Review* 4 (2004): 33.

6. Julie Peteet, "Male Gender and Rituals of Resistance in the Palestinian Intifada: A Cultural Politics of Violence," in *Imagined Masculinities: Male Identity and Culture in the Modern Middle East*, eds. Mai Ghoussoub and Emma Sinclair-Webb (London: Saqi Books, 2000), 120. Beatings and imprisonment by the Israeli military have been turned into "a cultural criterion of manhood" (ibid.). Indeed, "struggling against the Israeli occupiers and colonizers" is both an affirmation of nationalist agency and a masculinizing act, the two being closely paired. See Massad, "Conceiving the Masculine," 480.

7. Peteet, "Icons and Militants," 107. Hawari similarly emphasizes that masculine heroism during the Military Administration period was derived from a man's "capacity to provide for his family's subsistence needs (housing, food, drink)." See Hawari, "Men under the Military Regime," 33.

8. That Palestinian soldiering is discussed in highly gendered terms is not surprising. Daniel Monterescu argues that Palestinians living as a marginalized minority inside Israel—with "relentless contact with the occupying regime, and the 'local' other"—are continuously involved in a process of negotiating cultural boundaries. This negotiation is often expressed as "the intensive definition and redefinition of the sexual boundaries of manhood." See Daniel Monterescu, "City of 'Strangers': The Socio-Cultural Construction of Manhood in Jaffa," *Journal of Mediterranean Studies* 11, no. 1 (2001): 167.

The crossing of the boundaries of the collective is often linked with the crossing of boundaries of gendered morality. Deborah Bernstein, "Prostitution in Mandate Palestine: An Arab-Jewish-British Meeting Ground," paper presented at the annual meeting of the Middle East Studies Association, San Francisco (November 17–20, 2001). Members of the protest movement Women in Black who call for the end to the military occupation of the West Bank and Gaza Strip are showered by passersby "with sexist cat-calls and curses, in which national conflict [is] wedded to gender and ethnic conflict." See Helman, "Citizenship, Regime, Identity," 312.

Palestinian women suspected of "collaboration," that is, of working with the Israeli secret service, are often considered prostitutes, and some of the men suspected of collaboration are considered homosexual "deviants." B'Tselem, *Collaborators*; Tobias Kelly, "In a Treacherous State: The Fear of the Collaborator among West Bank Palestinians," paper presented at Treason and the Art of Politics: Anthropological and Historical Perspectives workshop, University of Edinburgh (December 7–9, 2006). The collaborators' questionable loyalties are linked to their so-called questionable sexualities. For example, a book about a man from the West Bank city of Jenin who set "honey traps" for men and women, took sexually "compromising" photos, and blackmailed them to work for the Israeli secret service was widely circulated during the first intifada and provided a popular image of collaborators as morally and sexually dubious. Kelly, "In a Treacherous State," 15.

Attempts by the Israeli government to settle collaborators from the West Bank and Gaza Strip in Arab communities within Israel are rejected and criticized on the basis of the corruptive influence of the agents—in terms of national identity, but also in terms of gendered morality. Mayors and other members of these communities often formulate their objections as fear that collaborators will corrupt the community morally and sexually. (This fear of the Western colonial deliberate use of sexual "corruption" to attack Arab culture is clearly articulated in Egypt for example. See Ted Swedenburg, "Saida Sultan / Danna International: Transgender Pop and the Polysemiotics of Sex, Nation and Ethnicity on the Israeli Egyptian Border," *Musical Quarterly* 81, no. 1 [1997]: 81–108.) Stories of the collaborators' wives having multiple, open extramarital affairs, of men prostituting their daughters, and of wife beating and abuse all indicate a conflation of crossing the boundaries of the collective with crossing the boundaries of gendered morality. "Hundreds of Residents from Makir and Jdaidi Demonstrate against Settling the Agents of the Occupation," *al-'Ittihad*, July 15, 2001, 7.

An emblematic image for many Palestinians of the political compromise embodied in the Oslo and subsequent accords is that of Yasser Arafat kissing Yitzhak Rabin. Although physical greetings among Arab men are standard, the emphasis on the "eagerness" and "cheapness" of the kiss in this case carries sexual homophobic undertones. "They sold Palestine for a kiss" again conflates national betrayal with so-called questionable sexuality. This is not to argue that the majority of Palestinians necessarily rejected the accords at the outset but that, when critical of them, they often used gendered tools. Five of the soldiers I interviewed used the image of the kiss; as one soldier told me, "If they sold the cause for an Israeli kiss, why should I fight for them?" In this sense, national honor is closely associated with gender and sexual honor. Discussions of whether Palestinian nationalism managed to prioritize land over honor (*al-'ard qabl al-'ard*) or failed to do so also emphasize the connection made between the two. Kitty Warnock, *Land Before Honor: Palestinian Women in the Occupied Territories* (New York: Monthly Review Press, 1990); Frances Hasso, "Modernity and Gender in Arab Accounts of the 1948 and 1967 Defeats," *International Journal of Middle East Studies* 32, no. 4 (2000): 491–510. The Arabic words *'ard* (land) and *'ard* (honor) begin with two different letters, transliterated as (') hamza and (') 'ayn respectively.

9. This is in addition to the common criticism of them as "sons of prostitutes; not one of them is moral or decent."

10. Another example of the attempted exploitation of weak masculinities comes from a conscientious objector I interviewed. The man refused to perform the mandatory military service imposed on him as a Druze and was imprisoned and harassed extensively as a result. The pressure tactics used against him included intimidation and threats, but also attempts to seduce him that imputed an immature masculine desire, "like promising candy to a little boy":

> At first, this officer tried to scare me. He threatened, "What do you think, prison is Coca-Cola? They are going to fuck you," and he used all the curse words you can think of—sexual threats. I was only eighteen and a nice studious boy. But I didn't let it get to me. Later they tried a different strategy: "They told us about you, how smart you are," and they described the ranks I could reach and the types of weapons I could get. They tried to seduce me with guns. But they came down from that tree very quickly.

Rape and sexual torture and harassment by Israeli prison authorities are widely reported. See for example, Human Rights Watch, "World Report 2001: Israel, the Occupied West Bank, Gaza Strip, and Palestinian Authority Territories," www.hrw.org/wr2k1/mideast/israel.html (accessed December 16, 2004); Palestinian Human Rights Information Center, *The Cost of Freedom* (Chicago: Palestinian Human Rights Information Center, 1991); and Peteet, "Male Gender."

11. Although ascertaining whether a given soldier received orders from state authorities to do this is difficult, this specific method of segmentation—enticement with gun permits—has been widely used. A security coordinating committee stated in 1950 that the distribution of weapons to "members of only a specific community is likely to benefit us, will create the desired tension between the different segments of the population and will allow us to control the situation." See Cohen, *Good Arabs*, 43.

12. I later came across a similar commentary in the *al-'Ittihad* newspaper: "My friends and I joke that the driver of the police patrol that weaves through the streets of Wadi Nisnas [the impoverished Arab neighborhood of Haifa] and disturbs its residents with its siren and lights, is sure to be an Arab. The police themselves make jokes about Arab 'volunteers,' likening their delight in driving a police patrol car to that of a lottery

winner." See Raja Zaʿatri, "Confrontation Is Not Only in Front of the Authorities," *al-ʾIttihad*, January 19, 2005, supplement, 8.

13. In contrast to the deployments of householder determinedly heterosexual masculinity I encountered in my interviews, an American colleague familiar with Israeli and U.S. military culture suggested that many Arab men who joined the Israeli military might be interested in having same-sex relationships there. With all the emphasis the soldier interviewees placed on provider masculinity, together with the stigma of homosexuality as well as the social distance built into my interviews, I did not find an appropriate context to pose this question to any of them. However, when I shared my colleague's suggestion with a Palestinian gay-identified man from Haifa, he retorted that "this is an American accusation. On the contrary, Arab men go looking for girls in the military. One of my classmates served and he told me the army is all fucking (*taʿarīs btaʿarīs*) with Jewish girls." A Palestinian gay activist argued that "there is no relationship between the decision to join the military and what is erroneously called 'sexual perversion'—serving in the military, *that* is perversion." Lisa Hajjar notes that many Druze men "cited army service as a first opportunity to have relationships of any kind with adult women 'strangers' (i.e. female soldiers), friendships as well as sexual relationships. Several interviewees were quite nostalgic about the social and sexual freedoms that they enjoyed during their military service, contrasting those experiences to their pre- and postarmy lives." See Hajjar, *Courting Conflict*, 143. This stark division is of course a product of the state policy of conscripting only Druze men. These relationships were also hinted at in some of my interviews, where soldiers specifically mentioned their increased access (though not totally unfettered) to Jewish discotheques and nightclubs, or in some giggling allusions to family objections to the socially "corrupting" influences of military service. While individual Palestinian soldiers might have had same-sex relationships in the military, it is heterosexual relationships and heterosexual commitments to building families that they highlight.

14. As is apparent, some of the soldiers' wives, wives-to-be, or mothers considered military service as holding the key to better family providers. Gill argues that many poor Bolivian women see military service as a guarantee that "a prospective husband will fulfill his social and economic responsibilities to the domestic unit," and as one woman explains, "The military booklet structures one's future and encourages responsibility." See Gill, "Creating Citizens," 543. However, some Muslim men in fact get engaged soon after enlistment because engagements for Muslim Palestinians usually involve the completion of the legal religious marriage contract, and thus allow soldiers to collect the higher stipends and salaries of married men. Several of my interviewees noted that some young Muslim men deceive girls and get engaged after a few months of service "for the salary," never intending to marry those girls. When they decide to get married, usually to other women, they then break up with these fiancées of convenience, creating social problems for them.

While some women saw military service as signaling a better male provider, other women I interviewed were not so supportive of their husband's or son's choices—including a woman from the Triangle who refused to touch, not to mention wash or iron, her husband's uniform, and another woman, in 'Ayn Rafa, who insisted on being present during an interview with her husband and prodded him, "Why are you giving her diplomatic answers? Give her a straight answer." Nawal told me, "I was so ashamed of my husband, what could I tell people he was doing? But I enjoyed the discounts and shopping promotions he received, it helped the family, and the children were so happy when we bought them things. Still I wish he could make money in a different way."

15. These middle-class aspirations echo Massad's description of the Palestinian nationalist agent as "bourgeois-in-the-making." See Massad, "Conceiving the Masculine," 479.

16. The diverse soldiers' statements reflect changing class-linked Palestinian conceptions of what being a good family man requires and deploy a particular "refrain of home." See Ilana Feldman, "Home as a Refrain: Remembering and Living Displacement in Gaza," *History and Memory* 18, no. 2 (2006): 10–47.

17. Wall hangings in Palestinian homes have been recognized as culturally significant. See Peteet, "Icons and Militants," 9; and Edward Said, *After the Last Sky* (London: Faber and Faber, 1986), 58. Ahlam Shibli's collection of photographs entitled "Trackers" includes several shots of the photos hung in trackers' homes. See Szymczyk, *Ahlam Shibli Trackers*, 85–89.

18. He used the Arabic term *titdahwar*.

19. Dayan, "Who Put Taysir el-Heyb in Charge?"

20. Ibid. Similarly, regarding Palestinian responses to Israeli proposals for national service, a commentator argued that national service is a slippery slope to military service and eventually to the worst situation conceivable in which Arab women become soldiers, the ultimate sign of the loss of social control. One commentator worries: "Are we before a new phenomenon of debauchery and are we before a scene in which a girl volunteers in spite of her father? Or are we in front of a scene in which the father encourages his daughter to perform national service? . . . Is the day that we will see Arab female soldiers carrying automatic weapons and strutting in the streets of the Arab sector far away?" See Yazid Dahamsheh, "Organizations and Institutions of Encouraging 'National Service' Pierces Arab Towns," *Hadith En-Nas*, October 22, 2004.

21. If my analysis here suggests that soldiers try to adhere to central elements of idealized Palestinian masculinity by incorporating its family focus into their narratives, this does not mean that all soldiers aspire to this dominant ideal in its totality. Indeed, some of the men I interviewed forcefully criticized other aspects of this ideal. Ramiz, one of the more vocal critics, described the nationalist masculinity idealized by politicians and members of Arab parties as outdated and impractical. He argued that

we live in this state, the state of Israel, and we have been living in Israel for over fifty years. [Palestinian] nationalism here is a self-delusion—nationalists shout a lot and get red in the face with absolutely no results. Look at the Arab Parliament members; what have they done for us lately? Everyone wants to live, and the way to live in Israel is to accept the reality we live in. The politicians know this, but they can't admit it, because then they won't have a role, they won't have a reason to stand up there on the stage and shout.

Ramiz, thus, describes himself as exceptional: "I'm not going to do something just because so and so tells me to. No, I look at the reality and reach my own conclusions." Indeed, many of the soldiers emphasized their independence as free thinkers, rather than as followers of cultural or national norms. One eloquent soldier explicitly argued that he "transcended taboos in pursuit of a higher personal dignity." This nonnationalist masculine dignity is built on commitments to the family, but also on the value of independence. Abu Mahmud, for example, told me that

the food is good, the dress is good, it is respect. This is my opinion, and that's all that matters. I'm not afraid of anyone except God. I don't care what anyone else thinks or says or threatens. I am in charge of recruiting [used Hebrew *giyyus*—a controversial act, indeed], and I put the new recruit in my car and I drive him in front of everyone all the way to Tiberias [to the enlistment center]. Imagine my courage! If you don't like it, this is my life and I'm free to do as I like.

It is, indeed, this courage to defy the local majority, the Palestinian communities in which the soldiers live, rather than acquiescence to the larger majority, the Israeli state and the greater Jewish population, that Abu Mahmud emphasized.

Many men stressed that they defied common norms by choosing to serve. Nihad said that many of his relatives and friends objected when they found out he was planning to join the army. "But they would talk in one ear, and I would let it fly out the other. Each person has a song (*mawwal*) in his head and he has to sing it. My whole dream was to be in the army, and I wasn't going to be weak and allow others to make decisions for me." Ramiz went so far as to see his defiance as pioneering new norms of behavior, akin to the feminist pioneers of older generations:

The first girls that went out of the village to study, everyone used to gossip about them. But they broke the ice [used Hebrew *shavru it ha-ḳerah*]. The same is true for the first girls who went out to work. But with time, these taboos were broken, and it's become more acceptable. After a few years everyone realized that these girls are right. In fact, now girls who don't study and work are considered not as good as those who do. Myself and the two others who were the first to serve in the village, we paid the price of this process of change. Now things are slowly becoming different.

Another interviewee, from another region of the country, used this specific argument as well: "A few years ago, if a girl said 'I want to learn to drive,' it was considered very strange. It was the same for me when I said I wanted to join the police force. Now it's very normal for girls to drive, and soon it will be very normal for men to join the police." Nonetheless, while emphasizing their ideological independence, Abu Mahmud, Nihad, and Ramiz also framed their accounts in terms of the support of families. Even while contesting nationalist masculinity, they continued to claim its family orientation and, in essence, reinforced the centrality of provider masculinity.

22. Martina Reiker, "Constructing Palestinian Subalternity in the Galilee: Reflections on Representations of the Palestinian Peasantry (Inscriptions 6)," http://humw-ww.ucsc.edu/CultStudies/PUBS/Inscriptions/vol_6/Reiker.html (accessed December 16, 2004); Ted Swedenburg, *Memories of Revolt: The 1936–1939 Rebellion and the Palestinian National Past* (Minneapolis: University of Minnesota Press, 1995). *Hanthala* is also transliterated as *Hanẓala*. The name refers to a bitter plant. This cartoon character is also widely graffitied and appears on shirts, buttons, rap CD covers, and tattoos. See Eqeiq, "Louder," 2.

23. Dan Rabinowitz, *Overlooking Nazareth: The Ethnography of Exclusion in the Galilee* (New York: Cambridge University Press, 1997); Arab Center for Alternative Planning, www.ac-ap.org/?lang=3 (accessed October 12, 2007).

24. Gill, "Creating Citizens"; and Linda Green, "Structures of Power, Spaces of Violence: Everyday Life in Post-Peace Accord Rural Guatemala," *Foccal European Journal of Anthropology* 39 (2002): 118.

25. Dan Rabinowitz describes, for example, how Riziq, a Palestinian coach of an Israeli Jewish basketball team in Upper Nazareth, drew in that Israeli Jewish context "his own discourse and metaphors from the domains of military valor" as well as military camaraderie and soldier-like responsibility, "thus effectively appropriat[ing] these values from their normal Israeli exclusivity." See Rabinowitz, *Overlooking Nazareth*, 126–27.

26. I use Israelization to refer to Palestinian assimilationist behavior in Israel and mimicry of Israeli (often Ashkenazi) Jewish culture as part of a colonizer–colonized relationship. This usage of the term is somewhat different than Israeli scholar Sami Smooha's. He defines Israelization in ideological rather than behavioral terms, as a compromising political stance and sees it as having a democratizing effect: for him it is "the adjustment of the Arabs to their minority status, the respecting of Israel's right to exist and its territorial integrity, the adoption of Hebrew as a second language and Israeli culture as a subculture, the conduct of struggle according to democratic procedures, and the viewing of their lot and future as firmly tied to Israel." See Sami Smooha, "The Advances and Limits of the Israelization of Israel's Palestinian Citizens," in *Israeli and Palestinian Identities in History and Literature*, eds. Kamal Abdel-Malek and David C. Jacobson (New York: St. Martin's Press, 1999), 28. Also see the section the Significance of Give and Take below for more on my use of Israelization.

27. In light of the harassment Arabs experience at the hands of the environmental protection agency, the residents of Bayt Jann referred to the national park surrounding their village as "'the choking ring,' perceiving it as a tool in the hands of the state to slowly diminish Druze life." See Yiftachel and Segal, "Jews and Druze," 494.

28. Arab gender norms are often mistakenly seen as ossified "traditions" that clash with the modern egalitarian ideals of the Israeli state. In a related argument, some scholars are convinced that after the establishment of the state of Israel in 1948, the domestic sphere was the only area remaining under the control of Palestinian men, thus increasing its importance. Mariam Marʿi and Sami Marʿi, "The Role of Women as Change Agents in Arab Society in Israel," in *Calling the Equality Bluff: Women in Israel*, eds. Barbara Swirski and Marilyn Safir (New York: Teachers College Press, 1993), 214; Barbara Swirski, "The Citizenship of Jewish and Palestinian Arab Women in Israel," in *Gender and Citizenship in the Middle East*, ed. Joseph Suad (Syracuse, NY: Syracuse University Press, 2000), 325. As a result, "cultural traditions" were supposedly seized on as the major vehicle for the maintenance of Palestinian identity and continuity. Marʿi and Marʿi, "Role of Women," 214.

While this may be true, this process radically transforms these so-called traditions. Far from being beyond the purview of the state, "the domestic" and "cultural traditions" are actually embroiled in the continued negotiations of citizenship in Israel. They should be understood as, in good part, products of state policies and practices.

An obvious example of the influence of the state on gender norms is the fact it has mostly recruited Palestinian men and not women into its security forces. As already noted, it formally conscripts Druze men only, thus changing and radically strengthening the contours of male dominance in that community. The state usually deploys a modernizing discourse vis-à-vis Palestinian women that it uses to patronize and control Palestinian citizens and to constitute itself in opposition to this Orientalized image as modern and Western. Abdo, "Honour Killing, Patriarchy, and the State"; Amalia Saʿar, "Contradictory Location: Assessing the Position of Palestinian Women Citizens of Israel," *Journal of Middle East Women's Studies* 3, no. 3 (2007); Gil Eyal, "The Discursive Origins of Israeli Separatism: The Case of the Arab Village," *Theory and Society* 25 (1996): 420. In this case, however, it adds a twist: it uses an argument of "pseudo cultural respect" to explain its conscription of Druze males only. Lauren Erdreich, "Marriage Talk: Palestinian Women, Intimacy, and the Liberal Nation-State," *Ethnography* 7, no. 4 (2006): 495. This attitude of uncharacteristic sensitivity and cultural relativism is convenient to the state in this case: it offers to support male dominance among the Druze—which Druze male leaders eagerly accept—allowing the state to continue to play its patronizing liberal role of modernizing the traditional Arabs. Abdo, "Honour Killing"; Manar Hassan, "The Politics of Honor: Patriarchy, the State and the Murder of Women in the Name of Family Honor," *Journal of Israeli History* 21, no. 1–2 (March–October, 2002): 1–37; Sharon Lang, *Sharaf Politics: Honor and Peacemaking in Israeli-Palestinian Society* (New York: Routledge, 2005); and Nadera Shalhoub-Kevorkian, "Racism, Militarisation and Policing: Police Reactions to Violence against Women in Israel," *Social Identities* 10, no. 2 (2004): 171–93. (I consider this so-called sensitivity uncharacteristic because the state usually has no problem being culturally imperialist.

This is the case, for example, in its attitude toward nomadism, which it stamped out by supposedly "modernizing" and sedentarizing Bedouins in the course of expropriating their land.)

When the state does recruit Palestinian women, it conveniently claims to do so with sensitivity to supposed Palestinian traditional (read: male dominant) cultural mores. Palestinian policewomen, for example, are often hired to intervene in family disputes and to offer a culturally sensitive alternative for battered Palestinian women and potential victims of so-called honor killings to turn to. The overall patronizing and oppressive nature of these interventions is made evident by the police force's record of dealing with Palestinian women accused of sexual transgressions who appeal to the police for help— they are regularly returned to their families, where they may face violent repercussions or even death. Abdo, "Honour Killing"; Hassan, "The Politics of Honor"; Lang, *Sharaf Politics*; and Shalhoub-Kevorkian, "Racism, Militarisation and Policing."

This gender violence in turn functions as a kind of "colonial scandal"; it is fetishized by the Israeli media and used as proof of Palestinian backwardness—justifying the supposedly liberal state's "salvation rhetoric" and control. Nicholas Dirks "The Policing of Tradition: Colonialism and Anthropology in Southern India," *Comparative Studies in Society and History*, 39, no. 1 (January 1997): 209; Lila Abu-Lughod, "Do Muslim Women Really Need Saving? Anthropological Reflections on Cultural Relativism and Its Others," *American Anthropologist* 104, no. 3 (2002): 788. Sherene Seikaly argues that it is no coincidence that Palestinian feminist work on domestic and sexual violence in particular has found such fertile ground among Israeli Jewish feminists (personal communication June 1, 2007). Recruitment to the security forces, as marginal and small a phenomenon as it is, thus shapes Palestinian masculinity and femininity and not only reacts to it.

29. According to Monterescu, the regime's policy toward Palestinian citizens "employed a combined tactic: drawing both nearer and farther away, offering citizenship while imposing martial ruling." See Monterescu, "City of 'Strangers,'" 162.

30. I borrow here from Bhabha's commentary on "mimic man." See Homi Bhabha, "Of Mimicry and Man: The Ambivalence of Colonial Discourse," *October* 28 (1984): 128.

31. Common questions researchers might raise include the following: Are assimilationists, or for that matter Palestinian soldiers, simply dupes operating under a form of false consciousness? Or is their behavior better understood as a form of resistance practiced by the weak? Or is such resistance overrated? Rather than look exclusively at the personal level at the soldiers' individual motivations, intentions, and backgrounds, I suggest an additional structural perspective. What are the motivations, intentions, and backgrounds of the state and its various organs and actors? This structural view would draw in additional questions such as, How interested is the state, in its fragmented contradictory forms, with multiple and overlapping institutions and actors, in duping

or assimilating these men, and how committed is it to this goal? Does the state see the men's behavior as a big help or as potentially subversive? Are the soldiers considered important to the state, or are they insignificant?

Chapter 9

1. Kenneth W. Grundy, *Soldiers without Politics: Blacks in the South African Armed Forces* (Berkeley: University of California Press, 1983).

2. There is no Palestinian military per se and certainly not much by way of a Palestinian state to manage it. The conflict has taken place between a state-organized, technologically advanced, well-funded military and unarmed citizens, guerilla groups, or more recently armed factions.

3. Martha Huggins, Mika Haritos-Fatouros, and Philip Zimbardo, *Violence Workers: Police Torturers and Murderers Reconstruct Brazilian Atrocities* (Berkeley: University of California Press, 2002). Huggins and her coauthors' term "violence worker" emphasizes that soldiering is a form of labor.

4. Myron Echenberg, *Colonial Conscripts: The Tirailleurs Senegalais in French West Africa, 1857–1960* (Portsmouth, NH: Heinemann, 1991), 113.

5. Mehdi Charef writes of his Harki character: "Il ne s'engagea pas contre quelqu'un, il s'engagea contre la terre: le ventre aride de sa terre" (He did not set out to fight against someone, he set out to fight against the land: the arid womb of his land). See Mehdi Charef, *Le Harki de Meriem* (Paris: Mercure de France, 1989), 74. Laura Reeck elaborates that the novel "describes the earth's barrenness, the animals' hunger, and the dried-out sources of water. . . . For [Azzedine], joining the French forces allows him to support his family. The character's joining a *harka* reflects the consequences of the colonial system on local practices: the novel evokes the 'déracinement' [uprooting] caused by the division and distribution of land among the colonials, and the subsequent end to the indigenous labor and farming that had once provided self-sufficiency. Azzedine in effect takes up arms against the dried earth or the negative consequences of the colonial system." See Laura Reeck, "Forgetting and Remembering the Harkis: Mehdi Charef's 'Le Harki de Meriem,'" *Romance Quarterly* 53, no. 1 (2006): 53.

6. Gill, "Creating Citizens," 537.

7. Keith Jeffery, "The British Army and Ireland since 1922," in *A Military History of Ireland*, eds. Thomas Bartlett and Keith Jeffery (Cambridge, UK: Cambridge University Press, 1996), 433.

8. Keith Jeffery, "The Irish Military Tradition and the British Empire," in *"An Irish Empire"? Aspects of Ireland and the British Empire*, ed. Keith Jeffery (Manchester: Manchester University Press, 1996), 97.

9. Pasha, *Colonial Political Economy*, 7.

10. Ibid.

11. Anthony Shadid, "Iraqi Security Forces Torn between Loyalties," *Washington Post*,

November 24, 2003, www.washingtonpost.com/wp-dyn/articles/A11809–2003Nov24
.html (accessed October 1, 2004).

12. Schirmer, *Guatemalan Military Project*, 58.

13. Gina Perez, "How a Scholarship Girl Becomes a Soldier: The Militarization of Latina/o Youth in Chicago Public Schools," *Identities: Global Studies in Culture and Power* 13 (2006): 54.

14. Ibid.

15. Andy Bickford notes that even the promise of 100 percent health care can serve as a powerful recruiting device. See Bickford, "Disposable," 15.

16. Andrew Gumbel, "Pentagon Targets Latinos and Mexicans to Man the Front Lines in War on Terror," *The Independent*, http://news.independent.co.uk/world/americas/story.jsp?story=441886 (accessed September 12, 2003).

17. American Broadcasting Corporation, *Nightly News*, April 5, 2003.

18. Gumbel, "Pentagon Targets Latinos."

19. Sylvia Moreno, "Injured Marines Get Wish: Citizenship," *Washington Post*, April 12, 2003, A21, A31.

20. Grundy, *Soldiers without Politics*, 29.

21. Green, "Structures of Power," 130. In the 1990s, Green witnessed the rounding up of all the young men in sight on a market day. They were then taken away on two-ton trucks with a "soldier posted in each corner of the truck with rifles pointed outward." Ibid.

22. Joe Lunn, *Memoirs of the Maelstrom: A Senegalese Oral History of the First World War* (Portsmouth, NH: Heinemann, 1999), 49. Lunn argues that "in scale the numbers of Senegalese exported overseas between 1914 and 1918 was substantially larger than the eighteenth-century trans-Atlantic slave trade had ever been during a similar period." Ibid., 5.

23. Green, "Structures of Power," 123.

24. Lunn, *Memoirs of the Maelstrom*, 41.

25. Amitav Ghosh, *The Glass Palace* (New York: Random House, 2001), 371.

26. Shira Robinson notes that dualistic models of power that are based on a "distinction between power that operates at the level of repression and power that operates at the level of persuasion (i.e. coercion versus consent)" are too simplistic. Robinson, "Occupied Citizens," 190.

A regime's symbols of domination, regardless of the degree to which subjects believe in them, can subordinate citizens by limiting their ability to "imagine alternative social, political or cultural orders" by being absorbed into a doxic, taken-for-granted realm. Ibid. See also Lori Allen, "The Polyvalent Politics of Martyr Commemorations in the Palestinian Intifada," *History and Memory* 18, no. 2 (Fall 2006): 127.

27. Grundy, *Soldiers without Politics*, 31.

28. Benedict Anderson stresses the importance of "the flow of subject populations

through the mesh of differential schools, courts, clinics, police stations and immigration offices" that the state organizes according to its imagined ethno-racial categories. This flow creates "traffic-habits," which over time give "real social life to the state's earlier fantasies." Benedict Anderson, *Imagined Communities: Reflections on the Origin and Spread of Nationalism* (New York: Verso, 1991), 169. The military, of course, is an important part of this mesh that creates "traffic habits." It involves mechanisms for the management of populations and subject-constituting disciplinary practices. Michel Foucault, *Technologies of the Self* (Amherst, MA: University of Massachusetts Press, 1988). Recruitment techniques, unit names, training, locations, tasks, composition, leadership, promotions, symbols, and benefits all produce particular myths of ethnicity and shared descent of Jew vs. Arab. Enloe, "Ethnic Soldiers."

29. Lunn, *Memoirs of the Maelstrom*, 125, 161. Similarly, black South African soldiers sent to fight in the Second World War were subject to social controls. They were not granted leave in many areas in order to minimize their contact with "the different values and lifestyles of the people in Europe and North Africa." Louis Grundlingh, "Non Europeans Should Be Kept Away from the Temptations of Towns: Controlling Black South African Soldiers during the Second World War," *International Journal of African Historical Studies* 25, no. 3 (1992): 546. South African authorities considered such contact with different social and political conditions dangerous because it might cause soldiers to reject their inferior status in South African society. Ibid., 541. Authorities also attempted to restrict the soldiers' access to other armies and communities by censuring the publications they had access to. Certain newspapers—such as the *London Picture Post*, which showed pictures of black American soldiers enjoying the hospitality of the British people—were banned. Ibid., 551.

30. Echenberg, *Colonial Conscripts*, 110.

31. Gill, "Creating Citizens," 534.

32. Jeffery, "British Army," 447.

33. Schirmer, *Guatemalan Military Project*, 114.

34. Grundy, *Soldiers without Politics*, 110.

35. Ghosh, *The Glass Palace*, 247.

36. Grundy, *Soldiers without Politics*, 110.

37. Echenberg, *Colonial Conscripts*, 84.

38. Ibid., 80; Lunn, *Memoirs of the Maelstrom*, 6.

39. Buffalo Soldiers Greater Atlanta Chapter, "History," www.buffalosoldiersatlanta.com/html/History/html (accessed June 6, 2007).

40. Pasha, *Colonial Political Economy*, 246.

41. Margot Canaday, "U.S. Military Integration of Religious Ethics, and Racial Minorities in the Twentieth Century," www.gaymilitary.ucsb.edu/Publications/canaday.htm (accessed February 9, 2005). There was apparently less racism in the South African military than in most other South African institutions. Grundy, *Soldiers without Politics*, 111.

42. Jeanette Steele, "Up in Arms against Bigotry: Arab-American Marine Forms Group to Send Patriotic Message," from *San Diego Tribune*, www.aaiusa.org/pressroom/1849/mustread07042002 (accessed June 7, 2007).

43. Echenberg, *Colonial Conscripts*, 64.

44. Lunn, *Memoirs of the Maelstrom*, 45.

45. Enloe, "Ethnic Soldiers."

46. Schirmer, *Guatemalan Military Project*, 72–73.

47. Ibid., 115–16.

48. Green, "Structures of Power," 130.

49. Gill, "Creating Citizens," 537.

50. Nadire Mater, "Mehmed's Book. Extracts Translated by Ertugrul Kürkçü," www.rsf.org/rsf/uk/html/mo/rapport/nadire.html (accessed April 28, 2004): 6. In Nazi Germany, racial status and the promise of literally being confirmed "of German blood" was used to manage part-Jewish *Mischlinge* in the military. Hitler signed exemption documents allowing some *Mischlinge* to serve: "After the war, I will decide whether to declare Whilhelm von Gwinner of German blood according to his performance as a soldier." Brian Mark Rigg, *Hitler's Jewish Soldiers: The Untold Story of Nazi Racial Laws and Men of Jewish Descent in the German Military* (Lawrence: University Press of Kansas, 2002), 18.

51. Jansson, "Bedouin Soldiers," 45. The ways militaries are able to radically reshape identities is dramatically illustrated in cases where former enemies of the state are rehabilitated into its most brutal soldiers. The apartheid-era South African police trained former members of the anti-apartheid ANC, placing them in a covert counter insurgency unit. Eugene DeKock, *A Long Night's Damage: Working for the Apartheid State as Told to Jeremy Gordin* (Saxonwold, South Africa: Contra Press, 1998), 18. Schirmer reports that former guerillas in Guatemala were tortured, interrogated for long periods, then amnestied on condition that they join the army, and were eventually selected as *jefes* of Civil Patrols to provide invaluable information to military units. Schirmer, *Guatemalan Military Project*, 82, 85. Military interventions in ethnicity and identity are, of course, not overdetermining. Some transformations in the opposite direction occur as well. Potlako Leballo, a former soldier in the South African military, received his "political baptism participating in a mutiny against the army's color bar regulations," and went on to become a leader in the Pan-Africanist Congress. Similarly, Herman Toivo Ja Toivo went from being a member of the Union's Native Military Corps to become a founder of the revolutionary SWAPO. Ibid. During World War II, Eric Dorman-Smith was a brilliant "Catholic Irish general" in the British army. After the war he changed his name to O'Dorman Gowan, returned to his family home in County Monaghan, and became an active supporter of the IRA, even offering his estate for training purposes. Jeffery, "British Army," 444; Jeffery, "Irish Military Tradition," 108. Soldiers in the British Indian Army later became leaders in the Indian Independence movement. Ghosh,

The Glass Palace. The examples of the former soldier in the Arab Liberation Army (ALA) who struck a bargain to serve in the Israeli Border Guard in exchange for citizenship in Israel, or the 500 Druze who deserted the ALA and joined the Jewish forces in the 1948 war, or the Bedouin soldier who is an activist on behalf of unrecognized villages, all demonstrate how military service can take on a life of its own, beyond the control of military planners. Pappe, *Ethnic Cleansing*, 114.

52. An incredibly similar scene is repeated in Rachid Bouchareb's 2005 film *Days of Glory*. North African soldiers in the French military are in a food line and are denied tomatoes, which are reserved for whites only. The soldiers dump the tomatoes and smash them saying "German bullets don't choose."

53. Echenberg, *Colonial Conscripts*, 102–3.

54. Ibid., 133.

55. Ibid., 128.

56. Ibid., 104; Lunn, *Memoirs of the Maelstrom*, 78.

57. Gerald Hynes, "A Biographical Sketch of W.E.B. DuBois," www.duboislc.org/man.html (accessed December 1, 2005).

58. Association of Patriotic Arab Americans in Military, "Arab American Generation-X Signing up to Serve America," www.apaam.com/aiman.htm (accessed February 14, 2008).

59. Arab American Institute, "Famous Arab Americans," www.aaiusa.org/arab-americans/23/famous-arab-americans (accessed February 14, 2008).

60. National Museum of American Jewish Military History, "Liberating the Concentration Camps: GIs Remember" (Washington, D.C., 1994), 4.

61. This link is so salient in certain contexts that the subjugated demand the right to join militaries, in the hope that this will lead to improvement in their status. Many African Americans demanded the right to fight, and specifically to engage in combat, in the American Civil War. As Frederick Douglass's widely used quote argues: "Once let a black man get upon his person the brass letters 'US,' let him get an eagle on his button and a musket on his shoulder and bullets in his pockets and there is no power on earth which can deny that he had earned the right to citizenship in the United States." However, these military aspirations were turned on their head at other times: if in one era black Americans were used as underpaid labor and were excluded from combat, in other eras, such as during the Vietnam War, they were overrepresented in the military and some would argue, served as cannon fodder. Irene Shigaki, "The Internment of Japanese Americans: A Multicultural Perspective," unpublished manuscript (nd), part 4, p. 13. Palestinians in Israel have never demanded as a community the right to military service, even though such words were put in the mouth of some Druze leaders. Hajjar, "Speaking the Conflict," 323. Yet some soldiers have at points pushed for the right to be involved in combat, and at others, questioned the dangerous posts they are assigned to.

62. Arlington Cemetery, "Felix Z. Longoria," www.arlingtoncemetery.net/longoria.htm (accessed February 14, 2008).

63. Ibid.

64. Patrick Carroll, *Felix Longoria's Wake: Bereavement, Racism, and the Rise of Mexican American Activism* (Austin: University of Texas Press, 2003). Kasuo Masuda, a Japanese American killed in action in Italy, was refused burial in the local cemetery in Santa Ana, California, in 1945. Outraged Japanese Americans brought it to the attention of General Stillwell, who "flew to California and personally presented the Masuda family with the soldier's posthumous Distinguished Service Cross." Shigaki, "Internment," part 3, p. 26. Part of a project to research and recognize black contributions to the Civil War actually involves marking formerly unmarked graves of the dead.

65. Begoña Aretxaga, "Maddening States," *Annual Review of Anthropology* 32 (2003): 403.

66. Szymczyk, *Ahlam Shibli Trackers*, 99.

67. Amos Harel, Nir Hasson, and Jack Khoury, "Five Soldiers Buried, Only One in Military Funeral," *Haaretz*, December 14, 2004, 1.

68. Gideon Alon, "Lawmaker Wants IDF to Recruit Non-Jewish Chaplains," *Haaretz*, www.haaretz.com/hasen/objects/pages/PrintArticleEn.jhtml?itemNo=434188 (accessed June 7, 2007). For more on Ministry of Religion posts, see Louer, *To Be an Arab.*

69. Hugh Schofield, "France's 'Harkis' File Suit for Crimes against Humanity," *Middle East Times*, www.metimes.com/2K1/issue2001–35/reg/frances_harkis_file.htm.

70. "Letter of the FLN to the Harkis," Marxist.org, www.marxists.org/history/algeria/1960/harkis.htm (accessed June 6, 2007).

71. Reeck, "Forgetting and Remembering," 51.

72. Schofield, "France's 'Harkis.'"

73. Echenberg, *Colonial Conscripts*, 97.

74. Ibid., 98–99.

75. Ibid., 104.

76. A. O. Scott, "Yes, Soldiers of France, in All But Name," *New York Times*, December 6, 2006.

77. Grundy, *Soldiers without Politics*, 45.

78. Adam Hochschild, *King Leopold's Ghost: A Story of Greed, Terror and Heroism in Colonial Africa* (New York: Houghton Mifflin, 1998), 123.

79. Frank J. Gaffney, Jr., "The 'Fifth Column' Syndrome," *Washington Times*, March 25, 2003.

80. Shigaki, "Internment," part 3, p. 10.

81. Daniel Pipes, "Murder in the 101st Airborne," published in the *New York Post*, www.danielpipes.org/article/1042 (accessed June 7, 2007).

82. Moustafa Bayoumi, "How Does It Feel to Be a Problem?" in *Asian Americans*

on War and Peace, eds. Russell C. Leong and Don T. Nakanishi (Los Angeles: UCLA Asian American Studies Center Press, 2002).

83. Echenberg, *Colonial Conscripts*, 35.

84. Ibid.

85. Lunn, *Memoirs of the Maelstrom*, 163

86. Chad Williams, "African-American Soldiers and the Constructions of Black Masculinity during WWI," paper presented at the Conference on Black Masculinities, CUNY Graduate Center, New York (February 4, 2005).

87. Julie Otsuka, *When the Emperor Was Divine* (New York: Alfred Knopf, 2002), 141.

88. See, for example, Ada Ushpiz, "Just Keep Them away from Our Daughters!" *Haaretz*, July 9, 2004, B4; Yuval Azoulay, "Lod Vice Mayor Calls for Transfer of Jews from Arab Neighborhood," *Haaretz*, www.haaretz.com/hasen/objects/pages/Print ArticleEn.jhtml?itemNo=508178 (accessed February 14, 2008).

89. Zvi Harel and Yuval Yoaz, "Colonel on Trial for Raping Soldier Says She Initiated Intimate Contact," *Haaretz*, June 16, 2005, www.haaretzdaily.com/hasen/pages/ShArt.jhtml?itemNo=588208 (accessed June 16, 2005).

90. William Wilson, "World War II: Navajo Code Talkers," *American History Magazine*, www.historynet.com/magazines/american_history/3038096.html?page=2&c=y (accessed February 14, 2008).

91. Katy Van Every, "Navajo Code Talkers: Life During and After World War Two," paper for graduate seminar on Minorities in the Military, American University, Washington, D.C. (2003), 14, 16.

92. Shigaki, "Internment," part 4, p. 9; Williams, "African-American Soldiers."

93. The soldier used the term *khawājāt*, referring to Jewish Israelis as foreigners.

94. At the same time that uniforms effectively fail to blur the boundaries between "wrong siders" with their militaries, the actions they are assigned make uniforms problematic symbols. A *New York Times* account of black soldiers in the South African military notes that a loyal and obedient black sergeant took off his uniform before setting off for his home on leave, explaining that "my friends don't like it." Grundy, *Soldiers without Politics*, 114. Bedouins in Israel who served under the education track are rewarded for wearing military uniforms while teaching in their village schools, but often feel pressure not to do so: "I only wear it when I know an official is coming to visit. I don't want to have problems with the parents," Samir told me. The actions of the state imbue the uniforms with negative meaning.

95. Peter Lennon, "Secret Army," *The Guardian*, August 23, 2002, http://arts.guardian .co.uk/fridayreview/story/0,,778833,00.html#article_continue (accessed February 14, 2008). One of these code talkers, Nez, ponders the irony: "Back in the 20s and 30s, we were told, 'Don't speak Navajo.' They washed our mouths out with [government-issue] soap. . . . Then Uncle Sam came along and told us to use our language in World War II."

Tom Gorman, "Navajos Honored for War of Words," *Los Angeles Times*, July 26, 2001. A commemorative website notes that at a time "when Navajos were not citizens of the United States and not allowed to vote, military recruiters were going throughout the federal board schools, recruiting young Navajos and [other] Native Americans to fight in a war that was foreign to them." Harrison Lapahie, Jr., "Harry Benally," www.lapahie .com/Harry_Benally.cfm (accessed February 14, 2008).

96. Gregory Mann, "Locating Colonial Histories: Between France and West Africa," *American Historical Review* 110, no. 2 (2005), www.historycooperative.org/journals/ ahr/110.2/mann.html (accessed October 10, 2007), par. 32.

97. Grundy, *Soldiers without Politics*, 102. In some cases, like that of noncitizens serving in the U.S. military or U.S. recruitment efforts in Mexico, the opening of the ranks to these groups is driven by military manpower considerations, that is, the need for more recruits. It is not part of a policy to encourage immigration, but an attempt to reach military staffing goals. The same can be said for the recruitment of blacks to the South African forces in the early 1970s. This recruitment was directly incompatible with the apartheid homeland scheme and merely signaled that "the time had arrived to defend the regime by any and all means." See ibid., 101. With the French African Conscription Laws of 1912 and 1919 "no egalitarianism was ever intended or extended. . . . The purpose of the entire military exercise was simple: to obtain more soldiers." See Echenberg, *Colonial Conscripts*, 84. According to Rhonda Evans, rates of discharge of homosexual service members in the U.S. military "have fluctuated relative to the manpower needs of the service. During periods of sustained conflict, when the need for good unit function and operational effectiveness [that the military argues homosexuality undermines] is at its zenith, the numbers of discharges for homosexuality decrease." See Rhonda Evans, "U.S. Military Policies Concerning Homosexuals: Development, Implementation and Outcomes," www.gaymilitary.ucsb .edu/Publications/evans1.htm (accessed January 12, 2003).

98. Grundy, *Soldiers without Politics*, 105.

99. Grundlingh, "Non Europeans," 553.

100. Deanne Stillman, "Uncle Sam's Jihadists: What's the U.S. Military Doing about Radical Muslim Soldiers? Not Enough," *Slate*, March 27, 2003, www.slate.com/ id/2080770/ (accessed February 14, 2008).

101. Earl Ofari Hutchinson, "Echoes of 'Fragging,'" *San Francisco Chronicle*, March 27, 2003, A19, www.sfgate.com/cgi-bin/article.cgi?f=/c/a/2003/03/27/ED279159.DTL& hw=vietnam+war&sn=714&sc=261 (accessed February 14, 2008). Often soldier resistance is viewed by militaries as an aberration, rather than "an expression of any deeper contradictions in the colonial project." See Pasha, *Colonial Political Economy*, 11. Their behavior is more likely labeled as mutiny rather than revolt. More minor rebellions against military discipline—often unjust—merely result in the labeling of soldiers as undisciplined, unruly, or "bad soldiers." See Grundy, *Soldiers without Politics*, 555.

102. Echenberg, *Colonial Conscripts*, 101.

103. Ibid., 100. The spark for the Great Revolt in the British Indian Army was the introduction of a new rifle, with cartridges that had to be bitten open, allegedly greased with the tallow of pigs and cattle, offensive to both Muslims and Hindus. At this particular moment, the balance of forces that kept Indians in the British Indian Army tipped so that soldiers believed that "the Christian colonizers had been deliberately planning to destroy the sepoys' religion and caste." To prevent this, the soldiers were willing to kill and die. Pasha, *Colonial Political Economy*, 139.

104. In 1945, 162 black Tuskegee airmen demanded lawful entry into the white officers club, were arrested and set to be court martialed. These events were subsequently linked to the initiation of the civil rights movement. "Who Were the Tuskegee Airmen?" Tuskegee Airmen, Inc., www.tuskegeeairmen.org/Tuskegee_Airmen_History .html (accessed June 6, 2007). Such acts of resistance can be celebrated retrospectively, sometimes in more coherent and nationalistic frameworks than initially seen by soldiers. In 1920, three hundred or so men in the Connaught Rangers mutinied in the Punjab "'in sympathy with their country' and . . . 'would do no more work until the British troops had been removed from Ireland.'" Jeffery, "Irish Military Tradition," 116. As Jeffery explains, in the years that followed, the mutineers were celebrated as Irish patriots and popular ballads were written about the mutiny. Ibid., 117.

105. Lunn, *Memoirs of the Maelstrom*, 76.

106. Ibid., 65–66.

107. Ibid., 84. Robinson notes that "European discourses of citizenship and political rights"—predicated as they were on racial exclusions institutionalized in the colonies— were "subject to reformulation by colonized peoples who demanded that their rulers make good on their liberal claims." Robinson, "Occupied Citizens," 26.

108. Lomsky-Feder and Ben-Ari, "People in Uniform," 166.

109. Cook, *Blood and Religion*, 4.

110. Tobias Kelly warns of the "danger of reifying categories of national difference as explanations for violence. . . . Studies have worked with the categories produced by the conflict rather than critically interrogated them. This has in part at least meant a reification of categories of difference, rather than an examination of how differences are produced, reproduced and take on meaning in processes of state formation, borders and the associated violence." Tobias Kelly, "Violent States: Work, Borders and Citizenship during the Palestinian Intifada," unpublished paper (nd).

111. Aretxaga, "Maddening States," 400

112. Dan Rabinowitz, "Eastern Nostalgia: How the Palestinians Became 'Israel's Arabs,'" *Theory and Criticism* 4 (Fall 1993): 144.

113. Lomsky-Feder and Ben-Ari, "People in Uniform," 162.

114. Jeff Halper quoted in Slyomovics, "Rape of Qula," 46.

115. *Istiqlal*, dir. Nizar Hassan (1994).

116. Abu-Lughod and Sa'di, "Claims of Memory," 11.

117. Sherene Seikaly, "From Haifa to Beirut," unpublished paper (nd).

Afterword

1. While non-Druze Palestinian service in the Israeli military is formally considered voluntary, the degree of choice involved is shaped by the combined pressures of, for example, discrimination against those who do not serve in the military, the dearth of other employment opportunities, the confiscation of land, and the promise of leasing land as a reward for service.

2. The Communist Party has been one of the major political parties representing Arab voters in the Israeli parliament. The Association of Forty is an NGO committed to gaining recognition for the unrecognized Arab villages (www.assoc40.org).

3. Ebtisam Mara'ana's 2003 documentary film *Paradise Lost* provides an excellent meditation on this fear and silencing. The shadow of the state, especially its secret service, looms over the village in the film, muting and contorting the public discourse of villagers on history and identity. See Rhoda Kanaaneh, "Review of *Paradise Lost*," *Journal of Middle East Women's Studies* 1, no. 2 (2005): 163–64.

4. Areen Hawari writes that one of the men she interviewed about the Military Administration period asked not to be recorded because "the texts you write, I can always deny but how can I deny my own voice." Hawari, "Men under the Military Regime." This too points to the fear of the surveilling authorities.

5. See Anton Shammas, "Mixed as in Pidgin: The Vanishing Arabic of a 'Bilingual' City," in *Mixed Towns, Trapped Communities: Historical Narratives, Spatial Dynamics, Gender Relations and Cultural Encounters in Palestinian-Israeli Towns*, eds. Daniel Monterescu and Dan Rabinowitz (Hampshire, England: Ashgate, 2007), 305.

6. Shammas, "Mixed as in Pidgin," 305–6.

7. Ibid., 308.

8. James C. Scott, *Weapons of the Weak: Everyday Forms of Peasant Resistance* (New Haven, CT: Yale University Press, 1985).

9. Pamela Ballinger, *History in Exile: Memory and Identity at the Borders of the Balkans* (Princeton, NJ: Princeton University Press, 2002), 10.

10. Stephen Schensul, Jean Schensul, and Margaret LeCompte, *Essential Ethnographic Methods: Observations Interviews and Questionnaires* (Walnut Creek, CA: AltaMira, 1999), 143.

11. As Blee describes in her interviews with white supremacists, the question of the researcher's position on the research subject tends to hang over the interview. See Kathleen Blee, "White on White: Interviewing Women in U.S. White Supremacist Groups," in *Racing Research, Researching Race: Methodological Dilemmas in Critical Race Studies*, eds. France Winddance Twine and Jonathan Warren (New York: New York University Press, 2000), 104.

12. See Seteney Shami, "Studying Your Own: The Complexities of a Shared Culture," in *Arab Women in the Field: Studying Your Own Society*, eds. Soraya Altorki and Cimillia Fawzi El-Solh (Syracuse, NY: Syracuse University Press, 1988), 124.

13. France Winddance Twine, "Racial Ideologies and Racial Methodologies," in *Racing Research, Researching Race: Methodological Dilemmas in Critical Race Studies*, eds. France Winddance Twine and Jonathan Warren (New York: New York University Press, 2000).

14. Laud Humphreys, *Tearoom Trade: Impersonal Sex in Public Places* (New York: Aldine de Gruyter, 1975), 202.

15. Huggins, Haritos-Fatouros, and Zimbardo, *Violence Workers*, 46; Antonius C. G. M. Robben, "The Politics of Truth and Emotion among Victims and Perpetrators of Violence," in *Fieldwork Under Fire: Contemporary Studies of Violence and Survival*, eds. Carolyn Nordstrom and Antonius C. G. M. Robben (Berkeley: University of California Press, 1995), 96.

16. Moslih Kanaaneh, "The 'Anthropologicality' of Indigenous Anthropology," *Dialectical Anthropology* 22 (1997): 5.

17. In contrast, many anthropologists of the Israeli military routinely provide the brigades and units of interviewees. See, for example, Lomsky-Feder and Ben-Ari, "People in Uniform"; and Helman, "Construction of Community."

18. Tamara Neuman, "Reinstating the Religious Nation: A Study of National Religious Persuasion, Settlement, and Violence in Hebron," Ph.D. diss. (University of Chicago, 2000), 237.

19. Avram Bornstein, "Ethnography and the Politics of Prisoners in Palestine-Israel," *Journal of Contemporary Ethnography* 30, no. 5 (2001): 550.

20. Neuman, "Reinstating the Religious Nation," 243.

21. "AAA Statements on Ethics—Principles of Professional Responsibility," American Anthropological Association, www.aaanet.org/stmts/ethstmnt.htm (accessed February 14, 2008), 2.

22. "Commission to Review the AAA Statements on Ethics—Final Report," American Anthropological Association, www.aaanet.org/committees/ethics/ethrpt.htm (accessed February 14, 2008), 10.

23. Neuman, "Reinstating the Religious Nation," 243.

24. Ibid., 245.

25. Schensul, Schensul, and LeCompte, *Essential Ethnographic Methods*, 77.

26. Blee, "White on White," 104.

27. Howard Becker, "Racism and the Research Process," in *Racing Research, Researching Race: Methodological Dilemmas in Critical Race Studies*, eds. France Winddance Twine and Jonathan Warren (New York: New York University Press, 2000), 253.

28. On a Google newsgroup (talk.politics.mideast) a reader uses the first paragraph of my 2002 book on reproductive politics to dismiss Palestinians as heartless fanatics:

"of course, how they're actually gonna CARE for these kids . . educate them . . . keep them in good health . . . is left unsaid. Typical fanatic. Uses other human beings . . . in this case babies . . . to achieve a political end. if they cared for freedom they'd educate the kids they got now." See Google Groups, "Newsgroups: Subject: Birthing the Nation," talk.politics.mideast, July 10, 2002.

Bibliography

500 Dunam on the Moon: The Story of Three Villages in One, Ain Hawd, Ein Hod and Ain Hawd al-Jadida. Dir. Rachel Leah Jones. Co-produced by RLJ Publications (New York), and Momento! (Paris), 2002.

"AAA Statements on Ethics—Principles of Professional Responsibility." American Anthropological Association. www.aaanet.org/stmts/ethstmnt.htm (accessed February 14, 2008). Adopted by the Council of the AAA in 1971.

Abdo, Nahla. "Honour Killing, Patriarchy, and the State: Women in Israel." In Shahrzad Mojab and Nahla Abdo, eds., *Violence in the Name of Honour: Theoretical and Political Challenges*, 57–90. Istanbul: Istanbul Bilgi University Press, 2004.

Abufarha, Nasser. "The Making of a Human Bomb: State Expansion and Modes of Resistance in Palestine." Ph.D. diss., University of Wisconsin, Madison, 2006.

Abu-Lughod, Lila. "Do Muslim Women Really Need Saving? Anthropological Reflections on Cultural Relativism and Its Others." *American Anthropologist* 104, no. 3 (2002): 783–90.

———, ed. *Remaking Women: Feminism and Modernity in the Middle East*. Princeton, NJ: Princeton University Press, 1998.

Abu-Lughod, Lila, and Ahmad Sa'di. "Introduction: The Claims of Memory." In Ahmad Sa'di and Lila Abu Lughod, eds., *Nakba: Palestine, 1948, and the Claims of Memory*, 1–24. New York: Columbia University Press, 2007.

Abu-Ras, Amneh. "The Number of Those Who Serve in the Military from Ein Mahel Has Increased." *Al-Sinnara*, February 18, 2005. (Arabic)

Ahmed, Leila. *Women and Gender in Islam: Historical Roots of a Modern Debate*. New Haven, CT: Yale University Press, 1992.

Algazy, Joseph. "In Israel Too." *Le Monde Diplomatique*. http://mondediplo.com/1997/09/israel (accessed December 16, 2004).

Allen, Lori. "The Polyvalent Politics of Martyr Commemorations in the Palestinian Intifada." *History and Memory* 18 (2006): 107–39.

Alon, Gideon. "Lawmaker Wants IDF to Recruit Non-Jewish Chaplains." *Haaretz*, June 2, 2004. www.haaretz.com/hasen/objects/pages/PrintArticleEn.jhtml?itemNo=434188 (accessed June 7, 2007).

"Amazon.com: Birthing the Nation: Strategies of Palestinian Women in Israel (California Series in Public Anthropology, 2): Books: Rhoda Ann Kanaaneh." www .amazon.com/birthing-nation-strategies-palestinian-anthropology/dp/0520229444/ ref=pd_bbs_sr_1/002-3310311-4626435?ie=UTF8&s=books&qid=1179874930&s r=8-1 (accessed May 11, 2007).

Anderson, Benedict. *Imagined Communities: Reflections on the Origin and Spread of Nationalism.* New York: Verso, 1991.

Another Road Home. Dir. Danae Elon. Qi films. 77 mins. 2005.

Arab American Institute. "Famous Arab Americans." www.aaiusa.org/arab-americans/ 23/famous-arab-americans (accessed September 22, 2004).

Arab Center for Alternative Planning. www.ac-ap.org/?lang=3 (accessed October 12, 2007).

Arbeli, Aliza. "Bedouin Soldiers Hold Protest against Home-Razing Orders." *Haaretz,* January 18, 2002, 3.

Arens, Moshe. "Criminal Negligence." *Haaretz,* January 15, 2002, 5.

———. "Our Brothers, the Bedouin." *Haaretz,* October 29, 2002, 5.

———. "The Wages of a Non-Policy." *Jerusalem Post,* April 10, 1998.

Aretxaga, Begoña. "Maddening States." *Annual Review of Anthropology* 32 (2003): 393–410.

———. *Shattering Silence: Women, Nationalism, and Political Subjectivity in Northern Ireland.* Princeton, NJ: Princeton University Press, 1997.

Arlington Cemetery. "Felix Z. Longoria." www.arlingtoncemetery.net/longoria.htm (accessed February 14, 2008).

Aronoff, Myron. *Israeli Visions and Divisions: Cultural Change and Political Conflict.* New Brunswick, NJ: Transaction, 1989.

Asad, Talal. "Anthropological Texts and Ideological Problems: An Analysis of Cohen on Arab Villages in Israel." *Economy and Society* 4, no. 3 (1975). 247–382.

Ashqar, Ahmad. *Self Destruction, the Nazareth Example: Conflict in Shhab EdDin Theater.* Ramallah: Al Mashriq, 2000. (Arabic)

Association for Civil Rights in Israel. "Katzir Case." www.acri.org.il/english-acri/engine /story.asp?id=177 (accessed May 7, 2005).

Association of Patriotic Arab Americans in Military. "Arab American Generation-X Signing up to Serve America." www.apaam.com/aiman.htm (accessed February 14, 2008).

"Attorney Rabi' Jahshan Prepares to Submit a Suit to Compensate the Residents of Maghar for the Damage to Their Property." *Kul al-'Arab,* February 25, 2005. (Arabic)

Azoulay, Yuval. "Lod Vice Mayor Calls for Transfer of Jews from Arab Neighborhood." *Haaretz,* December 1, 2004. www.haaretz.com/hasen/objects/pages/PrintArticleEn .jhtml?itemNo=508178 (accessed February 14, 2008).

Bailey, Clinton. "Lieberman and the Bedouin." *Haaretz,* February 24, 2002, 5.

Ballinger, Pamela. *History in Exile: Memory and Identity at the Borders of the Balkans.* Princeton, NJ: Princeton University Press, 2002.

Bardenstein, Carol. "Cross/Cast: Passing in Israeli and Palestinian Cinema." In Rebecca Stein and Ted Swedenburg, eds., *Palestine, Israel, and the Politics of Popular Culture*, 99–125. Durham, NC: Duke University Press, 2005.

Bar-Natan, Yaacov. "Arabs in the IDF: Is Conscription of Christians and Moslems to the Israeli Army a Realistic Proposition?" *Spectrum: Israel Labour Movement Monthly* 6, no. 1 (1988).

Bayoumi, Moustafa. "How Does It Feel to be a Problem?" In Russell C. Leong and Don T. Nakanishi, eds., *Asian Americans on War and Peace*. Los Angeles: UCLA Asian American Studies Center Press, 2002.

Becker, Avihai. "Unsweet Revenge." *Haaretz*, January 19, 2002, magazine section.

Becker, Howard. "Racism and the Research Process." In Twine and Warren, eds., *Racing Research, Racing Race*, 247–54.

Ben-Ari, Eyal, with Galeet Dardashti. "Tests of Soldierhood, Trials of Manhood: Military Service and Male Ideals in Israel." In Daniel Maman, Eyal Ben-Ari, and Zeev Rosenhek, eds., *Military, State, and Society in Israel: Theoretical and Comparative Perspectives*, 239–67. New Brunswick, NJ: Transaction, 2001.

Ben Simon, Daniel. "A Community on Trial." *Haaretz*, May 5, 2006. www.haaretz.com /hasen/objects/pages/PrintArticleEn.jhtml?itemNo=712637 (accessed May 8, 2006).

Bernstein, Deborah. "Prostitution in Mandate Palestine: An Arab-Jewish-British Meeting Ground." Paper presented at the annual meeting of the Middle East Studies Association, San Francisco, November 17–20, 2001.

Bhabha, Homi. "Of Mimicry and Man: The Ambivalence of Colonial Discourse." *October* 28 (1984): 125–33.

Bickford, Andy. "Disposable, Deployable, Forgettable: Race, Class and Health in the US Military." Paper presented at the American University Department of Anthropology, Washington, D.C., January 6, 2004.

Bishara, Amahl. "Examining Sentiments about the Claims to Jerusalem and Its Houses." *Social Text* 75, no. 21 (2003): 141–62.

Blee, Kathleen. "White on White: Interviewing Women in U.S. White Supremacist Groups." In Twine and Warren, eds., *Racing Research, Researching Race*, 93–110.

Bornstein, Avram. "Ethnography and the Politics of Prisoners in Palestine-Israel." *Journal of Contemporary Ethnography* 30, no. 5 (2001): 546–74.

B'Tselem. *Collaborators in the Occupied Territories: Human Rights Abuses and Violations.* Jerusalem: B'Tselem, 1994.

Buffalo Soldiers Greater Atlanta Area Chapter. "History." www.buffalosoldiers.com/ html/History.html (accessed June 6, 2007).

Caglar, Ayse. "Outline of a Transregional and Transdisciplinary Research Agenda Centered on Turkey." Unpublished paper, Free University of Berlin, May 2001.

Canaday, Margot. "U.S. Military Integration of Religious Ethics, and Racial Minorities in the Twentieth Century." 2001. www.gaymilitary.ucsb.edu/Publications/canaday .htm (accessed February 9, 2005).

Carroll, Patrick. *Felix Longoria's Wake: Bereavement, Racism, and the Rise of Mexican American Activism.* Austin: University of Texas Press, 2003.

Cassell, Joan, and Sue-Ellen Jacobs, eds. *Handbook on Ethical Issues in Anthropology: A Special Publication of the American Anthropological Association* no. 23. June 1998. www.aaanet.org/committees/ethics/toc.htm (accessed February 14, 2008).

Charef, Mehdi. *Le Harki de Meriem.* Paris: Mercure de France, 1989.

Chatterjee, Partha. *The Nation and Its Fragments: Colonial and Postcolonial Histories.* Princeton, NJ: Princeton University Press, 1993.

Cohen, Hillel. *Good Arabs: The Israeli Security Services and the Israeli Arabs.* Jerusalem: Ivrit Hebrew Publishing House, 2006. (Hebrew)

"Commission to Review the AAA Statements on Ethics—Final Report." American Anthropological Association, September 16, 1995. www.aaanet.org/committees/ethics/ethrpt.htm (accessed February 14, 2008).

Cook, Jonathan. *Blood and Religion: The Unmasking of the Jewish and Democratic State.* Ann Arbor, MI: Pluto, 2006.

———. "Divide and Destroy." *Al Ahram Weekly* issue 645 (July 3–9, 2003). http://jkcook.net/Articles1/0022.htm (accessed October 5, 2007).

———. "The Holy War Israel Wants." *The Electronic Intifada*, July 11, 2003. www.jkcook.net/Articles1/0023.htm (accessed October 5, 2007).

Dahamsheh, Yazid. "Organizations and Institutions of Encouraging 'National Service' Pierces Arab Towns." *Hadith al-Nas*, October 22, 2004. (Arabic)

Dallasheh, Leena. "The Bedouins in the Naqab: The Citizens Israel Would Rather Forget?" Unpublished paper written for New York University course on the Anthropology of Citizenship and Displacement, New York, December 25, 2006.

D'Amico, Francine. "Citizen-Soldier? Class, Race, Gender, Sexuality and the US Military." In Susie Jacobs, Ruth Jacobson, and Jennifer Marchbank, eds., *States of Conflict: Gender, Violence, and Resistance*, 105–22. London: Zed Books, 2000.

Davis, Rochelle. "The Attar of History: Palestinian Narratives of Life before 1948." Ph.D. diss., University of Michigan, 2002.

———. "Mapping the Past, Re-creating the Homeland: Memories of Village Places in Pre-1948 Palestine." In Ahmad Sa'di and Lila Abu Lughod, eds., *Nakba: Palestine, 1948, and the Claims of Memory*, 53–76. New York: Columbia University Press, 2007.

Dayan, Aryeh. "Who Put Taysir el-Heyb in Charge?" *Haaretz*, August 29, 2005. www.haaretz.com/hasen/objects/pages/PrintArticleEn.jhtml?itemNo=618220 (accessed September 5, 2005).

"Decline in the Percentage of Arab Bedouin Recruitment in the Military by 20% from Last Year." Arabs48. www.arabs48.com/display.x?cid=19%sid=57&id=44330 (accessed April 10, 2007).

DeGrazia, Victoria. *How Fascism Ruled Women: Italy, 1922–1945.* Berkeley: University of California Press, 1992.

DeKock, Eugene. *A Long Night's Damage: Working for the Apartheid State as Told to Jeremy Gordin.* Saxonwold, South Africa: Contra Press, 1998.

Dirks, Nicholas. "The Policing of Tradition: Colonialism and Anthropology in Southern India." *Comparative Studies in Society and History*, 39, no. 1 (January 1997): 182–212.

"Discrimination in Life and Death." Editorial in *Haaretz*, December 15, 2004.

Dominguez, Virginia. *People as Subject, People as Object: Selfhood and Peoplehood in Contemporary Israel*. Madison: University of Wisconsin Press, 1989.

Doumani, Beshara. *Rediscovering Palestine: Merchants and Peasants in Jabal Nablus, 1700–1900*. Berkeley: University of California Press, 1995.

Echenberg, Myron. *Colonial Conscripts: The Tirailleurs Senegalais in French West Africa, 1857–1960*. Portsmouth, NH: Heinemann, 1991.

Elbedour, Salman. "Who Are the Bedouins of the Negev? Are They Israelis or Palestinians or Both? Ethnicity and Ethnic Identity among Bedouin-Arab Adolescents in Israel." Unpublished paper, Howard University.

El-Okbi, Nuri. *Waiting for Justice: The Story of the Elokbi Tribe in Israel*. NP, 2004. (Arabic and English)

Enloe, Cynthia. *Does Khaki Become You? The Militarization of Women's Lives*. San Francisco: Harper Collins, 1988.

———. *Ethnic Soldiers: State Security in Divided Societies*. Athens: University of George Press, 1980.

Eqeiq, Amal. "Louder Than the Blue I.D.: Palestinian Hip-Hop in Israel." Paper presented at the Middle East Studies Association Conference, Boston, November 2006.

Erdreich, Lauren. "Marriage Talk: Palestinian Women, Intimacy, and the Liberal Nation-State." *Ethnography* 7, no. 4 (2006): 493–523.

Esmair, Samera. "Memories of Conquest: Witnessing Death in Tantura." In Ahmad Sa'di and Lila Abu Lughod, eds., *Nakba: Palestine, 1948, and the Claims of Memory*, 229–50. New York: Columbia University Press, 2007.

Evans, Rhonda. "U.S. Military Policies Concerning Homosexuals: Development, Implementation and Outcomes." www.gaymilitary.ucsb.edu/Publications/evans1 .htm (accessed January 12, 2003).

"Extension of Arrest of Lieutenant Colonel 'Omar al-Hayb Accused of Spying for 'Hizbollah." Al-'*Ittihad*, December 25, 2002, 4. (Arabic)

Eyal, Gil. "The Discursive Origins of Israeli Separatism: The Case of the Arab Village." *Theory and Society* 25 (1996): 389–429.

Falah, Ghazi. "How Israel Controls the Bedouin in Israel." *Journal of Palestine Studies*. Special Issue: The Palestinians in Israel and the Occupied Territories. 14, no. 2 (1985): 32–51.

———. "Israeli 'Judaization' Policy in Galilee and Its Impact on Local Arab Urbanization." *Political Geography Quarterly* 8, no. 3 (1989): 229–53.

———. "Israeli State Policy toward Bedouin Sedentarization in the Negev." *Journal of Palestine Studies* 18, no. 2 (1989): 71–91.

Farah, Ja'far. "The Other Side of Judaizing the Galilee." *Zavoni–Karmiel*, May 14, 1993, 15–17. (Hebrew)

Feldman, Ilana. "Home as a Refrain: Remembering and Living Displacement in Gaza." *History and Memory* 18, no. 2 (2006): 10–47.

Firro, Kais. "Reshaping Druze Particularism in Israel." *Journal of Palestine Studies* 30, no. 3 (2001): 40–53.

Fleischmann, Ellen. *The Nation and Its "New" Women: The Palestinian Women's Movement, 1920–1948*. Berkeley: University of California Press, 2003.

Foucault, Michel. *Technologies of the Self.* Amherst: University of Massachusetts Press, 1988.

"Frequently Asked Questions." Ministry of Defense. www.hachvana.mod.gov.il/pages/general/FAQ.asp?UN=9&HD=12 (accessed July 31, 2003).

Gaffney, Frank J., Jr. "The 'Fifth Column' Syndrome." *Washington Times*, March 25, 2003.

"Gag on Names of Bedouin Soldiers." *Haaretz*, June 21, 2001, News in Brief.

Ghanem, As'ad. *The Palestinian Arab Minority in Israel, 1948–2000: A Political Study*. Albany: State University of New York Press, 2001.

Ghosh, Amitav. *The Glass Palace*. New York: Random House, 2001.

———. "India's Untold War of Independence." *New Yorker* (June 23–30, 1997): 116.

Ghoussoub, Mai, and Emma Sinclair-Webb, eds. *Imagined Masculinities: Male Identity and Culture in the Modern Middle East*. London: Saqi Books, 2000.

Gill, Lesley. "Creating Citizens, Making Men: The Military and Masculinity in Bolivia." *Cultural Anthropology* 12, no. 4 (1997): 527–50.

———. *The School of the Americas: Military Training and Political Violence in the Americas*. Durham, NC: Duke University Press, 2004.

Giv'at-Haviva: Jewish Arab Center for Peace. *Attitudes of the Arabs to the State of Israel*. Giv'at-Haviva, 2001.

Global Jewish Agenda. "Interior Minister to Foreign Minister: Soldiers Who Are Not Halachically Jewish To Be Granted Israeli Citizenship." nd. www.jafi.org.il/agenda/2001/english/wk4-12/2.asp (accessed November 14, 2006).

Glory. Dir. Edward Zwick. Sony Pictures. 122 mins. 1989.

Golan, Avirama. "Where the 'Alliance of Blood' Has Led." *Haaretz*, February 17, 2005. www.haaretz.com/hasen/objects/pages/PrintArticleEn.jhtml?itemNo=541263 (accessed January 28, 2006).

Google Groups. "Newsgroups: Subject: Birthing the Nation." talk.politics.mideast, July 10, 2002.

Gorman, Tom. "Navajos Honored for War of Words." *Los Angeles Times*, July 26, 2001.

Green, Linda. "Structures of Power, Spaces of Violence: Everyday Life in Post-Peace Accord Rural Guatemala." *Foccal, European Journal of Anthropology* 39 (2002): 117–35.

Greenberg, Hanan. "Can Druze Soldiers Be Shot?" *Yedioth*, March 1, 2005. www.ynetnews.com/Ext/Comp/ArticleLayout/CdaArticlePrintPreview/1,2506,L-3052594,00.html (accessed September 28, 2006).

———. "Who Doesn't Want the Druze Widow in the Memorial Ceremony?" *Ynetnews*, April 17, 2006. www.ynet.co.il/articles/0,3740,L-3240614,00.html (accessed April 18, 2006).

Grundlingh, Louis. "Non Europeans Should be Kept Away from the Temptations of Towns: Controlling Black South African Soldiers during the Second World War." *International Journal of African Historical Studies* 25, no. 3 (1992): 539–60.

Grundy, Kenneth W. *Soldiers without Politics: Blacks in the South African Armed Forces.* Berkeley: University of California Press, 1983.

Gumbel, Andrew. "Pentagon Targets Latinos and Mexicans to Man the Front Lines in War on Terror." *The Independent.* http://news.independent.co.uk/world/americas/story.jsp?story=441886 (accessed September 12, 2003).

Gur, Batya. "Dancing in the Dark." *Haaretz*, February 8, 2002, Week's End.

Gutmann, Matthew. "Trafficking in Men: The Anthropology of Masculinity." *Annual Review of Anthropology* 26 (1997): 385–409.

Hajj, The, Smadar Lavie, and Forest Rouse. "Notes on the Fantastic Journey of The Hajj, His Anthropologist, and Her American Passport." *American Ethnologist* 20, no. 2 (1993): 363–84.

Hajjar, Lisa. *Courting Conflict: The Israeli Military Court System in the West Bank and Gaza.* Berkeley: University of California Press, 2005.

———. "Israel's Interventions among the Druze." *Middle East Report* 26, no. 3 (1996).

———. "Speaking the Conflict, Or How the Druze Became Bilingual: A Study of Druze Translators in the Israeli Military Courts in the West Bank and Gaza." *Ethnic and Racial Studies* 23, no. 2 (2000): 299–328.

Hamdan, Hana. "Individual Settlement in the Naqab: The Exclusion of the Arab Minority." *Adalah Newsletter* 10 (February 2005).

Harb, Husam. "For Twenty Years the Ministry of Defense Deprives the Ilias Family from Maghar of Benefits after the Death of the Father Who Served in the Border Guard." *Kul al-'Arab*, February 8, 2002. (Arabic)

Harel, Amos. "IDF to End Forced Druze Separation." *Haaretz*, November 20, 2001, 1.

———. "Stemming the Tide: Bedouin No Longer Flock to Join the Army." *Haaretz*, June 14, 2001, 1–2.

Harel, Amos, Jalal Bana, and Baruch Kra. "Bedouin Officer Says He's Innocent of Spying for Hezbollah, Drug Dealing." *Haaretz*, October 25, 2002.

Harel, Amos, Nir Hasson, and Jack Khoury. "Five Soldiers Buried, Only One in Military Funeral." *Haaretz*, December 14, 2004, 1.

Harel, Zvi, and Yuval Yoaz. "Colonel on Trial for Raping Soldier Says She Initiated Intimate Contact." *Haaretz*, June 16, 2005. www.haaretzdaily.com/hasen/pages/ShArt.jhtml?itemNo=588208 (accessed June 16, 2005).

———. "Fatwa Allows Bedouin Soldiers to Return Fire in Evacuation." *Haaretz*, March 3, 2005. www.haaretz.com/hasen/pages/ShArt.jhtml?itemNo=547219&contrassID=1&subContrassID=7&sbSubContrassID=0&listSrc=Y (accessed September 28, 2006).

Hassan, Manar. "The Politics of Honor: Patriarchy, the State and the Murder of Women in the Name of Family Honor." *Journal of Israeli History* 21, no. 1–2 (March–October, 2002): 1–37.

Hasso, Frances. "Modernity and Gender in Arab Accounts of the 1948 and 1967 Defeats." *International Journal of Middle East Studies* 32, no. 4 (2000): 491–510.

Havakook, Ya'cov. *Footprints in the Sand: The Bedouin Trackers in the IDF.* Tel Aviv: Israeli Ministry of Defense, 1998.

Hawari, Areen. "Men under the Military Regime." *Adalah's Review* 4 (2004): 33–44.

Helman, Sara. "Citizenship, Regime, Identity and Peace Protest in Israel." In Daniel Maman, Eyal Ben-Ari, and Zeev Rosenhek, eds., *Military, State, and Society in Israel: Theoretical and Comparative Perspectives*, 295–318. New Brunswick, NJ: Transaction, 2001.

———. "Militarism and the Construction of Community." *Journal of Political and Military Sociology* 25, no. 2 (1997): 305–32.

———. "Militarism and the Construction of the Life-World of Israeli Males: The Case of the Reserves System." In Edna Lomsky-Feder and Eyal Ben-Ari, eds., *The Military and Militarism in Israeli Society*, 191–221. Albany: State University of New York Press, 1999.

Herzfeld, Michael. *The Poetics of Manhood.* Princeton, NJ: Princeton University Press, 1988.

Hochschild, Adam. *King Leopold's Ghost: A Story of Greed, Terror and Heroism in Colonial Africa.* New York: Houghton Mifflin, 1998.

Huggins, Martha, Mika Haritos-Fatouros, and Philip Zimbardo. *Violence Workers: Police Torturers and Murderers Reconstruct Brazilian Atrocities.* Berkeley: University of California Press, 2002.

Human Rights Association (HRA). *By All Means Possible: A Report on the Destruction by the State of Crops of Bedouin Citizens in the Naqab (Negev) by Means of Aerial Spraying with Chemicals.* Arab Association for Human Rights, 2004. www.arabhra.org/ HraAdmin/UserImages/Files/CropDestructionReportEnglish.pdf (accessed February 14, 2008).

———. "Discrimination against Arabs on the Basis of Military Service." In *Weekly Review of the Arabic Press in Israel*, 195 (November 5–12, 2004). www.arabhra.org/ publications/wrap/wraphome2004.htm (accessed January 18, 2005).

———. "Land and Planning Policy in Israel." nd. www.arabhra.org/factsheets/factsheet2.htm (accessed December 16, 2004).

———. "On the Margins: Annual Review of Human Rights Violations of the Arab Palestinian Minority in Israel 2005." www.arabhra.org/HRA/SecondaryArticles/ SecondaryArticlePage.aspx?SecondaryArticle=1339 (accessed February 14, 2008).

Human Rights Watch. "Second Class: Discrimination against Palestinian Arab Children in Israel's Schools." 2001. www.hrw.org/reports/2001/israel2/ (accessed December 16, 2004).

———. "World Report 2001: Israel, the Occupied West Bank, Gaza Strip, and Palestinian Authority Territories." www.hrw.org/wr2k1/mideast/israel.html (accessed December 16, 2004).

———. "World Report 2006—Israel / Occupied Palestinian Territories (OPT)—January." www.unhcr.org/cgi-bin/texis/vtx/rsd/rsddocview.html?tbl=RSDCOI&id=43 cfaea22 (accessed October 9, 2007).

Humphreys, Laud. *Tearoom Trade: Impersonal Sex in Public Places*. New York: Aldine de Gruyter, 1975.

"Hundreds of Residents from Makir and Jdaidi Demonstrate against Settling the Agents of the Occupation." *al-'Ittihad*, July 15, 2001, 7.

Hutchinson, Earl Ofari. "Echoes of 'Fragging.'" *San Francisco Chronicle*, March 27, 2003, A19. www.sfgate.com/cgi-bin/article.cgi?f=/c/a/2003/03/27/ED279159.DTL& hw=vietnam+war&sn=714&sc=261 (accessed February 14, 2008).

Hynes, Gerald. "A Biographical Sketch of W.E.B. DuBois." Written in 1974, updated 2004. www.duboislc.org/man.html (accessed December 1, 2005).

"IDF Reserve Soldiers and Officers Say No to Disengagement." *Arutz Sheva: Israel National News*, June 22, 2005. www.israelnn.com/news.php3?id=84374 (accessed September 29, 2006).

Ilan, Shahar. "The Undocumented: Fifth in a Series—Bedouin Trackers: Israeli Enough for the IDF, but Not for an ID Card." *Haaretz*, October 10, 2006. www.haaretz .com/hasen/objects/pages/PrintArticleEn.jhtml?itemNo=772444 (accessed October 10, 2006).

"Israel Strips Citizenship from Arab Suspect." *New York Times*, September 10, 2002, late edition—final, A10.

Istiqlal. Dir. Nizar Hassan. Released in Israel. 25 mins. 1994.

Jabareen, Hassan. "On the Oppression of Identities in the Name of Civil Equality." *Adalah's Review (Politics, Identity and Law)* 1 (1999): 26–27.

———. "Towards a Critical Palestinian Minority Approach: Citizenship, Nationalism, and Feminism in Israeli Law." *Plilm* 9 (2000).

Jabareen, Yosef. "The Right to the City: The Case of the Shihab el-Din Crisis in Nazareth." In Suhad Bishara and Hana Hamdan, eds., *Makan: Adalah's Journal for Land Planning and Justice, Volume 1: The Right to the City and New Ways of Understanding Space*. Shafa-'Amr: Adalah—The Legal Center for Arab Minority Rights in Israel, 2006.

Jakubowska, Longina. "Finding Ways to Make a Living: Employment among Negev Bedouin." *Nomadic Peoples* 4, no. 2 (2000): 94–105.

———. "Resisting 'Ethnicity': The Israeli State and Bedouin Identity." In Carolyn Nordstrom and JoAnn Martin, eds., *The Paths to Domination, Resistance, and Terror*, 85–105. Berkeley: University of California Press, 1992.

Jamal, Amal. "Ethnic Nationalism, Native Peoples and Civic Equality: On Collective Rights in Israel." Paper presented at the Conference on the Legal and Socio-Economic Status of Arab Citizens in Israel, New York University, April 3, 2003.

Jansson, Maria. "Bedouin Soldiers—Loyal 'Israelis'? A Study on Loyalty and Identification among a Minority Group in a Nation Building Process." MA thesis, Gothenburg University, Sweden, 2004.

Jayyusi, Salma Khadra. Introduction to *The Secret Life of Saaed the Ill-Fated Pessoptimist*, by Emile Habiby. Columbia, LA: Readers International, 1989.

Jean-Klein, Iris. "Domestic Nationalism and Resistance: The Two Faces of Everyday Activism in Palestine during the Intifada." *Cultural Anthropology* 16, no. 1 (1992).

Jeffery, Keith. "The British Army and Ireland since 1922." In Thomas Bartlett and Keith Jeffery, eds., *A Military History of Ireland*, 431–507. Cambridge, UK: Cambridge University Press, 1996.

———. "The Irish Military Tradition and the British Empire." In Keith Jeffery, ed., *"An Irish Empire"? Aspects of Ireland and the British Empire*, 94–122. Manchester: Manchester University Press, 1996.

Jiryis, Sabri. *The Arabs in Israel*. New York: Monthly Review Press, 1976.

Kanaaneh, Hatim. *A Doctor in Galilee: The Story and Struggle of a Palestinian in Israel*. London: Pluto, 2008.

Kanaaneh, Moslih. "The 'Anthropologicality' of Indigenous Anthropology." *Dialectical Anthropology* 22 (1997): 1–21.

Kanaaneh, Rhoda. *Birthing the Nation: Strategies of Palestinian Women in Israel*. Berkeley: University of California Press, 2002.

———. "Embattled Identities: Palestinian Soldiers in the Israeli Military." *Journal of Palestine Studies* 32, no. 3 (2003): 5–20.

———. "In the Name of Insecurity: Arab Soldiers in the Israeli Military." *Adalah's Review* 4 (2004): 57–65.

———. "Review of *Paradise Lost*." *Journal of Middle East Women's Studies* 1, no. 2 (2005): 163–64.

Kaplan, Caren, Norma Alarcon, and Minoo Moallem, eds. *Between Woman and Nation: Nationalisms, Transnational Feminisms, and the State*. Durham, NC: Duke University Press, 1999.

Kaplan, Danny. "The Military as a Second Bar Mitzvah: Combat Service as Initiation to Zionist Masculinity." In Ghoussoub and Sinclair-Webb, eds., *Imagined Masculinities*, 127–44.

Kaplan, Danny, and Eyal Ben-Ari. "Brothers and Others in Arms: Managing Gay Identity in Combat Units of the Israeli Army." *Journal of Contemporary Ethnography* 29, no. 4 (2000): 396–432.

Kawano, Kenji. *Warriors: Navajo Code Talkers*. Flagstaff, AZ: Northland Publishing, 1990.

Kelly, Tobias. "In a Treacherous State: The Fear of the Collaborator among West Bank Palestinians." Paper presented at Treason and the Art of Politics: Anthropological and Historical Perspectives workshop, University of Edinburgh, December 7–9, 2006.

———. *Law, Violence and Sovereignty among West Bank Palestinians*. Cambridge, UK: Cambridge University Press, 2006.

———. "Violent States: Work, Borders and Citizenship during the Palestinian Intifada." Unpublished paper, nd.

Kemp, Adriana. "Managing Migration, Reprioritizing National Citizenship: Undocumented Migrant Workers' Children and Policy Reforms in Israel." *Theoretical Inquiries in Law* 8, no. 2 (2007): 663–91.

Kernochan, Julia, and Rina Rosenberg. "A Critique of Equal Duties, Equal Rights." *Adalah's Review* 1 (1999): 28–31.

Khalidi, Rashid. *Palestinian Identity: The Construction of Modern National Consciousness.* New York: Columbia University Press, 1997.

Khoury, Jack, and Fadi Eyadat. "An Intifada in the Carmel." *Haaretz*, Nov 1, 2006. www.haaretz.com/hasen/spages/782043.html (accessed November 1, 2006).

Korn, Alina. "Crime and Legal Control." *British Journal of Criminology* 40, no. 4 (2000): 574–94.

Lang, Sharon. *Sharaf Politics: Honor and Peacemaking in Israeli-Palestinian Society.* New York: Routledge, 2005.

Lapahie, Harrison, Jr. "Harry Benally." www.lapahie.com/Harry_Benally.cfm (accessed February 14, 2008).

Lennon, Peter. "Secret Army." *The Guardian*, August 23, 2002. http://arts.guardian.co.uk/fridayreview/story/0,,778833,00.html#article_continue (accessed February 14, 2008).

Leshem, Guy. "IDF Widows' Organization Blacklisted Minority Members." *Haaretz*, March 30, 2007. www.haaretz.com/*hasen*/objects/pages/PrintArticleEn.jhtml?itemNo=843940 (accessed April 10, 2007).

"Letter of the FLN to the Harkis." Marxist.org. First published in 1960. www.marxists.org/history/algeria/1960/harkis.htm (accessed June 6, 2007).

Levine, Mark. "Nationalism, Religion and Urban Politics in Israel: Struggles Over Modernity and Identity in 'Global' Jaffa." In Daniel Monterescu and Dan Rabinowitz, eds., *Mixed Towns, Trapped Communities: Historical Narratives, Spatial Dynamics, Gender Relations and Cultural Encounters in Palestinian-Israeli Towns*, 281–302. Hampshire, England: Ashgate, 2007.

Levy, Orna Sasson. "Constructing Identities at the Margins: Masculinities and Citizenship in the Israeli Army." Paper presented at the Princeton-Columbia Graduate Student Workshop: National Identity and Public Policy, September 29–October 1, 2000.

Lewin, Alisa, and Haya Stier. "Who Benefits the Most? The Unequal Allocation of Transfers in the Israeli Welfare State." *Social Science Quarterly* 83, 2 (June 2002): 488–503.

Lewin-Epstein, Noah, and Moshe Semyonov. *The Arab Minority in Israel's Economy: Patterns of Ethnic Inequality.* Boulder, CO: Westview, 1993.

Lockman, Zachary. "Arab Workers and Arab Nationalism in Palestine; A View from Below." In James Jankowski and Israel Gershoni, eds., *Rethinking Nationalism in the Arab Middle East*, 249–72. New York: Columbia University Press, 1997.

Lomsky-Feder, Edna, and Eyal Ben-Ari. "From 'The People in Uniform' to 'Different Uniforms for the People': Professionalism, Diversity and the Israeli Defense Forces." In Josep Soaters and Jan van der Meulen, eds., *Managing Diversity in the Armed Forces: Experiences from Nine Countries*, 157–86. Tilburg, Netherlands: Tilburg University Press, 1999.

Lomsky-Feder, Edna, and Tamar Rappoport. "'Homebred Masculinity' Resists the Local Model of Manhood: Russian-Jewish Immigrants Confront Israeli Masculinity." Unpublished paper, 2001.

Louer, Laurence. *To Be an Arab in Israel.* New York: Columbia University Press, 2007.

Lunn, Joe. *Memoirs of the Maelstrom: A Senegalese Oral History of the First World War.* Portsmouth, NH: Heinemann, 1999.

Lustick, Ian. *Arabs in the Jewish State: Israel's Control of a National Minority.* Austin: University of Texas Press, 1980.

Lutz, Catherine. *Homefront: A Military City and the American 20th Century.* Boston: Beacon, 2001.

Majali, Nazir. "Like in the Third World." *Haaretz,* February 15, 2005, editorial page.

Mann, Gregory. "Locating Colonial Histories: Between France and West Africa." *American Historical Review* 110, no. 2 (2005). www.historycooperative.org/journals/ahr/110.2/mann.html (accessed October 10, 2007).

Mar'i, Mariam, and Sami Mar'i. "The Role of Women as Change Agents in Arab Society in Israel." In Barbara Swirski and Marilyn Safir, eds., *Calling the Equality Bluff: Women in Israel,* 213–21. New York: Teachers College Press, 1993.

Marteu, Elisabeth. "Some Reflections on How Bedouin Women of the Negev Relate to Politics: Between Political Marginalisation and Social Mobilisation." *Bulletin du Centre de Recherche Français de Jérusualem* 16 (2005): 271–86.

Massad, Joseph. "Conceiving the Masculine: Gender and Palestinian Nationalism." *Middle East Journal* 49, no. 3 (1995): 467–83.

Mater, Nadire. "Mehmed's Book. Extracts Translated by Ertugrul Kürkçü." 1998. www.rsf.org/rsf/uk/html/mo/rapport/nadire.html (accessed April 28, 2004).

Meari, Lena. "The Roles of Palestinian Peasant Women, 1930–1960: Al-Birweh Village as a Model." Paper presented at the Middle East Studies Association annual meeting, Boston, 2006.

Ministry of Defense. *Bulletin for Released Soldiers 2001/2002: The Fund for Absorbing Released Soldiers and the Unit for Guidance of Released Soldiers.* Holon: Mieri Press, 2001.

Ministry of Housing. "Ministry of Housing." www.moch.gov.il/NR/rdonlyres/0F7 E9446–CBA8–411C-858A-FB40F89D0F1F/5347/2–1–4.pdf (accessed March 11, 2004).

Mitzna, Amram. "There Was a Pogrom in Maghar." *Haaretz,* February 16, 2005, editorial page.

Monterescu, Daniel. "City of 'Strangers': The Socio-Cultural Construction of Manhood in Jaffa." *Journal of Mediterranean Studies* 11, no. 1 (2001): 159–88.

Moreno, Sylvia. "Injured Marines Get Wish: Citizenship." *Washington Post,* April 12, 2003, A21, A31.

Mualem, Mazal. "Interior Minister Poraz Grants Citizenship to Ten Non-Jewish Soldiers." *Haaretz,* May 5, 2004. www.haaretz.com/hasen/objects/pages/PrintArticleEn .jhtml?itemNo=290230 (accessed November 14, 2006).

Naffa', Hisham. "The Dirty Military Mirror." *al-'Ittihad,* August 25, 1997. (Arabic)

———. "Maghar, the Responsibility of All of Us, and Not Only in Slogans." *al-'Ittihad*. February 18, 2005, 5. (Arabic)

Nagel, Joane. "Masculinity and Nationalism: Gender and Sexuality in the Making of Nations." *Ethnic and Racial Studies* 21, no. 2 (1998): 242–70.

Nahmias, Roee. "GDP Per Capita of Arab Israelis Third of That of Jews." *Ynetnews*, January 18, 2007. www.ynetnews.com/articles/0,7340,L-3354260,00.html (accessed April 18, 2006).

National Museum of American Jewish Military History. Exhibit guide: "Liberating the Concentration Camps: GIs Remember." Washington, D.C., 1994.

Negbi, Moshe. "Not Activist, But Phlegmatic." *Haaretz*, February 24, 2002, 5.

Nelson, Soraya Sarhaddi. "Is 'Capt. R.' a War Criminal or a Scapegoat?" *Honolulu Advertiser*, December 26, 2004, A21.

Neuman, Tamara. "Establishing Hebron's Jewish Enclave: The Tactical Use of the Mother-Child Bond." *Journal of Palestine Studies* 33, no. 2 (2004): 51–70.

———. "Reinstating the Religious Nation: A Study of National Religious Persuasion, Settlement, and Violence in Hebron." Ph.D. diss., University of Chicago, 2000.

"News." Ministry of Defense. 2003 www.hachvana.mod.gov.il/pages/news/news.asp?UN=9&HD=14 (accessed July 31, 2003).

"News Update: Adalah Asks Tel Aviv University to Cancel Discriminatory Application Policy." Adalah, March 27, 2003. www.adalah.org/eng/pressreleases2003.php (accessed October 19, 2006).

"News Update: Adalah Challenges Attorney General's Claim That Discriminatory Cuts in Child Allowances Are Legitimate and Proportional." Adalah, March 10, 2003. www.adalah.org/eng/pressreleases/pr.php?file=03_03_10 (accessed February 14, 2008).

"News Update: Jewish and Palestinian Academics Testify Before the Or Commission." Adalah, January 9, 2002. www.adalah.org/eng/pressreleases2002.php (accessed April 20, 2007).

Nir, Ori. "Alienation Rife in Once Quiet Community." *Haaretz*, May 29, 2001, 5.

———. "Bedouin Teens Reject Army, Not Wanting To Be 'Suckers.'" *Haaretz*, January 10, 2002. www.haaretzdaily.com/hasen/pages/ShArt.jhtml?itemNo=115747&contrassID=2&subContrassID=1&sbSubContrassID=0&listSrc=Y (accessed October 1, 2002).

Nusair, Isis. "Gendered Politics of Location: Generational Intersections." In Nahla Abdo and Ronit Lentin, eds., *Women and the Politics of Military Confrontation*, 89–99. New York: Berghahn Books, 2002.

'Odeh, Aiman. "Serving Which Nationality and Which Nationalism Exactly?!" *al-'Ittihad*, January 14, 2004, 2–4. (Arabic)

Otsuka, Julie. *When the Emperor Was Divine*. New York: Alfred Knopf, 2002.

Palestinian Human Rights Information Center. *The Cost of Freedom*. Chicago: Palestinian Human Rights Information Center, 1991.

Pappe, Ilan. *The Ethnic Cleansing of Palestine*. Oxford: One World Publications, 2006.

———. *The Making of the Arab-Israeli Conflict, 1947–1951*. London: I. B. Tauris, 1994.

Paradise Lost. Dir. Ibtisam Mara'ana. Released in Israel; distributed by Women Make Movies. 56 mins. 2003.

"The Parliamentary Committee on the Interior Studies the Acts of Violence in Abu Snan." *al-'Ittihad*, February 17, 2005, 5. (Arabic)

Parsons, Laila. "The Druze and the Birth of Israel." In Eugene L. Rogan and Avi Shlaim, eds., *The War for Palestine: Rewriting the History of 1948*, 60–78. Cambridge, UK: Cambridge University Press, 2001.

———. *The Druze between Palestine and Israel, 1947–1949.* New York: St. Martin's Press, 2000.

Pasha, Mustapha Kamal. *Colonial Political Economy: Recruitment and Underdevelopment in the Punjab.* Oxford: Oxford University Press, 1998.

Peled, Alon. *A Question of Loyalty: Military Manpower Policy in Multiethnic States.* Ithaca, NY: Cornell University Press, 1998.

Perez, Gina. "How a Scholarship Girl Becomes a Soldier: The Militarization of Latina/o Youth in Chicago Public Schools." *Identities: Global Studies in Culture and Power* 13 (2006): 53–72.

Peteet, Julie. "Icons and Militants: Mothering in the Danger Zone." *Signs* 23, no. 1 (1997): 103–29.

———. "Male Gender and Rituals of Resistance in the Palestinian Intifada: A Cultural Politics of Violence." In Ghoussoub and Sinclair-Webb, eds., *Imagined Masculinities*, 103–26.

Pfeffer, Anshel. "Double Vision." *Haaretz*. www.haaretz.com/hasen/objects/pages/PrintArticleEn.jhtml?itemNo=909583 (accessed October 7, 2007).

Pipes, Daniel. "Murder in the 101st Airborne." Published in *New York Post*, March 25, 2002. www.danielpipes.org/article/1042 (accessed June 7, 2007).

Power. Dir. Ayelet Bechar. Promoted by World Health Organization. Funded by the Turin Municipality and Rabinovitch Foundation, distributed by Cinephil. 2006.

National Insurance Institute of Israel (NII). "Quarterly Statistics." nd. www.btl.gov.il/english/rivon_E/htm/en_rivon_3_061.htm (accessed November 14, 2006).

———. "Quarterly Statistics." nd. www.btl.gov.il/english/rivon_E/htm/en_rivon_1_13.htm (accessed November 14, 2006).

Rabinowitz, Dan. "Eastern Nostalgia: How the Palestinians Became 'Israel's Arabs.'" *Theory and Criticism* 4 (Fall 1993): 141–51. (Hebrew)

———. *Overlooking Nazareth: The Ethnography of Exclusion in the Galilee.* New York: Cambridge University Press, 1997.

Rabinowitz, Danny. "Rights before Service." *Haaretz*, December 12, 2004, www.haaretz.com/hasen/pages/ShArt.jhtml?itemNo=517521 (accessed September 29, 2006).

Reeck, Laura. "Forgetting and Remembering the Harkis: Mehdi Charef's 'Le Harki de Meriem.'" *Romance Quarterly* 53, no. 1 (2006): 49–61.

Regional Council for the Unrecognized Villages in the Negev and the Arab Association for Human Rights. "The Unrecognized Villages in the Negev: Submission to the UN Committee on Economic, Social and Cultural Rights." 2003.

Reiker, Martina. "Constructing Palestinian Subalternity in the Galilee: Reflections on Representations of the Palestinian Peasantry (Inscriptions 6)." 1992. http://hum-www.ucsc.edu/CultStudies/PUBS/Inscriptions/vol_6/Reiker.html (accessed December 16, 2004).

"Ridiculous Answer from the Interior Security Ministry to the Questioning of Representative Dahamsheh on the Latest Violent Event in Bi'ni." *Sawt ul-Balad*, March 4, 2005, 19. (Arabic)

Rigg, Brian Mark. *Hitler's Jewish Soldiers: The Untold Story of Nazi Racial Laws and Men of Jewish Descent in the German Military*. Lawrence: University Press of Kansas, 2002.

Robben, Antonius C. G. M. "The Politics of Truth and Emotion among Victims and Perpetrators of Violence." In Carolyn Nordstrom and Antonius C. G. M. Robben, eds., *Fieldwork Under Fire: Contemporary Studies of Violence and Survival*, 91–103. Berkeley: University of California Press, 1995.

Robinson, Shira. "Occupied Citizens in a Liberal State: Palestinians under Military Rule and the Colonial Formation of Israeli Society, 1948–1966." Ph.D. diss., Stanford University, 2005.

Rosenberg, Jennifer. "Navajo Code Talkers." http://history1900s.about.com/od/world warii/a/navajacode.htm (accessed June 6, 2007).

Rosenhek, Zeev. "The Exclusionary Logic of the Welfare State: Palestinian Citizens in the Israeli Welfare State." *International Sociology* 14, no. 2 (1999): 195–215.

Rouhana, Nadim. *Palestinian Citizens in an Ethnic Jewish State*. New Haven, CT: Yale University Press, 1997.

Rouhana, Nadim, and Nimer Sultany. "Redrawing the Boundaries of Citizenship: Israel's New Hegemony." *Journal of Palestine Studies* 33, no. 1 (2003): 5–22.

Sa'ar, Amalia. "Contradictory Location: Assessing the Position of Palestinian Women Citizens of Israel." *Journal of Middle East Women's Studies* 3, no. 3 (2007).

Sa'ar, Amalia, and Taghreed Yahya-Younis. "Masculinity in Crisis: The Case of Palestinians in Israel." *British Journal of Middle East Studies* 35, no. 5 (2006).

Sabbagh-Khouri, Areej. "Palestinian Predicaments: Jewish Immigration and Refugee Repatriation." In Rhoda Kanaaneh and Isis Nusair, eds., *Blue ID: Palestinians in Israel Revisited*. Albany: State University of New York Press, forthcoming.

Sa'di, Ahmad. "Between State Ideology and Minority National Identity; Palestinians in Israel and Israel Social Science Research." *Review of Middle East Studies* 5 (1992).

———. "The Incorporation of the Palestinian Minority by the Israeli State, 1948–1970: On the Nature, Transformation, and Constraints of Collaboration." *Social Text* 75, no. 21, 2 (2003): 75–94.

———. "Introduction: The Claims of Memory." In Ahmad Sa'di and Lila Abu Lughod, eds., *Nakba: Palestine, 1948, and the Claims of Memory*, 1–24. (New York: Columbia University Press).

———. "Modernization as an Explanatory Discourse of Zionist–Palestinian Relations." *British Journal of Middle Eastern Studies* 24, no. 1 (1997): 25–48.

Said, Edward. *After the Last Sky*. London: Faber and Faber, 1986.

Sasson-Levy, Orna. "Constructing Identities at the Margins: Masculinities and Citizenship in the Israeli Army." Paper presented at the Joint Princeton-Columbia Graduate Student Workshop: National Identity and Public Policy in Comparative Perspective, Princeton, NJ, September 29–October 1, 2000.

Sawalha, Aseel. "Anthropology Faces a Crisis after Orientalism." *Al-Adab* 51 (November–December 2003): 15–18.

———. "'Healing the Wounds of the War': Placing the War-Displaced in Postwar Beirut." In Jane Schneider and Ida Susser, eds., *Wounded Cities: Destruction and Reconstruction in a Globalized World*, 271–90. New York: Berg Publishers, 2003.

Sayf, Ghalib. "Land and Military Recruitment." *al-'Ittihad*, November 23, 2001, 11. (Arabic)

Schensul, Stephan, Jean Schensul, and Margaret LeCompte. *Essential Ethnographic Methods: Observations, Interviews and Questionnaires*. Walnut Creek, CA: AltaMira Press, 1999.

Schirmer, Jennifer. *The Guatemalan Military Project: A Violence Called Democracy*. Philadelphia: University of Pennsylvania Press, 1998.

Schofield, Hugh. "France's 'Harkis' File Suit for Crimes against Humanity." *Middle East Times*, August 2001. www.metimes.com/2K1/issue2001-35/reg/frances_harkis_file.htm.

Scott, A. O. "Yes, Soldiers of France, in All But Name." *New York Times*, December 6, 2006.

Scott, James C. *Seeing Like a State: How Certain Schemes to Improve the Human Condition Have Failed*. New Haven, CT: Yale University Press, 1998.

———. *Weapons of the Weak: Everyday Forms of Peasant Resistance*. New Haven, CT: Yale University Press, 1985.

Seeds of Peace. *A Tribute: Memories of Our Friend Asel Asleh, 1983–2000*. n.p. 2000.

Seikaly, Sherene. "From Haifa to Beirut." Unpublished paper, nd.

Shadid, Anthony. "Iraqi Security Forces Torn between Loyalties." *Washington Post*, November 24, 2003. www.washingtonpost.com/wp-dyn/articles/A11809–2003Nov24.html (accessed October 1, 2003).

Shafir, Gershon, and Yoav Peled. *Being Israeli: The Dynamics of Multiple Citizenship*. Cambridge, UK: Cambridge University Press, 2002.

Shaked, Ronny. "Abu Gosh: Hummus and Coexistence." *Ynetnews*, September 26, 2006. www.ynetnews.com/Ext/Comp/ArticleLayout/CdaArticlePrintPreview/1,2506,L-3308173,00.html (accessed September 27, 2006).

Shalhoub-Kevorkian, Nadera. "Racism, Militarisation and Policing: Police Reactions to Violence against Women in Israel." *Social Identities* 10, no. 2 (2004): 171–93.

Shami, Seteney. "Studying Your Own: The Complexities of a Shared Culture." In Soraya Altorki and Cimillia Fawzi El-Solh, eds., *Arab Women in the Field: Studying Your Own Society*, 115–38. Syracuse, NY: Syracuse University Press, 1988.

Shamir, Rohen. "Suspended in Space: Bedouins under the Law of Israel." *Law and Society Review* 30, no. 2 (1996): 231–57.

Shammas, Anton. "Mixed as in Pidgin: The Vanishing Arabic of a 'Bilingual' City." In Daniel Monterescu and Dan Rabinowitz, eds., *Mixed Towns, Trapped Communities: Historical Narratives, Spatial Dynamics, Gender Relations and Cultural Encounters in Palestinian-Israeli Towns*, 303–11. Hampshire, England: Ashgate, 2007.

Shelach, Oz. *Picnic Grounds: A Novel in Fragments*. San Francisco: City Light Books, 2003.

Shigaki, Irene. "The Internment of Japanese Americans: A Multicultural Perspective." Unpublished manuscript, nd.

Shlezinger, Nadav. "Israeli Bedouins: Ishmael Khaldi Discusses Israel's Bedouin Minority." http://pnews.org/ArT/ExP/KHaldi.shtml (accessed October 6, 2006).

Shohat, Ella. *Taboo Memories, Diasporic Voices*. Durham, NC: Duke University Press, 2006.

Sinai, Ruth. "Court: IDF Service Not Necessary to Get Job." *Haaretz*, June 16, 2003, 2.

Sinha, Mrinalini. *The "Manly Englishman" and the "Effeminate Bengali" in the Late Nineteenth Century*. Manchester: Manchester University Press, 1995.

Slyomovics, Susan. *The Object of Memory: Arab and Jew Narrate the Palestinian Village*. Philadelphia: University of Pennsylvania Press, 1998.

———. "The Rape of Qula, a Destroyed Palestinian Village." In Ahmad Sa'di and Lila Abu Lughod, eds., *Nakba: Palestine, 1948, and the Claims of Memory*, 27–51. New York: Columbia University Press, 2007.

Smooha, Sami. "The Advances and Limits of the Israelization of Israel's Palestinian Citizens." In Kamal Abdel-Malek and David C. Jacobson, eds., *Israeli and Palestinian Identities in History and Literature*, 9–33. New York: St. Martin's Press, 1999.

———. "Ethnic Democracy: Israel as an Archetype." *Israel Studies* 2, no. 2 (1997): 128–241.

Sofer, Ronny "'Fire Back If Needed': New Edict Allows Bedouin (IDF) Soldiers to Kill Settlers Who Attack Them." *Yedioth*, March 3, 2005. www.ynetnews.com/articles/0,7340,L-3053327,00.html visited on march 15 2005

Stadler, Nurit, and Eyal Ben-Ari. "Other-Worldly Soldiers? Ultra-Orthodox Views of Military Service in Contemporary Israel." *Israeli Affairs* 9, no. 4 (2003): 17–48.

Steele, Jeanette. "Up in Arms against Bigotry: Arab-American Marine Forms Group to Send Patriotic Message." *San Diego Tribune*, July 4, 2002. www.aaiusa.org/press-room/1849/mustread07042002 (accessed June 7, 2007).

Stein, Rebecca Luna. *National Itineraries: Tourism, Coloniality and Cultural Politics in Contemporary Israel*. Durham, NC: Duke University Press, forthcoming.

Stillman, Deanne. "Uncle Sam's Jihadists: What's the U.S. Military Doing about Radical Muslim Soldiers? Not Enough." *Slate*, March 27, 2003. www.slate.com/id/2080770/ (accessed February 14, 2008).

Sultany, Nimer. "Palestinian Arabs in Israeli Universities." *Arab48*, July 15, 2002. (Arabic).

"Supreme Court Petitions: Land Rights." Adalah. www.adalah.org/eng/legaladvocacy land.php. (accessed February 14, 2008).

Swedenburg, Ted. *Memories of Revolt: The 1936–1939 Rebellion and the Palestinian National Past.* Minneapolis: University of Minnesota Press, 1995.

———. "Occupational Hazards: Palestine Ethnography." *Cultural Anthropology* 4, no. 3 (1989): 265–72.

———. "The Palestinian Peasant as National Signifier." *Anthropological Quarterly* 63, no. 1 (1990): 18–30.

———. "Saida Sultan / Danna International: Transgender Pop and the Polysemiotics of Sex, Nation and Ethnicity on the Israeli Egyptian Border." *Musical Quarterly* 81, no. 1 (1997): 81–108.

Swirski, Barbara. "The Citizenship of Jewish and Palestinian Arab Women in Israel." In Joseph Suad, ed., *Gender and Citizenship in the Middle East*, 314–44. Syracuse, NY: Syracuse University Press, 2000.

Szymczyk, Adam, ed. *Ahlam Shibli Trackers.* Cologne: Kunsthalle Basel, 2007.

Tagari, Hadas. "Petition 9173/96." Association of Civil Rights in Israel, 1996. (Hebrew)

Tamari, Salim. "Building Other People's Homes: The Palestinian Peasant's Household and Work in Israel." *Journal of Palestine Studies* 1, no. 41 (Autumn 1981): 31–66.

———. "Factionalism and Class Formation in Recent Palestinian History." In Roger Owen, ed., *Studies in the Economic and Social History of Palestine in the Nineteenth and Twentieth Centuries*, 177–201. London: Macmillan, 1982.

———. "Problems of Social Science Research in Palestine; An Over-view." *Current Sociology* 42, no. 2 (1994): 68–86.

Traubmann, Tamara. "Court Rules Haifa University Must Halt Housing Advantages for IDF Veterans." *Haaretz*, August 20, 2006. www.haaretz.com/hasen/objects/pages/PrintArticleEn.jhtml?itemNo=752686 (accessed August 21, 2006).

Tuba and Migdal. Dir. by Gil Karni. In Hebrew. 45 mins. 1998.

Tuma, Emile. *The Path of Struggle of the Arab Masses in Israel.* Acre: Dar Abu Salma Press, 1982. (Arabic)

Twine, France Winddance. "Racial Ideologies and Racial Methodologies." In Twine and Warren, eds., *Racing Research, Researching Race*, 1–34.

Twine, France Winddance, and Jonathan Warren, eds., *Racing Research, Researching Race: Methodological Dilemmas in Critical Race Studies.* New York: New York University Press, 2000.

"UN Human Rights Committee—Information Sheet #3." Adalah. www.adalah.org/eng/intladvocacy/unhrc_03_fam_uni.pdf (accessed February 14, 2008).

Union of Communist Youth. *al-Khizy wa-al-'Ār li-al-Mujannadīn* (The shame and dishonor of recruits). 'Arrabi: Union of Communist Youth, 2000. (Arabic)

Ushpiz, Ada. "Doves among the Druze." *Haaretz*, March 8, 2004. www.haaretz.com/hasen/objects/pages/PrintArticleEn.jhtml?itemNo=401368 (accessed February 14, 2008).

———. "Just Keep Them Away from Our Daughters!" *Haaretz*, July 9, 2004, B4.

———. "Tents of Mourning: Soul-Searching in the Bedouin Towns of Rahat and Kse-ifa Following the Death of Their Soldiers in Rafah This Week." *Haaretz*, December 17, 2004, B6.

Van Every, Katy. "Navajo Code Talkers: Life During and After World War Two." Paper for graduate seminar on Minorities in the Military, American University, Washington, D.C., 2003.

Warnock, Kitty. *Land Before Honor: Palestinian Women in the Occupied Territories*. New York: Monthly Review Press, 1990.

Weiss, Meira. *Chosen Body: The Politics of the Body in Israeli Society*. Stanford, CA: Stanford University Press, 2002.

"Who Were the Tuskegee Airmen?" Tuskegee Airmen, Inc. www.tuskegeeairmen.org/Tuskegee_Airmen_History.html (accessed June 6, 2007).

Wiemer, Reinhard. "Zionism and the Arabs after the Establishment of the State of Israel." In Alexander Scholch, ed., *Palestinians Over the Green Line*, 26–63. London: Ithaca, 1983.

Williams, Chad. "African-American Soldiers and the Constructions of Black Masculinity during WWI." Paper presented at the Conference on Black Masculinities, CUNY Graduate Center, February 4, 2005.

Wilson, William. "World War II: Navajo Code Talkers." *American History Magazine*, June 12, 2006. www.historynet.com/magazines/american_history/3038096.html?page=2&c=y (accessed February 14, 2008).

Woollacott, Martin. "War Comes Home: Israel's Killing of Its Own—Eight Israeli Arabs—Changes Everything." *The Guardian*, October 4, 2000. www.guardian.co.uk/Columnists/Column/0,5673,377059,00.html (accessed February 8, 2006).

Wynchank, Amy. "Sembene Ousmane: Breaking the Silence." University of Cape Town, South Africa. http://web.uct.ac.za/conferences/filmhistorynow/papers/awynchank.doc (accessed October 2004).

Yahya-Younis, Taghreed. "Between 'Normativity' and 'Violation': Women's Political Loyalty in Municipal Elections in Palestinian-Arab Society in Israel." In Rhoda Kanaaneh and Isis Nusair, eds., *Blue ID: Palestinians in Israel Revisited*. Albany: State University of New York Press, forthcoming.

Yehoshua, Yossi. "Arab Muslim Wants to Join IAF." *Ynetnews*. www.ynetnews.com/home/1,7340,3083,00.html (accessed January 26, 2006).

Yiftachel, Oren. "The Dark Side of Modernism: Planning as Control of an Ethnic Minority." In Sophie Watson and Katherine Gibson, eds., *Postmodern Cities and Spaces*, 216–42. Cambridge, UK: Basil Blackwell, 1995.

———. "State Policies, Land Control and an Ethnic Minority: The Arabs in the Galilee Region, Israel." *Environment and Planning D: Society and Space* 9 (1991): 329–62.

Yiftachel, Oren, and Hubert Law Yone. "Regional Policy and Minority Attitudes in Israel." *Environment and Planning A* 26, no. 4 (1993): 387–403.

Yiftachel, Oren, and Michaly Segal. "Jews and Druze in Israel: State Control and Ethnic Resistance." *Ethnic and Racial Studies* 21, no. 3 (1998): 476–506.

Yoaz, Yuval. "State Refuses to Register 'Israeli' Nationality." *Haaretz*, May 19, 2004. www.haaretz.com/hasen/objects/pages/PrintArticleEn.jhtml?itemNo=429149 (accessed February 14, 2008).

Yuval-Davis, Nira. "Front and Rear: The Sexual Division of Labour in the Israeli Army." In Haleh Afshar, ed., *Women, State and Ideology: Studies from Africa and Asia*, 186–204. Albany: State University of New York Press, 1987.

———. "The Jewish Collectivity and National Reproduction in Israel." In *Khamsin, Special Issue on Women in the Middle East*, 60–93. London: Zed Books, 1987.

Za'atri, Raja. "Confrontation Is Not Only in Front of the Authorities." *al-'Ittihad*, January 19, 2005, supplement, 8. (Arabic)

Zaydan, Nayif. "Yesterday I Went to Maghar to Record the Latest Pictures and Visit the Village's Schools and Car Cemetery." *Panorama*, February 25, 2005, 37. (Arabic)

"Ze'ev Hartman, Consultant to the Mayor of Mashhad: 'I Will Try to Enlist All the Young Men in the Village of Mashhad and One Day, an Arab Will Be the Commander In Chief.'" *Kul al-'Arab*, February 8, 2002. (Arabic)

Zo'bi, Sayf al-Din. *Eye Witness: Memoirs*. Shafa-'Amr: al-Mashriq, 1987. (Arabic)

Zureik, Raif. "The Unbearable Lightness of Enlightenment." *Adalah's Review* 1 (Fall 1999): 5–7.

Index

Abdo, Nahla, 153n33, 168n, 169n28
Abdullah, Timor, 78
Abu-'Atif, 23
Abu al-Hayja, Mohammad, 22
Abufarha, Nasser, 134n13
Abu Ghanim, Salami, 76
Abu Ghosh, 14, 35, 38
Abu Kishik, Nihad, 29
Abu-Lughod, Lila, 134n13, 136n1, 169n28
Abu Ras, Amneh, 146n1
Abu Saleh, Walid, 17
Abu Snan, 58, 59, 66
Acre, 107
Algeria: French colonialism in, 91, 92, 103, 170n5
Ali, Naji al-, 88
Allen, Lori, 171n26
American GI Forum, 102
Amir, Yigal, 29
Anderson, Benedict: *Imagined Communities*, 171n28
anthropological methods, 120–21, 123, 180n17
Arab al-Hayb, 150n28
Arab American Institute, 101
Arab Druze Initiative Committee, 137n14
Arabic, 4, 64, 97, 118–19, 146n46
Arab political parties, 25, 146n41, 165n21; Communist Party, 18, 65, 80, 81–82, 88, 116, 125, 179n2
Arab rebellion of 1936, 10

Arabs48 website, 125
Arafat, Yasser, 162n
Arens, Moshe, 77
'Arrabi, 16, 18, 58, 119, 142n50, 153n33
As'ad, Andy, 156n7
As'ad, As'ad, 159n27
Ashqar, Ahmad, 153n31
Ashkenazim, 66, 167n26; as soldiers, 54–55, 71
Asleh, Asel, 1, 16–17, 18
assimilation/Israelization, 89–90, 167n26, 169n31
Association for Civil Rights in Israel, 28, 33, 144n8
Association of Forty, 22, 116, 179n2
Association of Patriotic Arab Americans in the Military, 100–101
Atrash, Salim al-, 75–76
attitudes of Israeli Jews: regarding Palestinians in Israel, 2, 3–4, 7–8, 9–10, 13, 15–16, 48, 62–67, 71, 98, 104, 105, 106, 107, 116, 151n39, 153n12, 155n7, 156n22, 157nn10,11; regarding Palestinians in security forces, 8, 71, 90, 105, 106, 151n39, 153n12, 157nn10,11; as suspicious of Palestinians, 2, 3–4, 7–8, 13, 62–67, 90, 98, 104, 105, 106, 107, 116, 155n7, 156n22. *See also* Israeli state
attitudes of Palestinians in Israel: regarding Israeli state, 2–3, 5–6, 8, 23, 34, 91–92, 95, 116–17, 119; regarding Palestinians serving in Israeli security

forces, 6–7, 17, 18, 20, 21, 24, 25, 35,
47–48, 79, 80–83, 86, 87, 89, 90, 117,
119, 120, 121, 122–23, 134n13, 149n26,
152n24, 163nn9,12, 164nn13,14. *See
also* Palestinian identity; Palestinian
nationalism
attitudes of Palestinians in security
forces: regarding discrimination,
47, 49, 55–56, 64–66, 69, 70–74,
76–77, 90, 91–92, 96–97, 99, 107,
152n24; regarding economic conditions, 35–39, 41–43, 83–84, 87, 92,
94, 164n14, 165n15; regarding ethnic
identity, 14–15, 141n39; regarding
family commitments, 80, 82, 83, 94,
165nn16,21; regarding Israeli state, 8,
22, 34, 44, 47, 91–92, 95, 116–17, 119;
regarding Palestinian nationalism, 15,
18–19, 20, 165n21; regarding politics,
35–36, 38, 116; regarding promotion
practices, 19, 55–56, 64–65, 70–71, 77,
96–97; regarding violence, 17, 20–22,
121–22, 152n24; regarding Zionism,
19, 20, 65, 155n22
'Ayn Rafa, 14, 150n31, 165n14

Ballinger, Pamela, 120
Bardenstein, Carol, 154n3
B'ayni, 58
Bayt Jann, 73–74, 158n17, 167n27
Bayt Naquba, 14
Bechar, Ayelet: *Power*, 110–11, 149n26
Bedouins, 113; 'Azazme tribe, 28, 139n;
Desert Reconnaissance Battalion,
52, 55, 76; discriminated against after
service, 28–29, 74–77; education-military track for, 38, 40, 41, 56, 152n14,
176n94; ethnic identity among, 12,
99, 138n24; Fallen Bedouin memorial,
56; in the Galilee, 12, 13, 69, 137n20,
149n28; land confiscation involving,
12–13, 47, 69, 75–76, 107–8, 139n,
140n31, 158nn23,24; military assignments, 55; in the Naqab, 12–13, 27–28,
47, 52, 76, 99, 124, 137n20, 139n,
140n31, 149n28, 158n23; during 1948
war, 11, 12, 138n22; policies of Israeli
state regarding, 3–4, 10, 12–13, 27–28,
47, 62–63, 66–67, 74–77, 98, 107–8,
110, 138nn22,24, 139n, 140n31, 143n6,
144n8, 149n28, 151nn36,37, 152n14,
158nn23,24, 169n28; relations with
Circassians, 58; relations with Druze,
51, 53, 57; with stateless status, 27–28,
30, 143n6, 144n8; Trackers, 52, 53–54,
55, 70–71, 108; Tuba soccer team, 25;
as volunteers in Israeli security forces,
9, 12, 13, 15, 18, 28, 38, 39, 40–41,
44–45, 47, 51, 52, 53–54, 55, 61–62, 63,
70–71, 122–23, 147n8, 149nn26,27,
152n14, 154nn3,5, 155n22, 157n10,
158n27, 174n51
Belgian Congo, 104
Ben-Ari, Eyal, 160n3, 161n4, 180n17
Ben Gurion, David, 106
Bernstein, Deborah, 161n8
Bhabha, Homi, 169n30
Bickford, Andy, 171n15
Bir al-Sabi', 45, 51, 124
Birwe, al-, 23
Bishara, Amahl, 138n21, 139n
Bishara, 'Azmi, 1, 154n5
Blee, Kathleen, 179n11
Bolivian military: peasant conscripts in,
88, 92, 96, 99, 164n14
Border Guard, 39, 42–43, 46, 48, 73, 74,
113, 174n51; Druze in, 54; and infiltra-
tors, 16, 20, 29; vs. military and
police, 114–15; women in, 87
Bouchareb, Rachid: *Days of Glory*, 174n52
British colonialism: Great Revolt in
India, 98, 178n103; Indian Army
during, 16, 91, 92, 95, 97, 98, 148n20,
173n51, 178n103; Irish enlistment in
British Army, 92, 96, 173n51, 178n104;
vs. Israeli policies, 13, 16, 98, 148n20;
in West Africa, 98
B'Tselem, 162n

Bush, George W., 93
Buthelezi, Chief Gatsha, 107

Caglar, Ayse, 134n13
Camp Thiaroye, 99–100
Carmel region, 12
Charef, Mehdi, 170n5
Christians, 113, 140n34; in Israeli security forces, 9, 14; land confiscations involving, 14; during 1948 war, 13; in police force, 14, 54, 56, 66; policies of Israeli state regarding, 3–4, 10, 13–14, 51, 62, 98, 110, 140n37; relations with Druze, 54, 58; relations with Muslims, 14, 57–58
Circassians, 9, 58
Cohen, Geula, 30–31, 140n34
Cohen, Hillel, 58, 141n41, 148n20, 150n30, 158n12, 163n11
collaborators, 24, 25, 46, 141n41, 150n30, 152n17, 158n12, 162n; informers, 6, 45, 54, 148n20
Communist Party, 18, 65, 80, 81–82, 88, 116, 125, 179n2
conscription: of Druze, 4, 9, 11, 16, 33–34, 63–64, 73, 101, 134n13, 135nn15,23, 137nn11,14, 152n17, 158n18, 159n27, 164n13, 168n; of Jews, 4, 7, 133n3
construction work, 5, 22, 23, 38, 42
converts to Judaism, 136n28

Dahamsheh, Yazid, 165n20
Daliyat al-Karmil, 74
Dallasheh, Leena, 139n
Dardashti, Galeet, 160n3
Darwish, Mahmoud, 22
Davis, Rochelle, 139n
Dayr al-Asad, 17
Dayr Hanna, 58
deaths of Palestinians in security forces: Bedouins, 15, 55, 56; Druze, 74; fatality rates, 35, 55, 74; and IDF Widows' Organization, 71; memorials to the dead, 56, 75, 101–3, 151n40, 156n7;

relationship to enlistment, 146n1; widows of Arab soldiers, 71, 156n7
De Gaulle, Charles, 100, 103, 104
DeKock, Eugene, 173n51
Democratic Front for Peace and Equality, 125
Denogean, Guadalupe, 93–94
Diagne, Blaise, 108–9
Diaspora, Palestinian, 1, 9
Dirks, Nicholas, 169n28
Dorman-Smith, Eric, 173n51
Douglass, Frederick, 174n61
Doumani, Beshara, 134n13
Druze, 113, 115, 157n10, 174n61; in Border Guard, 54; conscription of, 4, 9, 11, 16, 33–34, 63–64, 73, 101, 134n13, 135nn15,23, 137nn11,14, 152n17, 158n18, 159n27, 164n13, 168n; discrimination against, 12, 72–74, 107; educational system for, 11, 12; Eid al-Fitir holiday, 137n14; ethnic identity among, 23–24, 98, 137n19, 155n5; land confiscations involving, 12, 49, 72–74, 77, 101, 158n17; military assignments, 55, 152n24; Nabi Sh'ayb holiday, 53; during 1948 war, 10–11, 137n14, 141n41, 174n51; in police force, 58, 64, 154n37; policies of Israeli state regarding, 3–4, 9, 10–12, 19, 23–24, 33, 51, 52–53, 62–64, 72–74, 98, 110, 152nn14,24, 167n27, 168n; relations with other Palestinians, 10–11, 51, 53, 54, 57, 58, 98, 137n14, 152n24; social status and military service among, 151n39; Sword Battalion, 52–53, 56
Druze Initiative Committee, 73
DuBois, W. E. B., 100

Echenberg, Myron, 177n97
economic conditions, 35–44; attitudes of Palestinians in Israeli security forces regarding, 35–39, 41–43, 83–84, 87, 92, 94, 164n14, 165n15; construction

work, 5, 22, 23, 38, 42; for Palestinians
vs. Jews, 37; poverty, 13, 39, 84, 88,
92–94, 120, 164n14; and provision
for family, 80, 82, 83–85, 87–88, 89,
90, 94, 161n7, 164nn13,14, 165nn16,21,
166n; unemployment, 13, 37, 40, 74,
84, 87, 88, 92, 147n5, 179n1
education, 4, 6, 37, 147n6, 148n17; for
Druze, 11, 12; education-military
track for Bedouins, 38, 40, 41, 56,
152n14, 176n94
Ein Hod, 22
Ein Mahel, 146n1
Eitan, Rafael, 158n24
Elbedour, Salman, 138n24
Eliezer, Benjamin, 46
employment: construction work, 5,
22, 23, 38, 42; discrimination in,
37, 39–40, 54, 74, 87; Palestinian
unemployment, 13, 37, 40, 74, 84, 87,
88, 92, 147n5, 179n1; relationship to
military service, 39–40, 54, 73, 74,
92–94, 147n11
Enloe, Cynthia, 172n28
equality, promises of, 6, 33–34, 71; role in
recruitment, 97–98, 101, 109
Esmair, Samera, 136n1
Ethiopian immigrants, 53–54
Evans, Rhonda, 177n97

family commitments: attitudes of Palestinians in security forces regarding,
80, 82, 83, 94, 165nn16,21; relationship to masculinity, 80, 82, 83–88, 89,
90, 161n7, 164nn13,14, 165n21, 166n
Faras, 'Imad, 72
fatality rates: of minority soldiers in colonial armies, 97; for Palestinians, 35,
55, 74. See also deaths of Palestinians
in security forces
Firro, Kais, 10, 135n23
first intifada, 16, 24, 152n24, 162n
Flame, 41
Foucault, Michel, 172n28

French colonialism: African Conscription Laws, 177n97; in Algeria, 91, 92,
103, 170n5, 174n52; vs. Israeli policies,
13, 95, 97, 98, 101–3, 109; in Lebanon, 13; in Syria, 13; in West Africa,
92, 94–96, 97, 98, 101, 103–4, 105,
107, 108–9, 171n22, 177n97; during
World War I, 94–96, 104, 105, 107,
108–9, 174n52; during World War
II, 99–100, 101, 103–4, 108, 171n22,
177n97
Front de Libération Nationale (FLN), 103

Galilee, the, 79, 81–82, 113; Bedouins
in, 12, 13, 69, 137n20, 149n28; Druze
in, 12; Fallen Bedouin memorial, 56;
regional planning in, 5, 41–42
Galon, Zahava, 145n33
Ganon, Col. Pini, 52
gender: and criticism of Palestinians in
Israeli military, 80–83, 84–87, 165n20;
gender norms, 84–87, 90, 168n; of
interviewer, 117–19; and national-
ism, 159n1, 162n, 163n9; patriarchal
relations, 80, 153n33, 168n, 169n28;
women in police force, 15, 34, 84–87,
115, 169n28. See also masculinity
Ghanaim, 'Imad, 17
Ghosh, Amitav, 16, 95, 173n51
Ghoussoub, Mai, 160n1
Gill, Lesley, 164n14
Givat Haviva, 23
Giv'ati Brigade, 46, 54, 72
Glory, 100
Golan, Avirama, 152n24, 157n8
Gorman, Tom, 177n95
Green, Linda, 171n21
Greenberg, Hanan, 157n10
Green Line, 15, 24, 141n40
Green Patrol, 151n36
Grundlingh, Louis, 172n29
Grundy, Kenneth W., 172n41, 176n94,
177nn97,101
Guantanamo Bay, 105

Guatemalan military: collaborators with, 148n20, 173n51; Mayan conscripts in, 88, 93, 94, 96, 98–99, 171n21
Gutierrez, José, 93
Gutmann, Matthew, 160n1

Haaretz, 28, 55, 71, 72, 76–77, 87, 125, 151n39, 152n24, 157n10
Habiby, Emile: *The Secret Life of Saeed*, 6, 111
Haifa, 18, 163n12; Haifa University, 41, 148n17
Hajjar, Lisa, 134n13, 135n23, 152n24, 164n13, 174n61
Halabi, Ahmad al-, 105
Halabi, Rafik, 155n5
Halusa, 139n
Hammer, Zevulun, 144n9
Hams, Iman al-, 17
Hanthala character, 88, 167n22
Haredim, 31, 145n19
Haritos-Fatouros, Mika, 170n3
Harkis, 103
Hartman, Za'ev, 46
Hason, Nir, 157n10
Hassan, Manar, 168n
Hassan, Nizar: *Istiqlal*, 150n31
Hasso, Frances, 163n8
Havakook, Ya'cov, 138n22, 147n8, 149n28, 151n37, 156n22
Hawari, Areen, 161nn5,7, 179n4
Hayb, Amira al-, 87
Hayb, Hasan al-, 15, 70–71
Hayb, Nayif, 102
Hayb, Omar al-, 66–67
Hayb, Taysir al-, 1, 72, 87, 157n10
Hazan, Naomi, 145n33
Hebrew, 4, 48, 64, 97, 118–19, 146n46, 147n3, 154nn1,3, 167n26
Helman, Sara, 155n13, 180n17
Herzfeld, Michael, 160n1
Hezbollah, 18, 66, 111–12, 122
Hitler, Adolf, 173n50
honor killings, 58, 153n33, 169n28

housing, 4–5, 36–37, 41–42, 44, 94, 142n52, 148n22; home demolitions, 47, 69, 75–76, 77, 114, 142n55, 158n23
Hozayyil, Ibrahim al-, 76–77
Huggins, Martha, 170n3
humanization of Palestinians, 124–25, 180n28
Human Rights Watch, 153n34, 163n10
Hurndall, Tom, 1, 7, 72, 87, 157n10
Hutchinson, Earl Ofari, 177n101

ID cards, 3–4, 12, 14–15, 28–29, 133n2
identity: and ethnicity, 23–24, 95–99; of Jews, 24–25, 97; of Palestinians, 14–15, 23–24, 25, 92, 98, 99, 137n19, 138n24, 141n39, 142n66, 155n5, 168n; relationship to military service, 23–24, 95–99
Ighbariyyi, Sa'id, 89
Ilan, Shahar, 143n6
impunity for soldiers, 58, 81, 120, 154n34
infiltrators, 16, 20
informers, 6, 45, 54, 148n20. *See also* collaborators
Interministerial Committee of 1949, 10
International Solidarity Movement (ISM), 1, 72, 87, 157n10
interviewees: and gender of interviewer, 117–19; interaction with interviewer, 15, 115–25, 141n39, 179n11; mediators, 89, 115–16, 117, 118, 124; sampling of, 115–17; socioeconomic class of, 38–39, 84, 113, 120
Iraq: non-citizens in U.S. military in, 93–94
Ireland, 92, 96, 173n51, 178n104
'Isifya, 56
Israeli, Raphael, 32
Israeli air force, 33, 52, 61–62, 65–66, 71, 97
Israeli-Arab conflict, 170n2; sources of, 91–92, 110
Israeli citizenship: for foreign immigrant laborers, 29–30; for Jews, 7, 27, 29,

30–32, 49, 62, 69–70, 77–78, 102–3,
109, 110, 133n2; for non-Arab non-
Jews, 29, 144n13; for Palestinians, 1–2,
3–4, 5, 8, 16, 27–30, 49, 62, 69–70,
77–78, 95, 102–3, 109, 110, 114–15,
144n9, 168n, 169n29, 174n51; relationship to military service, 7, 27–34, 37,
49, 62, 77, 103, 121, 155n13, 160n3
Israeli flag, 3, 89, 100
Israeli intelligence services, 52, 97
Israeli Labor Party, 111
Israeli national anthem, 1, 110–11
Israeli prisons, 163n10
Israeli state: Absentee Property Law,
139n; Black Goat Law, 151n37; vs. colonial powers, 13, 16, 95, 97, 98, 101–3,
104, 109, 148n20; democracy of, 6, 7,
19, 20; Expulsion of Intruders Law,
13; and gender norms, 90, 168n; High
Court/Supreme Court, 31–32, 133n2,
142n52; ID cards issued by, 3–4, 12,
14–15, 28–29, 133n2; independence
day, 3; Land Administration, 41–42,
73, 139n, 140n31; land owned by, 4;
Law of Return, 27; Military Administration period, 12, 43, 44, 139n,
149n28, 161nn5,7, 179n4; Ministry
of Defense, 28, 34, 39, 40, 43, 48, 53,
62, 122, 124, 147n7, 151n40, 155n22,
157nn7,10, 158n27; Ministry of Environmental Protection, 89, 167n27;
Ministry of Justice, 144n13; Ministry
of Religious Affairs, 11; Ministry of
the Interior, 11, 29, 37, 144nn9,13; Nationality and Entry into Israel Law,
144n13; Planning and Construction
Law, 139n; policies regarding child
allowances, 147n10; policies regarding
expansion of Arab communities, 36,
42; policies regarding Hebrew, 64;
policies regarding home demolitions,
47, 69, 75–76, 77, 114, 142n55, 158n23;
policies regarding land confiscation,
3, 4, 5, 13, 14, 19, 23, 37, 42, 44, 47, 49,
72–74, 75–76, 77, 101, 107–8, 139n,
140nn31,37, 148n20, 158nn12,17,23,24,
179n1; policies regarding movement
of Palestinians, 43, 44; policies regarding patronage, 43–44; policies regarding Russian Jews, 24–25; policies
regarding segmentation of Palestinians, 3–4, 10–15, 21, 23–24, 51, 52–54,
56–59, 72–74, 81, 96–97, 98, 110,
137n14, 138nn21,24, 152n14, 153n33,
163n11, 164n13; policies regarding
unrecognized villages, 4, 6, 13, 22,
62, 74–76, 77, 139n; Public Lands
Expulsion of Intruders Law, 140n31;
Shabak, 45, 65; taxation by, 4, 22, 44,
94; torture of political prisoners by, 5;
welfare agencies, 37; and Zionism, 3,
15, 16, 19, 20, 25, 31, 32, 43, 44, 62, 72,
90, 99, 110–11, 121, 158nn12,24
Israelization/assimilation, 89–90,
167n26, 169n31
Israel on Campus Coalition, 1
'Ittihad, al, 73, 125, 163n12
Ivri Commission, 145n33

Jabal al-Qarn, 139n
Jabara, James, 101
Jabareen, Hassan, 22
Jahaja, Yusif, 102
Jakubowska, Longina, 138n20
Janam, Husam, 53
Jansson, Maria, 99, 134n13
Jarra, Rami, 17
Jatt, 17, 150n31
Jayyusi, Salma Khadra, 134n12
Jean-Klein, Iris, 141n42
Jeffery, Keith, 92, 178n104
Jenin, 162n
Jerusalem, 14, 16, 65, 114
Jewish Agency, 29; Settlement Depart-
ment, 156n1
Jewish identity, 24–25, 97
Jewish immigrants, 53–54, 147n10
Jewish settlers, 142n52, 156nn1,3, 157n10

Jewish women: and military service, 30–31, 80; relations with Palestinian soldiers, 106, 164n13

Johnson, Lyndon, 102

Kammani, 69
Kaplan, Danny, 160n3
Kashua, Sayed, 1, 3
Katzir, 156n3
Kelly, Tobias, 162n, 178n110
Khader, Abd-al-Majid, 154n3
Khaldi, Ishmael, 1, 61–62, 154nn1,3,4
Khalidi, Rashid, 141n42
Khnayfis, Salih, 149n28
Kobati, ʻAbir, 1
Kseifa township, 74
Kufur Kanna, 35
Kufur Minda, 58

land confiscation: involving Bedouins, 13, 47, 69, 75–76, 107–8, 139n, 140n2, 158nn23,24; involving Christians, 14; involving Druze, 12, 49, 72–74, 77, 101, 158n17; Israeli state policies regarding, 3, 4, 5, 13, 14, 19, 23, 37, 42, 44, 47, 49, 72–74, 75–76, 77, 101, 107–8, 139n, 140nn31,37, 148n20, 158nn12,17,23,24, 179n1; Land Day of 1976, 19
Land Day protests, 19
Lang, Sharon, 168n, 169n28
Lapahie, Harrison, Jr., 176n95
Lapid Committee, 32
Leballo, Potlako, 173n51
Lebanon, 64, 102; Hezbollah, 18, 66, 111–12, 122; war in 1980s, 55; war in 2006, 111–12
Lewin, Alisa, 147n10
Lieberman, Avigdor, 76
Likud Party, 15, 24, 25, 146n1, 153n31, 159n27
Lockman, Zachary, 143n66
Lomsky-Feder, Edna, 161n4, 180n17
Longoria, Felix, 102
Lunn, Joe, 94–95, 171n22, 172n29

Lustick, Ian, 149n28
Lutz, Catherine, 160n3

Maccabi Sakhnin, 1
Maghar, 48, 58, 151n40, 154n37
Majd al-Krum, 79
Makhmunim, 69, 156nn3,5
Makhoul, Ameer, 145n28
Maraʻana, Ebtisam: Paradise Lost, 179n3
Marʻi, Mariam, 168n
Marʻi, Sami, 168n
Marteu, Elisabeth, 138n24
martyrs, Palestinian, 18–19, 65, 155n19
Martyrs of Israel building, 151n40
masculinity: as immature, pubescent, 80–83, 89, 90, 118; of Jews, 7, 79–80, 110, 160n3, 161n4; and nationalism, 160n1, 161n6, 165n21; of Palestinians, 79–84, 87–90, 118, 160n1, 161nn4,5,6,8, 163n10, 164n13, 165n21, 167n25, 168n, 169n28; relationship to providing for family, 80, 82, 83–88, 89, 90, 161n7, 164nn13,14, 165n21, 166n
Mashhad, 46, 111, 150n31
Massad, Joseph, 160n1, 161n6, 165n15
Masuda, Kasuo, 175n64
Mazarib, Ashraf, 71
Mazarib, Asri, 71
McCabe, William, 106
Mexico, 93, 177n97
Migdal soccer team, 25
military service: vs. alternative national service, 7, 32–34; assignments of minority units, 55; and becoming a state man (misudar), 42–43, 59, 83–84, 88, 90; benefits after, 4, 7, 36–37, 38, 39–49, 69, 74–75, 94, 101, 114, 122, 147nn7,10, 148n22, 179n1; central nation-building role of, 7; conscription of Jews, 4, 7, 133n3; discrimination against Palestinians in, 19, 90, 92, 97, 107; exemptions of Jewish women, 30–31; exemptions of Palestinians, 62; exemptions of

ultra-Orthodox Jews, 31–32, 145n19, 147n10; fatality rates for Palestinians, 35, 55, 74; gun permits for soldiers during, 58, 81, 163n11; impunity for soldiers during, 58, 81, 120, 154n34; vs. police, 39, 114–15, 135n14; promotions, 19, 55–56, 64–65, 70–71, 77, 96–97; relationship to basic services, 43–44, 74–75, 94, 149n26; relationship to education, 4, 41; relationship to employment, 39–40, 54, 73, 74, 92–94, 147n11; relationship to ethnic identity, 23–24, 95–99; relationship to masculinity, 79–90; relationship to rights, 7, 27–34, 37, 49, 62, 77, 99–100, 103, 109, 121, 145n28, 155n13, 160n3; relationship to social status, 47–48, 151n39; Widows' Organization, 71. *See also* recruitment

minorities units, 51, 52–54, 98; assignments of, 55, 152n24; Bedouin Desert Reconnaissance Battalion, 52, 55, 76; Bedouin Trackers, 52, 53–54, 55, 70–71, 108; discrimination against, 54–55, 96–97; fatality rates, 55; during 1948 war, 11, 137n7; Sword Battalion, 52–53, 56

Mizrahi soldiers, 24, 54–55, 71, 152n23

Mofaz, Shaul, 145n33, 157n10

Moledet party, 150n28

Monterescu, Daniel, 161n8, 169n29

Mossawa Advocacy Center for Arab Citizen of Israel, 141n45

movement of Palestinians, 43, 44

Muslims, 113, 164n14; Eid al-Fitir holiday, 137n14; policies of Israeli state regarding, 3–4, 10, 11, 13, 51, 62, 64–65, 98, 110; relations with Christians, 14, 57–58

Nablus, 2, 152n24

Nafar, Tamer, 5

Naffa', Hisham, 23–24, 63, 154n39, 157n11, 159n27

Nagel, Joane, 160n1

Nahariyya, 66, 116

Nakba, day of the, 3

Naqab, the, 45, 113, 116; Bedouins in, 12–13, 27–28, 47, 52, 76, 99, 124, 139n, 140n31, 149n28, 158n23; Druze in, 12; regional planning in, 5, 41–42

National Committee of Arab Mayors, 146n41

National Democratic Assembly Party, 125

National Insurance Institute, 159n32

national service: for Jewish women, 33; for Palestinians, 7, 32–34, 145n33, 146n41, 165n20

Na'ura, 154n3

Nazareth, 57–58, 153n31

Nazi Germany: *Mischlinge* in, 173n50

Negbi, Moshe, 145n33, 158n24

Nelson, Soraya Sarhaddi, 157n8

1948 war, 2, 5, 22–23, 168n; Arab Liberation Army during, 16, 29, 141n41, 174n51; Bedouins during, 11, 12; Christians during, 13; Druze during, 10–11, 137n14, 141n41, 174n51; Palestinian villages destroyed in, 133n4, 139n

1967 war, 34

Occupied Territories, 22, 27, 61–62, 142n53, 157n11; Gaza Strip, 1, 2, 3, 9, 15, 17, 20, 21, 23, 24, 55, 64, 78, 80, 114, 136n1, 144n13, 152n24, 156n1, 157n10, 162n; West Bank, 1, 2, 3, 9, 17, 23, 24, 49, 55, 64, 80, 81, 87, 114, 136n1, 141n40, 144n13, 152n24, 156n1, 162n

October 2000 demonstrations, 1, 5–6, 17–18, 32, 35, 66, 107, 134n11, 141n45

Ofek, 71

Or Commission of Inquiry, 32, 141n47

Organization of Negev Bedouin Heroes of Israel, 76

Orwell, George, 104

Oslo Accords, 20, 24, 35–36, 38, 162n

Otsuka, Julie, 105

Paebon, Bondi, 30
Palestine Liberation Organization
    (PLO), 24
Palestinian Human Rights Information
    Center, 163n10
Palestinian identity, 9–10, 25, 136n1,
    168n; attitudes of Palestinians in
    security forces regarding, 14–15,
    141n39; and Bedouins, 12, 99, 138n24;
    and Druze, 23–24, 98, 137n19, 155n5;
    policies of Israeli state regarding
    segmentation, 3–4, 10–15, 21, 23–24,
    51, 52–54, 56–59, 72–74, 81, 96–97,
    98, 110, 137n14, 138nn21,24, 152n14,
    153n33, 163n11, 164n13
Palestinian National Authority (PNA),
    22, 24
Palestinian nationalism, 79, 89, 114–15,
    134n13, 136n1, 143n66, 161n6, 165n15;
    attitudes of Palestinians in secu-
    rity forces regarding, 15, 18–19, 20,
    165n21; and gender, 159n1, 162n,
    163n9; and Hanthala character, 88,
    167n22
Palmach, 138n22
Pappe, Ilan, 174n51
Parsons, Laila, 137n14, 149n28
Pasha, Mustapha Kamal, 148n20,
    177n101, 178n103
patronage, 21, 43–47, 48, 69, 150nn28,30
Peled, Yoav, 145n19
Peteet, Julie, 161nn5,7, 163n10, 165n17
Pipes, Daniel, 105
PKK (Kurdistan Workers Party), 99
police force, 44, 113; Christians in, 14, 54,
    56, 66; corruption in, 21; Druze in,
    58, 64, 154n37; during first intifada,
    24; vs. military, 39, 114–15, 135n14;
    Muslims in, 64–65; number of Pal-
    estinians in, 135n15; during October
    2000 demonstrations, 1, 5–6, 17–18,
    32, 35, 66, 107, 141n45; Palestin-

ians in, 14, 15, 34, 35–36, 38, 47, 54,
    56, 58–59, 61, 66, 71–72, 84–87, 115,
    117, 135n15, 150n31, 163n12, 166n;
    patronage in, 21, 45–46, 150n31; and
    Sakhnin killings, 17, 141n47; women
    in, 15, 34, 84–87, 115, 169n28
Poraz, Avraham, 144n13
poverty, 13, 39, 84, 88, 92–94, 120, 164
Power, 110–11, 149n26
present absentees, 113

Qasim, Samih al-, 1, 22

R., Captain, 72, 142n55, 157n8
Rabin, Yitzhak: assassination of, 29; and
    Oslo Accords, 162n
Rabinowitz, Dan, 167n25
Rafah, 2, 55, 72, 142n55
Rahat, 47, 74, 76
Ramallah, 81
Rami, 58
Rashad, Murshad, 17
recruitment, 166n, 172n28; and gun
    permits, 58, 81, 163n11; number of
    Palestinians in Israeli security forces,
    6–7, 79, 135n15, 158n27; recruitment
    rates, 158n27; relationship to fatalities,
    140n1; role of coercion in, 94–95; role
    of disputes between Palestinians in,
    57–59; role of economic conditions in,
    35–39, 41–43, 83–84, 87, 91, 92–94,
    171n15, 179n1; role of ethnicity in,
    95–99, 98; role of patronage and in-
    fluence in, 44–45, 46, 149n28, 150n28;
    role of promises of equality in, 97–98,
    101, 109
Reeck, Laura, 170n5
refusal to serve, 49, 108–9, 178n104; by
    Druze, 11, 73, 78, 137nn11,14, 158n18,
    163n10; by Jews, 61–62, 63
Regev, Arik, 34
regional planning committees, 5
Reiker, Martina, 167n22
Rigg, Brian Mark, 173n50

righteous gentile status, 78, 107, 159n32
Robinson, Shira, 141n41, 171n26, 178n107
Rouhana, Nadim, 144n13, 150n28
Rubenstein, Amnon, 32
Russian Jews, 24, 155n18

Sa'ar, Amalia, 168n
Sa'di, Ahmad, 134n13, 136n1, 137n19
Said, Edward, 165n17
Sakhnin, 17, 141n47
Sani', Talab al-, 28
Sasson-Levy, Orna, 160n3
Saturday Night Live: Eddie Murphy skit
    from, 49
Sawa'id, Khalid, 69, 77, 156nn3,5
Sawa'id, 'Omar, 18, 122–23
Sawalha, Aseel, 134n13
Schirmer, Jennifer, 148n20, 173n51
second intifada, 19, 72; October 2000
    demonstrations, 1, 5–6, 17–18, 32, 35,
    66, 107, 134n11, 141n45
Segal, Michaly, 135n23, 167n27
Seikaly, Sherene, 112, 169n28
"Serving Which Nationality and Which
    Nationalism Exactly?!," 34
sexuality, 164n13; gay Israeli men, 24–25;
    homosexuals in U.S. military, 177n97;
    sexualized fears, 105–6
Seyag area, 139n
Shafa-'Amr, 75
Shafir, Gershon, 145n19
Shalhoub-Kevorkian, Nadera, 168n,
    169n28
Shammas, Anton, 119
Sharon, Ariel, 32, 147n10, 151n36
Sheikh Muwannis, 133n4
Shekem department store, 147n7
Shhab al-Din conflict, 57–58, 153n31
Shibli, Ahlam, 102, 165n17
Shigaki, Irene, 174n61, 175n64
Shlezinger, Nadav, 154n5
Shohat, Ella, 136n1
Shougri-Badarneh, Banna, 144n8
Sinclair-Webb, Emma, 160n1

Sinha, Mrinalini, 160n1
Sinnara, al-, 125
Slyomovics, Susan, 139n
Smooha, Sami, 167n26
social networks, 40–41
Sofer, Ronny, 157n10
South African military: black service
    under apartheid, 91, 94, 95, 96, 97,
    107, 108, 172nn29,41, 173n51, 176n94,
    177n97
South African police: former ANC mem-
    bers in, 173n51
Srahin, Shtewi, 28
Stein, Rebecca Luna, 140n34
Stier, Haya, 147n10
Stillwell, Joseph, 175n64
Stone, Harlan Fiske, 104
suicide/martyr operations, 65, 66, 116
Sulieman, Elie, 1
Sultany, Nimer, 144n13, 150n28
Swedenberg, Ted, 134n13, 162n, 167n22
Swirski, Barbara, 168n
Szymczyk, Adam, 134n13

Tel Aviv University, 133n4, 148n17
Tiberias, 18, 107
Tirailleurs Sénégalais, 95–96, 97,
    99–100, 105, 107
Tnuva, 37
Toivo, Herman Toivo Ja, 173n51
Triangle region, 46, 113, 165n14
Tuba, 44
Tuba soccer team, 25
Turkish military: Kurds serving in, 91, 99

ultra-Orthodox Jews, 31, 145n19
Unified National Command of the
    Uprising, 24
United Nations' Human Development
    Index, 37
United States: African Americans
    in military, 96, 97, 100–101, 105,
    108, 174n61, 175n64, 178n104; Arab
    Americans in military, 97, 100–101,

105; Citizenship and Immigration Services, 93; civil rights movement, 178n104; Civil War, 100, 174n61, 175n64; Gulf War, 108; homosexuals in military, 177n97; Japanese Americans, 104, 105, 175n64; Jewish Americans in military, 101; Junior Reserve Officer Training Program, 93; Mexican Americans, 96, 102; military recruitment in, 93; Native Americans/Navajos, 96, 106, 107, 176n95; noncitizens in military, 30, 93–94, 96, 177n97; racial discrimination in, 49; second Iraq war, 93–94; September 11th attacks, 101, 104, 105; University Students for Israel, 61; Vietnam War, 108, 174n61; during World War I, 100, 105, 107; during World War II, 101, 102, 104, 105, 106, 107, 175n64, 176n91
unrecognized Arab villages, 69, 110, 116, 120, 149n26, 174n51, 179n2; Israeli state policies regarding, 4, 6, 13, 22, 62, 74–76, 77, 139n
Upper Nazareth, 46, 167n25

Wadi al-Na'im, 139n
Wadi Hamam, 72, 87
Wahib, Mahmoud, 157n10
Wailing Wall, 110–11
Warnock, Kitty, 163n8

Wiemer, Reinhard, 156n1
Women in Black, 162n

Yad Vashem Memorial Authority, 159n32
Yanuh, 137n14, 158n18
Yarka, 152n24
Yedioth, 125
Yee, James, 105
Yiftachel, Oren, 135n23, 167n27
Yishai, Eli, 29
Yuval-Davis, Nira, 160n3

Za'atri, Raja, 164n12
Zahir, 'Atif, 72, 106
Zarazir, 15, 66–67, 70–71, 116
Ze'evi, Raḥav'am, 150n28
Zimbardo, Philip, 170n3
Zionism, 124, 134n13, 138n21; attitudes of Palestinians in security forces regarding, 19, 20, 65, 155n22; and Christians, 14; and confiscation of Arab land, 3, 76, 77, 158n12; and the Druze, 10–11; and Israeli state, 3, 15, 16, 19, 20, 25, 31, 32, 43, 44, 62, 72, 90, 99, 110–11, 121, 158nn12,24; and ultra-Orthodox Jews, 31, 145n19
Zo'bi, Sayf al-Din, 150n31
zoning policies, 4, 42, 75
Zubud, 158n17
Zureik, Raif, 133n8

Stanford Studies in Middle Eastern and Islamic Societies and Cultures